ROY DOUGLAS is Emeritus Reader at the Univer
number of historical books. These include four
covering between them the period 1848–1945; a
study of the Land Question in UK politics; and fi
diplomatic history. He has almost completed a hi
was on five occasions a Liberal parliamentary candidate, and is active in the land
reform movement.

LIAM HARTE was born in County Mayo and he graduated from University
College Galway with a degree in English and Modern History. He
subsequently won a postgraduate scholarship to Trinity College Dublin, where
he completed a doctoral thesis on the Irish poet Louis MacNeice in 1991. He is
Senior Lecturer in Irish Studies at St Mary's University College, Strawberry Hill,
Twickenham, specialising in twentieth-century Irish literature and history. He
has published articles and reviews on Irish literature in *Irish Studies*, *Krino* and
Critical Survey and is the contributing co-editor of *Contemporary Irish Fictions: A
Collection of Critical Essays* (Macmillan, due for publication in 1999).

JIM O'HARA was born in Belfast in 1943. He graduated from Queen's University
Belfast and was later awarded an MA in Modern History at Queen Mary College,
London University. He has been a history lecturer in various universities in
Britain, and in 1990 established the Irish Studies Centre at St Mary's University
College. A founder member of the British Association for Irish Studies as well as
the European Federation of Centres for Irish Studies, he also chairs the Advisory
Committee of the Irish Youth Federation in the United Kingdom and is a
member of the Irish Government's DION committee. His articles have been
published in *Irish Studies*, *Fortnight*, *Ouest-France* and *Éire-Ireland*, and he contributed to *All Ireland* (New Burlington Books, 1988).

Jim O'Hara currently lives in Richmond, Surrey, and is Principal Lecturer in
Irish Studies at St Mary's University College, Strawberry Hill.

Martyn Turner's response to the referendum vote on the Good Friday Agreement; the cartoon appeared in the *Irish Times* on 25 May 1998.

DRAWING CONCLUSIONS

A Cartoon History
of Anglo-Irish Relations
1798–1998

ROY DOUGLAS • LIAM HARTE

JIM O'HARA

THE
BLACKSTAFF
PRESS

BELFAST

First published in 1998 by
The Blackstaff Press Limited
3 Galway Park, Dundonald, Belfast BT16 2AN, Northern Ireland

This book has received support from the
Cultural Diversity Programme of the Community Relations Council,
which aims to encourage acceptance and understanding of cultural diversity.
The views expressed do not necessarily reflect those of the
NI Community Relations Council.

Typeset by Techniset Typesetters, Newton-le-Willows, Merseyside

Printed in Northern Ireland by W. & G. Baird Limited

A CIP catalogue record for this book
is available from the British Library.

ISBN 0-85640-624-4

To the cause of peace and justice
in Ireland and Britain

CONTENTS

ACKNOWLEDGEMENTS

The authors wish to make grateful acknowledgement to the following individuals, newspapers and institutions whose help and co-operation have made this book possible:

Mary Dolan of the Library of Queen's University Belfast; Mary Doran of the British Library; John Gray, John Killen, Yvonne Murphy and Ciaran Crossey of the Linen Hall Library, Belfast; Brigit Istin of the *Punch* Library, London; Beryl Mason of St Mary's University College, Strawberry Hill; Jane Newton and the staff of the Centre for the Study of Cartoons and Caricature at the University of Kent at Canterbury; Colette O'Daly and Noel Kissane of the National Library of Ireland.

The British Library for permission to reproduce material from the Newspaper Library at Colindale; the librarian and staff of the Central Library, Belfast; the Keeper of Prints and Drawings at the British Museum; Peter Brookes and Richard Willson, Times Newspapers Limited; Frank Kelly for permission to use the cartoons of Charles E. Kelly of *Dublin Opinion*; Ewan MacNaughton Associates for permission to use cartoons by Nicholas Garland from the *Daily Telegraph* and the *Independent*; Mirror Syndication International for permission to reproduce material from the *Daily Mirror* and *Sunday Mirror*; the Trustees of the National Library of Ireland; Solo Syndication Limited for permission to use cartoons by David Low and JAK from the *Star* and the *Evening Standard*; the librarian and staff of St Mary's University College Library; the librarian and staff of the University of London Library at Senate House.

The authors also wish to express particular thanks and admiration to the following cartoonists for generously allowing their work to be reproduced: Steve Bell; Phelim Connolly; Bernard Cookson; Cormac; Michael Cummings; Fitz; Rowel Friers; Les Gibbard; Draper Hill; Ian Knox; Mac; Oisín; Chris Riddell; Nick Robinson; Martin Rowson; Gerald Scarfe; Peter Schrank and Martyn Turner.

Grateful thanks are due to the editorial staff at Blackstaff for their active interest, endless patience and constant support during the writing of this book.

The authors and publisher have made every effort to obtain permission to reproduce copyright material throughout the book. If any proper acknowledgement has not been made, or permission not received, we would be grateful to be notified of any corrections that should be incorporated in the next edition or reprint of this volume.

Most of the cartoons have been reproduced from contemporary prints and newspapers, the print quality of which was occasionally poor. The authors apologise for these imperfections and hope that they will not mar the reader's enjoyment and appreciation of the book.

INTRODUCTION

For several decades now, historians have recognised the value of cartoons as historical documents which contain important political and cultural insights into the complex and often problematic relationship between Ireland and Britain in recent centuries. We can trace the beginning of this awareness to the pioneering work of L.P. Curtis in the late 1960s, which brought a keen analytical understanding to bear on the nature and function of Victorian representations of the Irish and Irishness. Since then, historians have examined the insights political cartoons offer into such topics as British anti-Irish racism, the Great Famine of the 1840s and the Northern Ireland conflict, while numerous other writers have made occasional illustrative use of cartoons in individual historical studies. This book aims to extend further the use of political cartoons as a means of historical and cultural analysis by examining Anglo-Irish relations over the past two centuries through this richly instructive medium. It is our hope that this analysis will contribute to a greater, more informed understanding between the two peoples and help dispel some of the myths and prejudices which have been built up over the centuries.

Beginning with the eighteenth-century background and the rising of the United Irishmen in 1798, the book examines some of the many ways in which key issues and events in Anglo-Irish politics, up to and including the Northern Ireland peace process of the 1990s, have been represented by political cartoonists from Ireland, Britain, America, France, Germany and the Soviet Union. Each chapter combines a concise interpretation of the main historical developments with a generous selection of graphic, witty, polemical and often highly provocative cartoons, representing a wide range of national and political opinion. Every cartoon is accompanied by a detailed explanatory annotation which helps the reader to view it in its proper historical context. It is hoped that such an approach will be of value both to those with little or no knowledge of the historical narrative of Anglo-Irish relations and to specialist students who wish to learn more about the relationship between political history and cultural representation.

By correlating visual images with historical developments, we hope to cast new and revealing light on the beliefs, assumptions and prejudices that have characterised political, cultural and economic interaction between Ireland and Britain over the past two hundred years. Cartoons, in the words of L.P. Curtis, are 'multilayered graphic texts filled with values and beliefs of political import' which hold vital clues to the ideological forces at work in society. Political cartoonists at once reveal and reinscribe prevailing ideologies by reflecting back at us ideas and attitudes which we already hold, but with such piquancy that our beliefs and prejudices may become graphically reinforced or challenged. They claim the right to simplify and exaggerate in order to illuminate, denigrate and, of course, titillate. As such, they enjoy a unique degree of freedom of expression, at least in democratic societies. Even in these politically correct times, the cartoonist can still say – or rather draw – the unsayable with virtual impunity, making him or her the most dangerous of iconoclasts. It is equally true that for all the power of the camera lens and computer graphic, the cartoonist's imagination retains exclusive access to the innermost sanctums of the political realm to capture the secret handshake, the private thought, the covert deal.

Measuring the extent of the cartoonist's influence on public opinion is a much more difficult, if not impossible task. While some have made rather large claims for the ability of graphic satire to influence public opinion, others, including many cartoonists, are more dubious about its power. What cannot be gainsaid, however, is that historically, the cartoonist's pen has often been perceived as a potent weapon by governing élites. Recognising the power of the caricaturist to wound as well as amuse, authoritarian regimes have vigilantly policed the border between the belly laugh and the subversive snigger.

There are examples of what might be called cartoons dating right back to Tudor times, but the spate of cartoons of an essentially modern kind, deeply satirical of contemporary events and personalities, really begins in the 1730s, when critics of Sir Robert Walpole found them a very useful medium for lampooning 'the first British prime minister'. The embarrassed authorities discovered that there was no effective way of controlling the flow, which has continued without interruption ever since. French caricaturists of the 1830s who dared mock King Louis Philippe were fined and imprisoned; New York cartoonists' criticisms of municipal corruption prompted government officials to attempt to pass an anti-cartoon law in 1897; and even in the modern era, when political cartoonists are awarded prizes rather than prison sentences, satirists in totalitarian states have suffered harsh censure. In Ireland, the publishers rather than the producers of cartoons have tended to be the targets of official repression, as evinced by the imprisonment of Watty Cox, editor of the anti-establishment *Irish Magazine*, in the early 1800s, and A.M. Sullivan, editor of the nationalist *Weekly News*, in 1868.

Not all artists are dissidents, however, and political cartoonists can support as well as subvert establishment values, a point perfectly illustrated by British artists of the Victorian era. Principal *Punch* cartoonists such as John Leech and John Tenniel, several of whose drawings are featured here, were staunch defenders of respectable middle-class values and of Britain's imperial integrity who reserved their most venomous ink for those, such as Irish separatists, who threatened to disrupt both. That such prolific artists were in a position to influence and reflect the views of the ruling élite which determined the political trends of Victorian society seems highly probable, though it is impossible to gauge the extent of their influence on the wider public with any degree of accuracy. The converse, however, is not true; for what cartoons tell us about the attitudes of their audience reveals an enormous amount about contemporary assumptions and prejudices. One may be tolerably certain that successful cartoonists did not stray far from the general ideas of their likely readers.

The drawings reproduced in the following chapters reflect a multiplicity of political perspectives, ranging from the vigorously radical to the highly reactionary. In each case, we try to decode the cartoon's political message, interpret its allusions and reveal the underlying assumptions, motives and insights of the cartoonist. We realised from the outset that comprehensive coverage of the huge volume of Anglo-Irish political cartoons was an impossible ideal, and that the best we could hope for was to assemble a representative selection of cartoon opinion. As it is, the images reproduced here are culled from over fifty original sources, from eighteenth century prints to the modern mass-produced newspaper cartoon. The diversity of artists whose work is represented is equally broad, ranging from

James Gillray's savage caricatures of the late 1790s to Martyn Turner's acerbic satires of the late 1990s.

Our primary emphasis throughout is on the major political developments in Anglo-Irish relations since the late eighteenth century, though cartoonists' attitudes to some related social, cultural and economic issues are also represented. Throughout our research, our chief criteria for selection have been the relevance and the acuity of a cartoon's political or cultural message, rather than its degree of artistic merit, allegorical sophistication or sheer funniness. Adhering to this principle has not always been easy, and each of us has reluctantly had to jettison personal favourites along the way. It has also meant that the work of certain cartoonists proliferates over others, and that some deserving artists are underrepresented, features which are ultimately attributable to the authors' taste and judgement. The fact that no cartoon by a female artist has been included will not, we hope, be seen as a sign of the authors' incorrigible chauvinism, but rather as a reflection of the fact that political cartooning in Ireland and Britain has been and continues to be an almost exclusively male profession.

Our original aim of devoting a roughly equal amount of cartoon space to each historical period, reflecting a reasonably balanced range of national and political perspectives, proved unworkable in practice because of gaps in the source material. The most obvious anomaly is that the British tradition of political caricature predates the emergence of cartoon art in Ireland by well over a century. Indeed, by the time the first Dublin comic journal appeared in 1870, London was enjoying a renaissance of cartoon art under the auspices of *Punch* magazine, the city having earlier been the epicentre of the golden age of English caricature between 1790 and 1820. The views of British artists necessarily dominate the early chapters, therefore, resulting in an inevitable but unavoidable degree of political bias in the representation of Anglo-Irish affairs. This is especially pronounced in the chapter dealing with the Irish Famine, where the absence of Irish cartoons leaves the historian heavily dependent upon *Punch* for satirical comment, much of which is stridently indifferent to the plight of the starving peasantry. This itself is remarkable, for it suggests strongly that a large section of British middle-class opinion either did not know what was going on in Ireland during the Famine, or did not much care, or possibly both. By contrast, however, the *Illustrated London News* and the *Graphic* carried dramatic sketches of famine suffering, but these have been omitted because they do not fall within the cartoon category.

The late blossoming of Irish artistic talent in the closing decades of the nineteenth century brought to the fore several political cartoonists of the first rank who quickly set about reversing some of the harsh Irish stereotypes of the British comic weeklies. Accomplished Dublin artists such as John F. O'Hea and Thomas Fitzpatrick produced dozens of politically trenchant cartoons which both mocked the simian Irish caricatures of British imaginations and gave graphic legitimacy to Irish nationalists' grievances and aspirations. Some of their most penetrating cartoons are reproduced in chapters seven, eight and nine, along with several perceptive political sketches from the Belfast-based *Nomad's Weekly*, an independent satirical magazine which appeared between 1905 and 1914. Yet, in a curious way, nineteenth-century Irish cartoons featuring Irish people are almost as unrepresentative as their British counterparts. Whereas the latter oscillate violently between representing Irishmen as homicidal apes and as loyal, but somewhat dim, subjects of Queen Victoria, the former usually portray Irish opinion either in the iconic form of an allegorical Erin, or else as Pat, a comfortable peasant farmer, probably from the Irish midlands. Neither side makes much effort to understand or portray the urban worker, the landless farm labourer, the almost landless peasant, or the middle-class town dweller.

This vibrant era of Irish political satire effectively came to an end following the death of Fitzpatrick in 1912 and the subsequent demise of the *Lepracaun*, the monthly satirical journal which he founded in 1905. His immediate successors failed to match his technical skill and incisive political intelligence at a time when both were required to capture the realities and complexities of the bloody revolutionary drama being played out on the streets of Ireland. Instead, some of the most acerbic cartoon comment on the political turbulence of the 1916–23 period comes from the pen of *Punch* cartoonists Bernard Partridge and Leonard Raven-Hill. The two men were by no means identical in their outlook, for *Punch* sometimes allowed considerable licence to its artists. Partridge is much the gentler, and has nothing of the racist bitterness which sometimes enters the work of Raven-Hill. Yet, both of them took a benign view of Britain's handling of Irish rebellion, unlike the *Star*'s David Low, one of the very few British cartoonists who dared denounce the government's repressive Irish policy. An instructive contrast to these British images may be seen in the polemical cartoons of the New York-based *Irish World*, which represent a strongly republican perspective on the violent Anglo-Irish conflict of this period.

The partition of Ireland in 1920, which brought the Northern Ireland state into being, and the 1921 Anglo-Irish Treaty, which created the twenty-six-county Irish Free State, marked a dramatic decline in the popularity of Ireland as a cartoon theme in Britain, with a mere handful of drawings on the subject appearing between 1923 and 1939. Just as British politicians quickly seemed to lose interest in Irish affairs, so too did cartoonists. Partition also brought about a significant change in the nature and practice of political cartooning in Ireland, north and south. The emergence of conservative, inward-looking societies in both parts of Ireland marginalised the voices of dissent and provided little encouragement for the critical vision of the cartoonist. Thus, independence for the south produced a much less acerbic form of cartoon humour than that which had gone before, epitomised by the gentle satire of *Dublin Opinion*, Ireland's only popular satirical magazine between 1922 and 1972. Northern Ireland was distinguished by its lack of any such journal during this period. In fact, there was an almost complete absence of graphic political satire during the Stormont years, a feature which partly reflected defensive Protestant fears of weakening the unionist state through criticism, while alienated Catholic opposition was too insecure and unorganised to pose a sustained cultural critique. The result is a paucity of cartoon material, as the relatively narrow range of sources represented in chapters eleven and twelve attest.

Whereas cartoon scarcity presents difficulties for the historian in the period before 1970, superfluity becomes a problem thereafter. The eruption of violent civil conflict in Northern Ireland in 1969 heralded a predictably dramatic increase in the number of cartoons dealing with the issue in British and Irish newspapers, and in the international press. The rapid escalation of the crisis amidst a rising toll of violent death and human suffering provided contemporary cartoonists with unprecedented opportunities for comment. Each successive act of this unfolding political tragedy – the arrival of British troops, the emergence of republican and loyalist paramilitaries, the introduction of internment, the imposition of direct rule and the continuing violence – seemed to elicit ever more polemical cartoon responses, which were themselves part of the wider propaganda war being fought through the media for the hearts and minds of the British and Irish people. One notable feature of some British cartoons about the Troubles is their tendency to resurrect the simian stereotype to present a view of republican and loyalist paramilitaries as sub-human psychopaths, a feature which merely served to perpetuate British ignorance and misunderstanding of the complex nature of the conflict. The more incisive cartoonists, however, frequently reveal a depth of knowledge and an instinctive subtlety which greatly illuminate the tangled Anglo-Irish relationship. As this relationship continues to improve, especially in the context of European co-operation, Northern Ireland remains the only substantial issue which causes serious political friction between London and Dublin.

Chapter fourteen, therefore, represents our personal choice of the most piquant political cartoons on the Troubles, made with difficulty from a bewildering range of material. This is also true of the final chapter in the book, which deals with the Northern Ireland peace process since 1993. The sudden political shifts, tortuous manoeuvrings and tedious wranglings which have characterised the Anglo-Irish talks process during the last five years have been brilliantly caricatured by such perceptive political cartoonists as Steve Bell, Ian Knox, Martin Rowson and Martyn Turner, some of whose shrewdest sketches are reproduced here. Indeed, the comic energy and sardonic commentary of their pungent satires occasionally recall the robust wit of the etchings of Gillray and Cruikshank, a fitting reminder, perhaps, of the continuing vitality and importance of the cartoonist as an analyst of political change.

1

THE
EIGHTEENTH-CENTURY BACKGROUND

The decisive victory of King William of Orange, a Dutch Protestant, over the Catholic King James II at the battles of the Boyne in 1690 and Aughrim in 1691 laid the foundation for almost two centuries of Protestant rule in Ireland. During this period the country was governed by a small landowning class known as the Protestant ascendancy, amounting to no more than five thousand families, in whose hands power, wealth and privilege were concentrated. The members of this governing élite were mostly descended from English colonists of the sixteenth and seventeenth centuries and adhered to the Established Church of Ireland, a body in full communion with the Church of England and the official religion of the state. They dominated the Irish parliament, which was still subordinate to Westminster, and used it to enact legislation designed to curtail the political, economic and religious freedoms of Catholics, who comprised about 75 per cent of the population, and, to a lesser extent, of Presbyterians and other non-Anglicans, collectively known as Dissenters.

A series of penal laws was introduced between 1695 and 1729 which severely restricted the rights of Catholics to practise their faith, receive an education, hold public office, bear arms, vote, sit in parliament, possess a horse worth more than five pounds and, above all, buy, lease or inherit land. Though not all these statutes were fully enforced, this last prohibition drastically reduced the proportion of Catholic landownership from approximately 22 per cent in 1688 to about 5 per cent in 1775, thereby swelling the ranks of the Catholic poor, described by Viscount Townshend, the English viceroy, in 1770 as 'amongst the most wretched people on earth'.

The legal and social persecution under which this wretched mass laboured was exacerbated by the exploitative activities of rapacious landlords. Many eighteenth-century Irish landlords were absentees who delegated control of their estates to agents or middlemen whose overriding concern was to extract the maximum amount of rent possible in the short term. Such people had little interest in the welfare of their tenant farmers, most of whom lacked any incentive to carry out improvements to their holdings. The abject condition of the poorer peasantry deteriorated further from mid-century when a rapid rise in population intensified the competition for land. This led to a growth in agrarian unrest which manifested itself in the formation of secret societies with names like the Whiteboys and Oakboys dedicated to seeking summary redress for the local grievances of the poor by means of intimidation and violence. Bands of armed peasants regularly carried out nocturnal attacks against landlords' property and livestock and disrupted the collection of the much-resented tithe, an annual payment made by Catholics and Dissenters, as well as members of the Established Church, for the upkeep of the Church of Ireland.

The political horizons of such groups were narrowly parochial; they lacked any wider national aims or objectives. In Ulster, however, agrarian violence assumed an increasingly sectarian complexion in the closing decades of the century as Catholic Defenders fought

Protestant Peep o' Day Boys. This rivalry reached its climax in 1795 at the 'Battle of the Diamond' in Armagh, after which the Protestant forces reconstituted themselves as the Orange Order, named after their deliverer of 1690, and dedicated themselves to the defence of Protestant supremacy. This development was to have profound importance for the subsequent history of Ulster and the Orange Order remains a formidable force in the politics of contemporary Northern Ireland.

The Anglo-Irish relationship in the eighteenth century was quintessentially a colonial one. Although Ireland had its own parliament, its powers were severely curtailed by Westminster under a fifteenth-century statute known as Poynings' Law which prescribed that no legislative initiative should be taken in Ireland without the authority of the British king and privy council. In 1720 a Declaratory Act went further still and affirmed the British parliament's full right to legislate for Ireland. By then, almost all important government and ecclesiastical positions were held by British appointees and, most important of all, Ireland's commerce and trade were strictly regulated and restricted in the interests of the imperial power, especially the export of wool and cattle. In short, Britain controlled Ireland's political and economic destiny.

As the century unfolded, the Anglo-Irish Protestant community's resentment at British economic exploitation combined with a growing sense of their cultural distinctiveness to produce a desire for parliamentary independence. Jonathan Swift, dean of St Patrick's Cathedral in Dublin, emerged in the 1720s as one of the most eloquent advocates of this Protestant Irish 'nationalism'. Speaking on behalf of what he termed 'the whole people of Ireland' (in fact, the Protestant colonial élite), he wrote a series of brilliant political pamphlets in which he savagely attacked Britain's maltreatment of the country and angrily rejected the right of the Westminster parliament to legislate for Ireland. Hailed as the first 'Hibernian patriot', it was he who coined the slogan 'Burn everything English except their coal!', a nationalist catchcry which has echoed down the centuries. Swift and his fellow colonial nationalists, however, were careful to distinguish between their opposition to the British parliament and their loyalty to the British crown. Their claim to be treated as an equal nation was based on the argument that as descendants of English settlers in Ireland they were entitled to the same rights as their fellow subjects in England and that these rights were being denied them by an interfering British parliament. In short, they saw themselves as Irish men with English civil rights. Thus, the desire for legislative independence was entirely compatible with loyalty to monarchical government in the minds of the eighteenth-century Irish Protestant.

The idea of a 'Protestant nation' was significantly boosted by the American War of Independence in the 1770s. Discontented Anglo-Irishmen readily identified with the political aspirations of the American colonists, many of whom were Ulster Presbyterian immigrants, frustrated by their exclusion from active citizenship in Ireland by the harsh penal code. However, sympathy for the rebels was counter-balanced by fear of invasion by enemies closer to home. With Britain's military forces redeployed across the Atlantic, Irish Protestants rallied to defend the country against an opportunistic attack from France which was at war with Britain. Starting in Ulster in 1778, they began forming themselves into companies of armed 'Volunteers' – the eighteenth-century equivalent of a paramilitary group – which by 1780 contained over forty thousand men. Of course, such a formidable show of defensive strength also had enormous offensive potential, particularly if used to exact constitutional concessions from a vulnerable British government. This recognition led the parliamentary leaders of the Volunteer movement, Henry Flood and

Henry Grattan, to push for economic and political reforms. In 1779 Grattan's Patriot 'party' forced England to lift its restrictions on Irish trade and three years later succeeded in winning legislative independence from Westminster when his Declaration of Independence was unanimously accepted by the Dublin parliament. Thus began eighteen years of partial Irish parliamentary autonomy (1782–1800), known to history as the era of 'Grattan's Parliament'.

The independence of the Irish parliament was more nominal than real, however, because of its corrupt and unrepresentative nature. In a political culture where parliamentary seats were openly bought and sold, two-thirds of the elected members of the Irish House of Commons were controlled by British government patronage. Westminster also retained control of the appointment of the Irish executive, including the lord lieutenant, which meant that British ministers continued to be the de facto governors of Ireland. Support for reform among Irish MPs was far from unanimous, however. In a parliament entirely composed of a wealthy, conservative Protestant élite, few were willing to contemplate changes which would endanger their powerful position, especially if this involved extending voting rights to the disenfranchised mass, comprising all three million Catholics, Presbyterians and the Protestant poor.

Then, in 1789, the outbreak of revolution in France delivered a dramatic stimulus to this moribund Irish polity. Stirring, momentous ideas circulated: the 'rights of man' to 'liberty, property, security and resistance to oppression'; the notion that 'sovereignty resides in the nation' rather than the king; the view that a people has the moral right to decide its own destiny. Inspired by these revolutionary ideals and eager to adapt them to Irish conditions, a group of educated, mostly middle-class Church of Ireland and Presbyterian radicals formed the Society of United Irishmen in Belfast, a hotbed of radical thought, and in Dublin, in 1791. A young Dublin Protestant lawyer, Theobald Wolfe Tone (1763–98), emerged as the leader of this radical organisation, which aimed to unite Irishmen of all religions behind a programme of parliamentary reform, including the enfranchisement of Catholics, and so end Britain's domination of Irish affairs. After 1795 the movement assumed an overtly republican and separatist character. Tone himself outlined his political motives in his autobiography with succinct eloquence:

> To subvert the tyranny of our execrable Government, to break the connection with England, the never-failing source of all our political evils, and to assert the independence of my country – these were my objects. To unite the whole people of Ireland, to abolish the memory of all past dissensions, and to substitute the common name of Irishman in place of the denominations of Protestant, Catholic and Dissenter – these were my means.

His espousal of such radical separatist ideals led to Tone becoming the acknowledged founder of Irish republican nationalism, whose grave at Bodenstown in County Kildare is still the site of an annual pilgrimage by Irish nationalists of all shades of opinion.

The renewed outbreak of war between Britain and France in early 1793 prompted the authorities to take action to curb the spread of revolutionary republicanism in Ireland and so prevent the French from capitalising on Irish disaffection. Irish Catholic discontent was appeased by the passing of two Relief Acts which enfranchised Catholic smallholders and removed more of the existing penal laws, though the prohibition on Catholics entering parliament remained. In 1795 the Irish parliament, prompted by the British government, was even prepared to support the establishment of a national Catholic seminary at

Maynooth in County Kildare, thus obviating the need for priests to go to the Continent to be educated, where they might be contaminated by republicanism. Fears that republican radicals might win over the Catholic peasantry led to the establishment of a government militia which many Catholics joined. The United Irish movement was itself declared illegal in 1794 and driven underground.

Meanwhile, Tone had left Ireland for France, where his persistent attempts to persuade the government to sanction an expeditionary Irish force eventually bore fruit in December 1796 when a large fleet of forty-four ships carrying an army of fourteen thousand men set sail under General Lazare Hoche. However, when they arrived at Bantry Bay in County Cork they were prevented from landing by a strong headwind which turned into a gale. After a frustrating ten-day wait, they were forced to abort the attempted invasion and returned to France. As in 1688, a 'Protestant wind' exerted a decisive effect upon the course of history, causing some devout Protestants to discern a mark of divine intervention. It is indeed arguable that the elements saved Britain from military defeat at the hands of one of the largest invasion forces ever to threaten the British Isles.

The government's relief was only temporary, however. Since their suppression in 1794, the United Irishmen had reorganised themselves as a secret oath-bound society intent upon building up a nationwide military network in preparation for an insurrection. In addition to canvassing French support, they sought to mobilise the formidable but fragmented forces of the mainly rural Catholic Defenders behind their revolutionary agenda. One common means of mustering Defender support was to appeal to their crude sectarian instincts by invoking the spectre of Orange terror, since many Orangemen were now taking the government side and joining the ranks of the newly formed, overwhelmingly Protestant, yeomanry. Thus, ancient sectarian prejudices among the peasantry were beginning to dilute the original egalitarian aspirations of the intellectual middle class. The radical republican theory of a national rebellion transcending cleavages of class and creed was beginning to unravel in the face of intractable Irish realities.

2

REBELLION AND UNION
1797–1800

In the immediate aftermath of the failed invasion at Bantry Bay in 1796, the British authorities stepped up their attempts to suppress the United Irishmen. In 1797 General Gerard Lake, commander of the crown forces in Ireland, conducted a campaign of military repression against republican radicals in Ulster, using a regular army augmented by a forty thousand strong yeomanry force and twenty thousand militia. The United Irishmen's organisational coherence and rebellious resolve were seriously undermined by a series of arrests, the seizure of large quantities of arms and the killing or transportation of those found guilty of administering or taking an illegal oath. The indiscriminate brutality of the troops drove many out of the organisation, while creating a lasting hatred in the hearts and minds of others. Lake's terror tactics were backed up by the government's effective spy and informer network, which meant that the identity of most of the leaders of the United Irishmen was known to the authorities in Dublin Castle by the time they had finalised their plans for rebellion in 1798. These plans were dealt a severe blow in March of that year when fourteen of the principal conspirators were seized in Dublin. Lord Edward Fitzgerald, one of the chief rebel organisers, escaped, but was later apprehended and fatally wounded. Despite this setback, sufficient leaders and organisation remained and in late May an uprising began in several parts of Leinster with its epicentre at Wexford.

The Wexford rising of mainly Catholic peasants with local middle-class leadership was initially successful. For a short while a republic was established in Wexford town, where the people addressed each other as 'Citizen' and changed the calendar to the 'Year One' after the manner of the French. On 21 June, however, the insurgents were crushed by superior government forces at the Battle of Vinegar Hill. Recent historical scholarship has refuted much of the conventional interpretation of the Wexford revolt as one of ignorant, disorganised peasants, goaded into rebellion by sectarian hatred. Certainly opportunities were taken to settle old scores and Protestants were gruesomely massacred at Scullabogue and on Wexford Bridge after the discipline of the United Irishmen had broken down. Rumours of sectarian atrocities quickly spread to Ulster where they played a large part in alienating Protestants from the United Irish insurrection. After the rebellion ended, the authorities played up this aspect and played down the republican and democratic elements; the cartoons of both Cruikshank and Gillray, incidentally, help to endorse this sectarian interpretation of the rising. In early June in the north-eastern counties of Antrim and Down an uneasy coalition of Presbyterians and Catholics tried to assert the 'rights of man' and bring about an Irish republic through force. Within a week, however, Henry Joy McCracken's band of rebels had been defeated at Antrim and a similar fate befell those led by Henry Munro at Ballynahinch in County Down. In the north as in the south, the government militia carried out savage reprisals in the wake of the rebels' defeat.

The final episode of the 1798 rebellion took place in County Mayo. In August a long-awaited contingent of French soldiers, a little over a thousand strong, under General Jean

Humbert, arrived at Killala Bay to raise a revolt in the west. Three or four months earlier, French intervention might have proved decisive; now it was too late. Mayo was one of the poorest Irish counties and Connacht was the province where the United Irishmen had made least headway. The French were joined by a number of poorer Gaelic speaking peasants who helped Humbert's army to rout Lake's forces at Castlebar and set up a republic of Connacht. Substantial rebel support proved unforthcoming, however, and the French surrendered to the combined forces of Generals Lake and Cornwallis at Ballinamuck, County Longford, on 8 September. By the time a second fleet arrived in October, carrying Theobald Wolfe Tone and three thousand French troops, the initiative was firmly with the government militia, who captured them at Lough Swilly in County Donegal. Anticipating execution, Tone, a figure much influenced by the ideals of the eighteenth-century Enlightenment, asked that he be shot as a soldier rather than hanged as a common criminal, in keeping with his rank of general in the French army. The refusal of his request led him to take his own life in prison in November 1798.

The 1798 rising failed for a number of reasons. Rebel organisation and co-ordination were poor, government military strength was vastly superior and French aid was inadequate and ill-timed. At an ideological level, the secular, nonsectarian republican ideals of Tone and the United Irishmen were not borne out in practice. Though the rebellion witnessed the involvement of Catholic peasants, Presbyterian merchants and a Protestant aristocrat, their motives and objectives were disparate and contradictory, ranging from separatist nationalism to social grievance. Indeed, it could be said that a movement which set out to ameliorate the existing divisions in Irish society ended up exacerbating them. Undoubtedly, the whole process of mass politicisation is a key element in helping to explain the causes of the rising. Like many revolutions, it was marked by savage brutality on both sides, often going far beyond the military interests of the contestants. The defeated troops of Humbert were afforded full military honours and permitted to return to France, while the Irish rebels were punished ruthlessly.

Inevitably the rebellion left its legends and its martyrs, none more revered than Tone. Nationalists would remember the rising for the merciless behaviour of government troops; unionists for the anti-Protestant atrocities of Wexford. It remains one of the bloodiest episodes in modern Irish history, with an estimated thirty thousand deaths in total, many more than died during the Terror in France. The ideological legacy of 1798 was certainly profound. It established the concept of a republic as the holy grail of Irish nationalists, a political aspiration pure enough to die for. Yet because the original republican ideal was heterogeneous, even contradictory, in nature, Irish republicanism, in the words of one historian, 'became an extremely eclectic phenomenon from which almost all groups could pick what they wanted and reject what they disliked'. The ambiguous legacy of what has been called 'the Tone cult' is still in evidence today, as constitutional Irish nationalists honour Tone's nonsectarian radicalism, while militant republicans invoke his revolutionary separatism.

The most immediate consequence of the 1798 rebellion was the passing of the Act of Union between Great Britain and Ireland in 1800. The arguments in favour of legislative union – which, after all, had worked in the case of England and Scotland – were compelling from a British government perspective. With the war against France still going on, the strategic defence interests of Britain could not afford to allow a semi-independent, rebellious Ireland to continue to pose a threat to its security. Not only was direct control from Westminster considered the most effective means of keeping Ireland quiescent, the prime minister, William Pitt (1759–1806), believed that the abolition of the ineffectual and sometimes obstinate Irish parliament would remove a major source of Catholic disaffection, especially if coupled with a measure of emancipation for Catholics in a new constitutional arrangement.

As the cartoons of the period vividly attest, the idea of union was far from universally popular on either side of the Irish Sea. Many people in Britain had the deepest distaste for Pitt and all his works and in this particular case considered he was encumbering them with a potentially dangerous liability. Many Irish parliamentarians, Protestant to a man, were initially outraged by this gross infringement of their constitutional independence, but gradually realised that in the new structure they would be part of a large Protestant majority in the United Kingdom rather than a minority in Ireland. Orangemen opposed Pitt's proposals because they saw in them the seeds of Catholic hegemony in Ireland. Many Irish Catholics, on the other hand, were encouraged to support the proposed Union because it promised emancipation, though the issue was of little relevance to the peasant majority for whom parliamentary representation was a distant dream.

The government's first Union Bill was narrowly defeated in the Irish parliament in 1799. Pitt pressed ahead, however, making full use of his most effective weapon, the power of the purse. Though his methods would be scandalous in the modern era, government patronage was an accepted part of eighteenth-century political culture. Sinecures, pensions and direct money payments were commonly used to ensure electoral support and reward parliamentary allies. That said, the scale of government-sponsored bribery and fraud employed to persuade the Irish parliament to vote itself out of existence in February 1800 was unprecedented. (It is ironical that Pitt, who used this power of bribery to such tremendous effect upon others, was personally incorruptible and eventually died with large debts.) The resultant Act of Union decreed that Ireland would henceforth send one hundred MPs to the British House of Commons and thirty-two peers (including four bishops) to the House of Lords. The Established Church of England and Ireland was created, as was a free trade area between the two countries. But though the parliament at College Green was abolished, the executive at Dublin Castle was retained, indicating that Ireland's integration was destined to be less than complete and its distinctiveness a source of continual political tension. Britain's attitude to Ireland was to be confused and ambiguous throughout the nineteenth century; at times it was viewed as an integral part of the United Kingdom, at other times as a half-alien dependency.

Where Pitt failed disastrously was in his aim to reconcile the large Catholic majority in Ireland to the Union by Catholic emancipation, which would have removed the disabilities under which they laboured and would have given them, among other things, the right to sit in the United Kingdom parliament. Pitt was a man of large vision and he realised that the success of the Union would ultimately depend on the willingness of people on both sides of the Irish Sea to accept it as a sensible and equitable arrangement. The rock on which emancipation foundered was King George III. Integrity and obstinacy were two of the most marked features in his character and both were brought into full play when he decided that assenting to emancipation would violate his coronation oath. He was prepared to abdicate, but not to sign. In the end it was Pitt who went. A few weeks after the Union was set up, the prime minister surrendered his seals of office and the king selected the utterly undistinguished Henry Addington, later Viscount Sidmouth, to take his place. Pitt returned to office in 1804 but by that time Catholic emancipation was no longer a political possibility.

Though its short-term impact was slight, the Act of Union fundamentally altered the relationship between Britain and Ireland in the longer term. It was no love match, but a shotgun marriage, sadly lacking in connubial bliss, designed to control Ireland. Whereas the Union and its undoing became the singular obsession of nationalist Ireland over the next 120 years, the settlement of 1800 held no such significance for Britain, being but one of London's many imperial preoccupations. Within Ireland, the Union polarised political opinion in ways few could have foreseen in 1800. Pitt's failure to deliver on his promise of emancipation engendered feelings of betrayal among many Catholics and predisposed them to support campaigns for repeal and independence, thereby leading to the exclusive identification of the Irish nation with the Catholic nation. Protestants and Presbyterians, conversely, developed strong pro-Union sympathies as the century unfolded, especially in the north-east, the region which prospered most under the Union. Thus, the settlement which was intended to unite hearts and minds proved to be deeply divisive for Irish and Anglo-Irish political relations.

Pub.d Jan.y 20.th 1797.
Now bond.

G.y inv.t & f.t   *End of the Irish Invasion:___ or ___ The Destruction of the French Armada.*

2.1 'End of the Irish Invasion . . .', Gillray, 20 January 1797, British Museum (BM) 8979

This cartoon was drawn by James Gillray (1757–1815), widely regarded as the greatest of all English caricaturists. He was the first truly professional cartoonist whose graphic, sometimes outrageous, political parodies were often openly propagandistic. Indeed, during the Napoleonic Wars Gillray acted as the unofficial propagandist of Pitt's government, whose scathing anti-French satires led to him being described by one French historian as the 'veritable incarnation of John Bull, who roused the fires of patriotism'.

Gillray's ostensible subject in this cartoon is the wreck of the French invasion fleet which sought to initiate a rising in Ireland in December 1796. His main concern, however, was to make a British political point. Some of the government's principal political critics in Britain, including leading Whig radical Charles Fox, had given support to the French Revolution in its initial stages, and while they later expressed revulsion at the bloody violence which supervened, they remained hesitant about supporting Britain's war with France. This print, therefore, views the events of Bantry Bay, which were disastrous from an Irish republican perspective, through the prism of English parliamentary politics. The storm clouds blasting the French fleet to destruction bear the faces of Prime Minister William Pitt, his secretary of war, Henry Dundas, and other ministers. The anxious figurehead of the foundering French flagship, *Le Revolutionaire*, is Fox, the government's most powerful critic. A revolutionary jolly boat also founders nearby, while other opposition politicians drown in the turbulent waters. Neither side of the English political divide doubted that French fortunes at Bantry had immense implications for Britain.

2.2 'We fly on the Wings...', Gillray, 6 March 1798, BM 9183

This Gillray print appeared as part of a short series of drawings entitled 'Consequences of a Successfull French Invasion' two months before the rising of the United Irishmen began. Unusually for a London cartoon, it is addressed to Irish Catholics. Sympathy for the Catholic cause, whether in Ireland or elsewhere, was rarely expressed in British cartoons of the eighteenth and early nineteenth centuries. There was a widespread fear among all levels of British society that concessions to the Catholic minority might lead to violent persecution of Protestants and cartoonists often exploited this fear to make political points. In the present case, however, traditional hostility to Catholics has been supplanted by greater and more immediate fears of a French invasion.

The cartoon is intended to warn Irish Catholics of the dire threat posed to their religion by atheistic republican France and so deter them from revolutionary conspiracy. A defenceless priest is about to be murdered by two French soldiers, while a third gleefully tramples on sacred Catholic objects. The soldiers' iconoclastic fury has led them to desecrate statues and cover the portal cross with the revolutionary *bonnet rouge*. A passing French high court judge observes the scene with a malign, approving glance, suggesting

Dalrymple inv.   London. Pub.d March 6.th 1798. by J.s Gillray, 27 S.t James's Street.   *J.s Gillray fecit.*

N.o VI. Plate 1.st — *We fly on the Wings of the Wind to save the Irish Catholics from Persecution.* — Scene. The Front of a Popish Chape[l]

...tion. A Priest driven out of his Chapel, A French Sol-: | has learnt to speak the English Language well, by going | "thus, that, the Gratitude, of the French Republic
...ampling on Crucifixes & Mitres, another kicking the | much to the Play House, (having been long a Player | "always pays Three Favours for One." —
a Gracefull Old Man; & a third stabbing him with a | himself,) says in the words of Othello "Good,
...behind: A Membre de la haute Cour de Justice, (in English | "very Good, the Justice, of it pleases, even on the
...er of the high Court of Justice, in his habit of Office, who | "Stage of his own Imposition," — and it is

the absence of legal redress for persecuted Catholics. The clear implication is that while Irish Catholics might not like the Anglo-Irish Protestant establishment, they would find the French revolutionary alternative far worse.

Significantly, French degeneracy is signified by the soldiers' bestialised gait and appearance, especially their grotesquely enlarged facial features. Such negative stereotyping was far from mere harmless fun. It simultaneously drew on and reinforced prevailing British prejudices about the brutish nature of the revolutionary French and as such carried a powerful political and ideological depth charge. As the next cartoon reveals, Gillray's satirical wrath was not confined to French Jacobins – he reserved some of his most vitriolic ink for the enemies of British order in Ireland, the United Irishmen.

2.3 'United Irishmen upon Duty', Gillray, 12 June 1798, BM 9228

This Gillray cartoon appeared some weeks after the 1798 rising began and was aimed primarily at a British audience. It depicts the rebel United Irishmen as mere agents of destruction and pillage, without political or moral principles. The 'Liberty' legend on the rebel's sabre is intended as a barbed ironic comment on the debasement of the concept by radical republican revolutionaries in Ireland, as in France. The cartoon is one of several in which Gillray simianises the belligerent Irish. Not only is there a marked facial similarity between these brutish rebels and the marauding French soldiers of the previous print, the hunched figure with the wheelbarrow has a distinctly apelike posture and profile. These images originate in the widespread British conviction that the Irish were an inherently inferior race who were fundamentally unsuited to self-government, hence the need for firm but benign mastery by the superior Britons. This equation between militant Irish nationalism and a savage, bestial nature achieved its apogee a half-century later in the *Punch* cartoons of the Victorian era.

2.4 'The Allied Republics of France and Ireland', Sansom, 17 October 1798, BM 9254

This London cartoon represents a common English reaction to the 1798 rising, one of horror, revulsion and contempt. It depicts a Jacobin French soldier mounted on a donkey, representing Ireland, being goaded on by the devil. The animal tramples on the insignia of royalty and established religion and carries Irish plunder in the form of barrels of whiskey, a sack of potatoes and other provisions. In the background are scenes of revolutionary atrocity. The political implication is that the Irish radicals are merely the instrument of the opportunistic, self-aggrandising French, and ultimately of Satan himself. There is little evidence of republican brotherhood here, only economic exploitation. In the accompanying ballad, Irish rebel leaders Lord Edward Fitzgerald and Arthur O'Connor are ironically praised for bringing about such an iniquitous alliance. The legend 'Erin go Bray' is a disparaging corruption of 'Erin go Bragh' ('Ireland for Ever'), the catchcry of the United Irishmen.

2.5 'Conciliation–Reconciliation . . .', Ansell, 12 November 1798, BM 9265

This cartoon is by a London caricaturist named Charles Williams, much of whose work was published anonymously or, as in this case, pseudonymously. It appeared a few weeks after the collapse of the United Irish rebellion in October 1798 and shows John Bull, as a soldier in uniform, generously offering the hand of friendship to a frightened, uncertain Irishman in a war-torn landscape. The message appears temperate and sympathetic. The Irish are seen not as monsters but as misguided victims whom Britain is now prepared to befriend in a spirit of goodwill. Yet John Bull's resolute bearing and vastly superior military strength suggest that the proposed reconciliation between these two 'brothers' – the precise political form of which was not yet clear at the date of the cartoon – will not be one of equals. Indeed, as the Act of Union was to prove, Britain neither forgot nor forgave 'Brother Paddy' for his recalcitrance and presumption. Nevertheless, the theme of attempted reconciliation, in one form or another, was to appear repeatedly in British cartoons about Ireland for many years to come.

Conciliation–Reconciliation–or John Bull and his Brother Paddy

Horrors of the IRISH-UNION; — Botheration of poor Pat: or — a Whisper across the Channel

2.6 'Horrors of the Irish Union . . .', Gillray, 24 December 1798, BM 9284

Most of the British and Irish cartoons which have been preserved from the period when the Act of Union was being negotiated are hostile to the idea. This Gillray drawing is something of an exception, therefore, in that it conveys a sense of uncertainty about the alleged benefits of the Union for Ireland. It appeared at the end of 1798 at an early stage in the political discussions about parliamentary union. It shows a suppliant Britannia tempting an impoverished Irish peasant into union by offering him economic and military security. At her back, 'Charley' Fox and other British critics of Pitt's government urge Pat to resist her blandishments by all means available, claiming that her offer conceals much more sinister motives. The Irishman appears confused by these conflicting messages, not knowing whom to trust. Britannia's offer appears superficially attractive, but he is worried by Fox's dire warnings that all kinds of 'horrors' will follow if he accepts it, hence his 'botheration'.

2.7 'An Irish Union!', Cruikshank, 30 January 1799, BM 9344

Isaac Cruikshank (1756–1811) ranks alongside Gillray in the pantheon of early English caricaturists. His loyalty to the British cause in the Napoleonic Wars and opposition to the United Irishmen were as strong as that of Gillray, but unlike the latter, Cruikshank had not been bribed by Pitt and so felt free to criticise his policies. Here Cruikshank attacks Pitt's recent proposal of legislative union between the English and Irish parliaments. It shows the prime minister presiding over the union of a sceptical Irishman and a bewildered Englishman, assisted by his friend and political ally Henry Dundas (Viscount Melville). While Dundas, a Scot, encourages 'Paddy' to emulate the Scots of 1707 and enter union with England, a shadowy figure waits out of sight holding the 'wet blanket' of raised taxes. English cartoons of the period often show deep antipathy towards Scots, and Dundas was distrusted as much for his race as for his policies or conspicuous personal avarice. The subtitle points up the cartoonist's reservations about the efficacy of the whole enterprise: the enforced marriage of unwilling partners is likely to increase rather than lessen the mutual suspicion and antipathy of the parties involved.

2.8 'Peep of Day Boys . . .', Cruikshank, 2 March 1799, BM 9351

The Act of Union divided Irish Protestant opinion. Many ascendancy landowners, businessmen and lawyers opposed it because they feared it would erode their monopoly of power and influence. Others supported it, seeing in union a guarantee of protection against the potentially dangerous Catholic threat. In Ulster, Presbyterian commercial interests favoured the Union on economic grounds, but there was strong opposition from other Orangemen. The anti-unionism of the last group is the subject of this Cruikshank cartoon. It features the Peep o' Day Boys, an agrarian secret society of Ulster Protestant peasants who re-formed themselves as the Orange Order in 1795. They feared that the loss of Irish parliamentary autonomy would seriously undermine Protestant ascendancy and lead to tyrannical Catholic dominance. Here they are shown dragging the sun, which carries the features of Pitt, to a bonfire. The figure on the cliff labelled 'Holy Head' is Charles Fox, who is cheering on the mob. As in the previous print, Cruikshank's contempt for his subjects is conveyed by his subtitle, which in this case highlights the irrational and futile nature of Orange protests.

Ways & Means or Vox Populi !!

2.9 'Ways & Means . . .', *Hibernian Journal*, Dublin, January 1800

This cartoon by an unknown Irish artist presents a scathing view of the corrupt means by which the Act of Union was secured. The periodical in which it appeared was addressed to educated Irishmen, who in this period would be mainly Protestants. The drawing refers to the fact that majority support for the Union in the Irish parliament was obtained largely by bribery and the creation of peerages. It features the Irish viceroy, Lord Camden, and his retinue openly canvassing support for the Union among the poor and criminal classes, while a town crier blatantly announces the price of support: 'Hear ye! Hear ye! Wanted immediately a few hundred persons of any description to sign for a Union. 2*s*. 2*d*. a head for those who can write and 1*s*. 1*d*. for those who can scratch their mark. God save the King and his Majesty's subjects of west Britain that is to be — !!!' Camden's chief steward's claim that he is 'anxious to collect the sense of such respectable persons' as are assembled here is laden with bitter irony, since the Irish poor were the least of the government's concern at the time.

2.10 'The Modern Gulliver Removing the P-rl-t of Lilliput, Cruikshank, January 1800, BM 9507

This striking Cruikshank cartoon appeared during the last stages of the Irish parliamentary debates which ended in acceptance of the Union. The giant figure of Pitt, stripped to the waist and sweating, is shown carrying the Irish parliament on his back from Dublin to London, urged on by the Lilliputian Dundas. The sketch is based on Jonathan Swift's famous political satire, *Gulliver's Travels* (1726), a work suffused with irony, ambiguity and paradox. The target of Cruikshank's satire would appear to be Pitt himself, whose physical bulk, the cartoon suggests, is in inverse proportion to his political stupidity, as evidenced by his attempt to transplant the Dublin parliament to London. Perhaps Cruikshank had in mind Gulliver's observation about the gigantic inhabitants of Brobdingnag that 'reason did not extend itself with the bulk of the body; on the contrary we observed in our country that the tallest persons were usually least provided with it'. In any case, the words ascribed to Pitt by Cruikshank may well represent his true sentiments at this time.

CARRYING the UNION

2.11 'Carrying the Union', March 1800, BM 9529

This drawing by an unidentified cartoonist depicts a distressed Ireland being carried off to Britain by Pitt and Lord Clare, the Irish lord chancellor, astride an English lion. St Patrick is in hot pursuit, followed by his 'wild Irish pat–riots', including Henry Grattan and John Foster, Speaker of the Irish parliament. Significantly, the Irish are all mounted on bulls, which had various connotations when associated with Ireland in cartoons of the time. They were often used as symbols of Ireland, sometimes because of their pugnacious disposition, sometimes – especially when Irish Catholics were targeted – for their association with papal bulls. In more benign moments they were used to suggest that 'Paddy Bull' was a brother of John Bull.

More significant, perhaps, is the fact that by the early nineteenth century the racist term 'an Irish bull', meaning a ridiculously illogical statement or expression, was in common English usage. Implicit in the term was a view of the Irish as an idiotic, backward and violent people who were inherently incapable of political self-government. This derogatory stereotype had a theatrical equivalent in the character of the stage Irishman, a temperamental buffoon popular with British audiences, and was later repeatedly invoked by Victorian cartoonists to ridicule Irish nationalist aspirations. This cultural tradition was revived by British cartoonists in the 1970s following the eruption of violence in Northern Ireland, and lives on in the form of the contemporary anti-Irish joke.

2.12 'Hepenstall the walking gallows', Brocas, *Irish Magazine*, Dublin, January 1810

The preponderance of British cartoons in this chapter reflects the fact that there are few, if any, strictly contemporary Irish cartoons that view the events of 1798 from a republican perspective. Less than a decade after the rebellion, however, graphic depictions of British atrocities carried out against the native Irish population during 1798 began to appear in the *Irish Magazine*, an acerbic anti-government publication founded by Walter (Watty) Cox, a journalist from County Westmeath. Cox, who was a member of the United Irishmen, edited the magazine between 1807 and 1815 in spite of frequent fines and imprisonment for sedition. One of the most innovative features of the magazine was a series of striking cartoons by Henry Brocas (1766–1838), whose aggressive indictment of government brutality is conveyed in explicit images and spare, ironic titles, qualities which readily explain why the authorities wished to suppress the publication.

This Brocas cartoon is gruesome in its stark representation of the activities of the notorious Lieutenant Hempenstall, who specialised in this grotesque form of intimate execution. An accompanying commentary explains that the cartoon is based on the hangman's visit to the Westmeath village of Moyvore, during which 'he ordered the cord of a drum to be taken off, and with his own hands hung each of the young men successively

2.13 'Plan of a Travelling Gallows...', Brocas, *Irish Magazine*, Dublin, July 1810

across his athletic shoulders until the spark of life was completely extinguished'. A second Brocas drawing shows government troops enthusiastically carrying out reprisals against the native Irish by means of the travelling gallows, a crude instrument of torture and execution. Both cartoons provide a striking counterpoint to Gillray's forceful anti-republican cartoons such as 'United Irishmen upon Duty' (2.3), though it is notable that Brocas makes no attempt to bestialise the English soldiers in the way Gillray dehumanises the Irish rebels.

3

EMANCIPATION AND REPEAL
1801–1848

Among the arguments advanced by William Pitt in favour of the Act of Union was his contention that this was the constitutional arrangement 'most likely to give Ireland security, quiet, and internal repose'. The vanity of his hopes was to be repeatedly exposed as the nineteenth century unfolded, beginning with the ineffectual rising of Robert Emmet (1778–1803) in 1803. Emmet, a middle-class Dublin Protestant, was a member of the fragmented United Irish network which survived the purges of 1798. Encouraged by the renewal of the Anglo-French war in May 1803 and hoping for a Napoleonic invasion of England, he led an attack on Dublin Castle on 23 July which was intended to act as a catalyst for a spontaneous nationwide insurrection to establish 'a free and independent republic'. The rising was quickly aborted, however, largely because of Emmet's inept organisational and leadership skills. He was captured, convicted of treason and publicly hanged in Thomas Street in Dublin in September. Though Emmet's rebellious gesture changed nothing at the time, later revolutionaries such as Patrick Pearse would cherish 'the memory of a sacrifice Christ-like in its perfection' and draw inspiration from the mythic power of his speech from the dock, in which he declared: 'Let no man write my epitaph . . . When my country takes her place among the nations of the earth, then, and not till then, let my epitaph be written.'

If Emmet's rising proved anything, it was that radical republicanism had lost its popular appeal in early-nineteenth-century Ireland. Political discourse was becoming focused instead on an altogether different constitutional issue, that of Catholic emancipation. Although Irish Catholics had been granted the right to vote on the same terms as Protestants in the 1790s, they remained excluded from parliament and from state and municipal office. When Prime Minister Pitt's support for the inclusion of some measure of Catholic emancipation in the Act of Union foundered on parliamentary and royal opposition, Irish Catholic disaffection was left to simmer into the 1800s. Initially, the issue of emancipation was primarily of concern to a minority of Catholics, mainly those ambitious members of the middle class whose professional advancement was impeded by discriminatory laws. Such restrictions were largely irrelevant to the impoverished peasant majority, desperately trying to eke out a livelihood on subdivided plots of land. By the 1820s, however, a leader had emerged who was capable of uniting these disparate Catholic classes behind a revitalised crusade for emancipation, thereby transforming the character of the campaign from a polite sectional pressure group into a vigorous mass movement. This leader was Daniel O'Connell (1775–1847).

Born into a Catholic landowning family in County Kerry, O'Connell established a national reputation as a lawyer before turning his attention to the emancipation issue in the early 1800s. Staunchly royalist and socially conservative, he abhorred the revolutionary separatism of the United Irishmen, while sympathising with their desire for parliamentary reform. It was O'Connell's passionate belief that Irish Catholics would be loyal subjects of the king if they were granted equality of status with their Protestant compatriots. In 1823 he established the Catholic Association to agitate for emancipation using all available constitutional means. The most striking feature of the association was the admission of the Catholic poor as associate members for a subscription of one penny per month, a fee known as the 'Catholic rent', which was used to provide legal assistance and compensation for victimised freeholders. This innovation led to the unprecedented mass mobilisation of the Irish peasantry as a coherent, disciplined non-violent political force. For the first time in modern Irish history the democratic potential of Catholic Ireland was harnessed in the pursuit of fundamental political change. The association also secured the active support of the influential Catholic clergy, thereby forging a new and powerful alliance between Catholicism and nationalism, which proved to be of enduring importance in Ireland's subsequent historical development.

By the mid-1820s the campaign for Catholic emancipation had acquired an irresistible national momentum under O'Connell's radical, charismatic leadership. The first demonstration of the electoral power of this dynamic new movement came in the general election of 1826, when large numbers of tenant farmers defied their landlords by voting for liberal, pro-emancipation Protestant candidates. The obstinacy of this hitherto biddable electorate sent a tremor through the ranks of the Protestant oligarchy in Ireland and worried the British government.

Two years later, O'Connell himself took the remarkable step of standing for election against a government candidate in a County Clare by-election. His resounding victory marks the birth of Irish democracy, for it was this event that finally forced the government's hand. Alarmed by the unprecedented expression of popular feeling and fearing its translation into violent rebellion – a fear shrewdly exploited by O'Connell – the Duke of Wellington, supported by Sir Robert Peel, decided to submit to the democratic will. In April 1829 the Catholic Emancipation Act was passed into law, thus clearing the way for Catholics to enter parliament and hold high civil and military office. Though the tangible benefits of the Act were confined to a small minority of Irish Catholics, its symbolic significance had a much wider resonance. It represented a striking psychological role reversal for those who seemed forever destined to play the part of the vanquished in Ireland's historical drama and bequeathed an instructive moral to later nationalists. As Gearóid Ó Tuathaigh has written: 'The Government had yielded through fear what it had refused to the force of rational argument or basic justice. The lesson was obvious – Britain would not concede anything to Ireland except under the threat of revolution.' The Catholic masses were beginning to come into their own.

Following this historic victory, Ireland's 'Liberator', as O'Connell came to be affectionately known, turned his attention to his second great political objective and the one that dominated his parliamentary career: the repeal of the Union and the restoration of the Irish parliament. In 1830 he formed the Society for the Repeal of the Union and set about seeking parliamentary support for the creation of an independent Irish legislature under the British crown. It should be stressed that O'Connell was no separatist; on the contrary, he argued that repealing the Union would strengthen the people's loyalty to the British monarch by removing a festering grievance. But whereas emancipation could be conceded, albeit reluctantly, by Westminster, the repeal of the Union was non-negotiable because it would threaten the fundamental unity of the United Kingdom.

The futility of O'Connell's campaign was confirmed in 1834 when his pro-repeal motion was heavily defeated in the House of Commons. Chastened by this experience, he turned instead to the pursuit of Irish reforms under the existing Union framework through a parliamentary alliance with the ruling Whig Party. His abandonment of the repeal issue was merely temporary, however, and in July 1840 he renewed his agitation with the foundation of the Loyal National Repeal Association.

After a sluggish start, the campaign gathered momentum in 1842, aided by a group of new allies known as the Young Irelanders. These were a band of idealistic middle-class intellectuals led by Thomas Davis (1814–45), a Protestant barrister from Cork, who in 1842 co-founded the *Nation* newspaper with Charles Gavan Duffy (1816–1903), a northern Catholic, to spread the gospel of repeal and promote their pluralist, nonsectarian, nationalist views. The trusted tactics of the emancipation campaign were revived. A 'repeal rent', modelled on the Catholic rent of the 1820s, was collected, and the support and participation of the Catholic priesthood again enlisted. The year 1843 witnessed the emergence of 'monster meetings', a powerfully effective new tactic. These were vast, open-air political rallies, often held at places of historic significance, at which O'Connell would stir his massive audiences to euphoric heights with his militant rhetoric, while simultaneously stressing his allegiance to the British crown and constitution.

Despite O'Connell's sincere disavowal of violence as a means to political ends, the government saw the alarming spectre of mass revolt behind such demonstrations of moral force and decided to exorcise it. The moment of confrontation came in October 1843 when Prime Minister Peel banned a monster meeting scheduled for Clontarf near Dublin. Reluctant to risk violence and bloodshed, O'Connell cancelled the rally, though this did not prevent his subsequent arrest and imprisonment on a spurious conspiracy charge. If the momentum of the repeal movement seemed irresistible before this confrontation, it lost its essential impetus after Clontarf and led some of his supporters to question the capacity of O'Connell's constitutional methods to bring about change on this key issue. O'Connell had certainly miscalculated and his commanding leadership of Catholic Ireland had been fatally undermined.

Having failed in his bid to bring extra-parliamentary pressure to bear on the government, O'Connell gravitated towards more conventional parliamentary tactics to achieve his goal of repeal. As in the 1830s, he sought to further his cause by forging an alliance with the Whig Party which came to power in June 1846. This strategy, however, alienated many idealistic Young Irelanders, who accused O'Connell of compromise. He, in turn, resented their purist aloofness and resolved to reassert his authority over them. At a meeting of the Repeal Association in July 1846 he demanded from all members an absolute renunciation of violence as a political weapon.

Though still committed to non-violent methods in practice, the Young Irelanders refused to rule out the use of physical force in theory. One radical voice, that of Thomas Francis Meagher (1822–67), even went so far as to eulogise the sword as 'a sacred weapon'. Such language was anathema to O'Connellites and their protests led to the secession of the Young Irelanders from the association. The bond between Young and 'Old' Ireland was finally, and irrevocably, broken. In 1847 O'Connell died. No other Irish politician would be able to aspire to a fraction of his authority for many years to come.

In early 1847 the disaffected Young Irelanders formed a new association, the Irish Confederation, under William Smith O'Brien (1803–64), a Protestant landlord and MP. The confederation differed little in aims or objectives from the Repeal Association, being committed to the restoration of Irish self-government by non-violent means. Its united front was short-lived, however. With the country ravaged by chronic starvation, a rift developed between pro-landlord moderates like Smith O'Brien and more radical thinkers like James Fintan Lalor (1807–49), who espoused the revolutionary theory of land reform based on peasant proprietorship, claiming that 'the entire ownership of Ireland, moral and material, is vested of right in the people of Ireland'.

Lalor's social radicalism attracted the support of a minority of confederation members, notably John Mitchel (1815–75), who left the organisation in December 1847 and founded the *United Irishman* newspaper, through which he sought to inspire a revolutionary nationalist fervour. His efforts were greatly enhanced by the popular rising which swept the monarchy from power in France in February 1848 and radiated a mood of revolutionary excitement across Europe. Hitherto cautious confederation members were imbued with a new spirit of defiance and Mitchel himself openly called for the establishment of an Irish republic by force of arms.

Alarmed by this revolutionary ferment, the British government arrested Mitchel, Smith O'Brien and Meagher on sedition charges in March. In May, Mitchel was sentenced to fourteen years' transportation to Australia. Two months later, after further arrests, the government declared membership of the confederation illegal, thus provoking the rebel leadership to attempt a desperate act of insurrection. Without any proper military or tactical planning, Smith O'Brien tried to rouse a starving and dispirited Munster peasantry into rebellion in the closing days of July. His efforts proved pathetically fruitless and culminated in a farcical skirmish with police at Ballingarry, County Tipperary. Smith O'Brien himself referred to the incident as an 'escapade', though the event subsequently acquired the more disparaging epithet of 'the battle of the Widow McCormick's cabbage patch', in memory of the owner of the garden where the fiasco occurred. At the time, the 1848 'rising' merely marked the humiliating demise of the Young Irelanders. Later, however, it assumed a somewhat mythic significance in the historical continuum of revolutionary nationalism stretching back to Emmet and Tone, not least because among those wounded at Ballingarry was a young man named James Stephens (1825–1901), who would shortly resuscitate the corpse of revolutionary nationalism by helping to found a far more enduring militant movement, Fenianism.

'And now St PETER at heav'n's wicket seems | 'A violent cross-wind from either coast | [End of the Irish Farce of | 'Cowls, hoods & habits, with their wearers, tost, | 'The sport of winds! All these whirl'd up
'To wait them with his keys, & now at foot | 'Blows them transverse, ten thousand leagues awry | CATHOLIC- | 'And flutter'd into rags; then Reliques, Beads, | 'Fly o'er y backside of the world far off,
'Of heav'ns ascent they lift their feet :- when lo! | 'Into the devious Air: then might ye see | EMANCIPATION- | 'Indulgences, Dispenses, Pardons, Bulls, | 'Into a Limbo large, & broad, since call'd
Pub.d May 17th 1805 by H Humphrey 27 S.t James's Street | | | 'The Paradise of Fools' ____ Milton.

3.1 'End of the Irish Farce of Catholic Emancipation', Gillray, 17 May 1805, BM 10404

This savage Gillray cartoon expresses the virulent anti-Catholic feeling which prevailed in England in the early nineteenth century. In particular, it suggests the force of opposition to Pitt's attempt to introduce Catholic emancipation at the time of the Union, quite apart from the antipathy of King George III. Gillray's subject is a petition in favour of Catholic emancipation which was introduced in the Commons by Fox and in the Lords by Grenville in May 1805. By this date, events had moved on considerably from 1801. Pitt had resigned in that year because he favoured Catholic emancipation and was unable to win the king's approval. Following a short period out of office, he returned to power in 1804, having promised George III that he would no longer press for emancipation during the king's lifetime.

Hence, in this cartoon Pitt appears as an opponent of Catholic emancipation, alongside Henry Addington (later Viscount Sidmouth) and Lord Hawkesbury (later Lord Liverpool), both of whom were to become prime minister. All three are shown blasting a procession of Catholic petitioners as they approach their political heaven, emotively entitled 'Popish Supremacy'. In the vanguard of the petitioners are opposition politicians Grenville, in bishop's robes, a bespectacled Marquis of Buckingham, a sprawling Earl Moira and Fox, dressed as an abbess and mounted on the 'Bull of St Patrick'. Henry Grattan kneels in their wake, swinging a censer. Prominent also is the prostrate figure of

Mrs Dorothy Jordan, Irish mistress of the Duke of Clarence, the future King William IV. He appears opposite her, holding a chamber pot containing holy water from the River Jordan (a 'jordan' was a slang term for a chamber pot). But the most decisive intervention of all is made by the shadowy figure of the Almighty who is shown to be a resolutely Protestant God, as He too blasts the serried Catholic ranks into 'The Paradise of Fools'.

3.2 'The Merry Thought . . .', Cruikshank, 1 March 1814, BM 12016A

Although anti-Catholic legislation in Britain affected only a small minority of the population, the Union with Ireland meant that the issue became increasingly significant for the British political agenda throughout the early decades of the nineteenth century. Parliamentary motions in favour of Catholic relief arising from popular petitions were heavily defeated in both Houses between 1805 and 1808, to the dismay of the Irish Catholic Committee led by Daniel O'Connell. Irish Catholics' hopes were revived in 1811 when the 'madness' of George III, an intransigent opponent of Catholic emancipation, led to the appointment of his son, the future George IV, as prince regent, and his investiture with most of the power of the sovereign. However, the illusion that the prince regent was the Catholics' ally was quickly destroyed by his acceptance of Lord Liverpool's anti-Catholic ministry in 1812, which provoked an angry response from O'Connell and dimmed the prospects of emancipation once more.

This cartoon by George Cruikshank (1792–1878), son of Isaac, summarises a popular British – or at least English – view of the unresolved Catholic question in 1814. It shows a group of English Protestants (right), comprising John Bull, two Anglican bishops and a parson, struggling with a group of unruly Irish Catholics over a giant merrythought or wishbone. At its apex are the Bible and John Foxe's *Book of Martyrs*, a much-read work which describes the fate of Protestants who suffered for their faith at the hands of Catholics. This work, and the background image of a gibbet, suggest that the fear that any kind of toleration of Catholics would eventually lead to persecution of Protestants remained widespread at this time. Under the merrythought, the prince regent rides on the Pope's back, an allusion to the presumed Catholic sympathies of the former. Cruikshank suggests that if Catholic emancipation is granted, the regent will go to Ireland, become a monk and, given his well-known history of female liaisons, will generously dispense forgiveness to Irish female sinners. However, John Bull's cry of 'Long live *old* George our King' is a pointed expression of sympathy for the anti-Catholic views of the mentally incapable monarch, rather than for those of the regent and heir apparent.

The Two Irish Labourers.

3.3 'The Two Irish Labourers', Cruikshank, 1818, BM 13152A

This George Cruikshank cartoon illustrates the antiquity of the English view of the Irish as objects of laughter and derision. It is one of a series of small prints produced in 1818 which portray Irish people as stupid, backward and lacking in intelligence. One, for instance, shows an 'Irish gentleman' cutting off an apple tree branch on which he is sitting, with predictable results. Another depicts an Irish woman administering medicine to her ill husband, who is seated in a wheelbarrow, the humour evidently stemming from the sick man having misunderstood the advice to take his medicine 'in a vehicle', that is, mixed with another substance.

The cartoon reproduced here is another example of what were then called 'Irish bulls' and which today are known as 'Irish jokes'. It mocks the stupidity of Irish building labourers by showing one workman carrying another up a ladder in a hod designed to carry mortar, bricks or stones. Not only does the drawing exemplify the nature of anti-Irish prejudice in English culture at this time, the labouring theme reflects the fact that a great many Irishmen were engaged in such unskilled work as early as the first quarter of the nineteenth century. Almost two centuries later, Irish labourers continue to feature prominently in the British construction industry and in English anti-Irish jokes. As many people now recognise, however, such jokes are often far from being harmless. They are frequently intended to demean their targets, thereby asserting the superiority of the teller and, as such, are latently racist.

DANIEL the GREAT *entring* CLARE *preceeded by the* AMATEUR BAND.

Published by Hillrich & Son 12 Anglesea Street Dublin.

3.4 'Daniel the Great entring Clare ...', July 1828, BM 15540

This Dublin cartoon, which is evidently aimed at Irish Protestant sympathisers, satirises the tremendous reception Daniel O'Connell received following his 1828 by-election victory in Clare. In barrister's attire, he is shown in jubilant mood astride a donkey, propelled by a pair of wings, a 'clerical wing' and a '40-shilling freeholder wing'. These refer to the prevailing Protestant view that O'Connell's victory was built upon his strategic appeal to two main categories of voters: Catholics who were influenced by clerical opinion, and tenant freeholders who feared the government might soon introduce legislation which would disenfranchise them. O'Connell is preceded by a group of musical cats, symbolising the Catholic Association. As in cartoon 2.4 (see p. 17), the patriotic slogan 'Erin go Bragh' is translated into the rather crude pun 'Erin go Bray', which may strike the reader as asinine in more than one sense.

CATHOLIC PETITIONERS or SYMPTOMS of a PEACEABLE APPEAL.

3.5 'Catholic Petitioners . . .', Jones, February 1829, BM 15662

This London print, possibly by Thomas Howell Jones, takes a deeply cynical and hostile view of O'Connell's successful emancipation campaign of 1829. It would appear to be pandering to the widespread fear of many English and Irish Protestants that emancipation would usher in an era of tyrannical Catholic rule. It depicts O'Connell as an untrustworthy and dangerous demagogue whose protestations of loyalty to the king and disavowal of violence are mere rhetorical ploys to mask an aggressive Catholic bigotry. Thus he is shown at the head of a bellicose Catholic mob on his way to Westminster, trampling upon the 'Oath of Allegiance' and brandishing the 'Catholic Rent roll', the source of funds for the Catholic Association which had supported his candidature. O'Connell's political strategy, the cartoon suggests, is based on cunning, stealth and a cynical manipulation of the violent potential of the Irish Catholic masses. Hence his explicit advice to them to conceal their weapons and their aggression until emancipation is achieved; only then can they reveal their true colours and unleash the dragon of 'persecution' upon 'heretical' Protestants.

3.6 'The Apostates and the Extinguisher...', Williams, 23 February 1829, BM 15665

This cartoon, by an artist about whom little is known, is a waspish satire on the obsequiousness of British politicians in the face of Catholic agitation. It expresses the widespread Protestant fury which greeted Wellington's government's decision to take up the cause of Catholic emancipation in the late 1820s. The Dublin-born Wellington is shown kissing the Pope's toe and professing loyalty to Rome, while an equally deferential Home Secretary Robert Peel proffers the Anglican liturgy and the crown to the pontiff. The prime minister prepares to set the papal tiara upon both of them, thereby extinguishing the flame of Protestantism in Britain. The provocative identification of Wellington with Guy Fawkes, the alleged agent of the 1605 Gunpowder Plot, in the book lying open beside the Pope underscores the traitorous nature of his machinations. The plinth labelled 'Candi[e]d Orange Peel' signifies Peel's treachery, as he had earlier acquired the nickname 'Orange Peel' because of his strong Protestant views. The list of papal conditions is designed to reinforce Protestant fears of persecution in a future Catholic state, as is the symbolic image of a (papal) bull goring a helpless muzzled (British) dog.

3.7 'Terrors of Emancipation...', Williams, April 1829, BM 15711

Many British cartoons of this period were hostile to Catholic emancipation. This one, however, although apparently by the same artist as cartoon 3.6, is strongly sympathetic in that it derides the notion that emancipation would inevitably lead to the persecution of Protestants. At the centre of the cartoon is a straw bugaboo, an Irish manifestation of the Spanish Inquisition, which terrifies opponents of emancipation, including Lord Eldon, the former lord chancellor and a particularly bitter opponent of Wellington's proposals. Pro-emancipation Wellington and Peel, on the other hand, regard such exaggerated fears as the reflex reaction of Protestant bigots, and confidently assert that emancipation will strengthen the loyalty and obedience of Catholics.

3.8 'Real Union with Ireland', Seymour, *Figaro in London*, 31 October 1835

Not long after Catholic emancipation was granted, a new style of cartoon began to appear in Britain, inspired by the rise of French political caricature in the early 1830s. These new cartoons differed significantly from the broadsheet satirical prints of Gillray and Cruikshank. They were more restrained in political comment, less sophisticated in artistic style and more popular in appeal, being published in cheap weekly satirical magazines. One such magazine which flourished in the 1830s was *Figaro in London*, which, at one penny per copy, was accessible to many working-class readers. Its politics were radical; it was critical of Whigs and Tories alike, and sometimes of O'Connell as well.

REAL UNION WITH IRELAND.

'Real Union with Ireland' appeared in the autumn of 1835, a year after the resounding defeat of O'Connell's pro-repeal parliamentary motion. In the meantime, he had entered into the so-called Lichfield House compact, whereby O'Connellite MPs agreed to support the Whigs in return for reforms of the tithe system and municipal government. 'A real Union or no Union' was O'Connell's new motto, and this provided Robert Seymour, *Figaro*'s principal cartoonist, with his inspiration and title.

The sketch shows O'Connell advancing across the Irish Sea in the direction of the Whig government, using the heads of Wellington and that great controller of 'rotten boroughs', the Duke of Newcastle, as stepping stones. In his hands he carries the head of the much-hated and deeply reactionary Duke of Cumberland, brother of the king. The Whigs, led by Lord Melbourne, are advancing towards Ireland by similar means, though their progress over the heads of Irish Anglican bishops is slower, a metaphor perhaps for the government's reluctance to appropriate the surplus revenues of the Church of Ireland. Dissatisfied with the slow pace of Whig reforms, the Irish leader threatens to disrupt the Union unless they improve. The implication that O'Connell has separatist tendencies is misleading, however, since he never envisaged a complete severance of the British connection, believing instead that repeal would actually consolidate the Anglo-Irish relationship.

REBECCA AND HER DAUGHTERS.

3.9 'Rebecca and her Daughters', Leech, *Punch*, London, 1 July 1843

In 1841 a new satirical journal, *Punch*, appeared in London, founded by radical journalists Henry Mayhew, Douglas Jerrold and Joseph Sterling Coyne, a native of Birr in County Offaly. In its early years *Punch* adopted a radical satiric stance on English social issues such as urban poverty and sweated labour. This radicalism did not extend to O'Connell's campaign for the repeal of the Union, however, as this cartoon vividly demonstrates. The artist, John Leech, who was of Irish extraction, was one of *Punch*'s leading cartoonists from the early 1840s until his death in 1864. It was he who established the magazine's trademark weekly editorial cartoon, the 'big cut', based on the social or political issue currently dominating the news.

This is one of Leech's early *Punch* sketches which draws an analogy between the Irish repeal movement and the Rebecca riots which occurred in Wales in 1843–44. The Rebecca rioters, who derived their name from the biblical wife of Isaac, protested against the tolls imposed on turnpike roads by demolishing tollgates in south Wales. Here, O'Connell is cast as the leader of the rioters, who is dressed as a woman, and his followers as Rebecca's daughters. The toll-taker is Prime Minister Peel and the face of the Duke of Wellington appears on the gatepost on the right. The labelled bars of the gate all refer to policies which were criticised by O'Connell, including, of course, the Union itself, which is being sawn in two by one of his 'daughters'.

THE IRISH FRANKENSTEIN.

3.10 'The Irish Frankenstein', Meadows, *Punch*, London, 4 November 1843

In this arresting cartoon Joseph Kenny Meadows vilifies the repeal movement as a violent Irish peasant who is both bestial and diabolical. This creature shares a clear facial resemblance with Gillray's 1798 rebels, a similarity which conveniently obscures the very important distinction between the militant separatism of the United Irishmen and the non-violent constitutionalism of O'Connell's campaign.

3.11 'The Modern Sisyphus', Doyle, *Punch*, London, 16 March 1844

In Greek mythology Sisyphus was a king of Corinth who became infamous for his acts of deceit, robbery and murder. He was consequently given an exemplary punishment in Hades, which was to push uphill a huge stone which rolled down again as he reached the summit, thereby forcing him to begin the task all over again. In Richard Doyle's cartoon Peel is cast as the modern Sisyphus whose punishment stone is Ireland, which bears the features of O'Connell. Peel's Whig opponents, in the shape of the three Furies, headed by Lord John Russell, taunt him in the background, while a young Queen Victoria looks on in dismay and apprehension. The clear implication is that Peel can neither remedy nor rid himself of the problem of Ireland, and so must endure this unceasing, fruitless labour.

THE MODERN SISYPHUS.

" Sisyphus is said to be doomed for ever to roll to the top of a great mountain a stone, which continually falls down again."

SISYPHUS . . SIR R. P—L.   THE STONE . . D. O'C——L.   THE FURIES . . LORD J. R——L, S——L, &c.

This cartoon represents an early recognition that the Irish question would be a perennial problem for any British government so long as the Union persisted. It would not be resolved by merely treating some immediate grievance – as Peel himself had done at the time of Catholic emancipation – or by applying coercion, as he was soon to discover. Nor indeed would it be resolved by granting self-government to part of the island, as Peel's successors were later to learn to their cost. It is hardly surprising, then, that successive British and Irish cartoonists from the 1840s to the 1990s should return to the myth of Sisyphus at key historical moments to express their sense of the seemingly insoluble nature of the fraught Anglo-Irish relationship.

3.12 'The *Trumpeter* taken Prisoner', *Puck*, London, 15 May 1844

Puck was a short-lived London satirical magazine of the 1840s which adopted a similar anti-repeal stance to its much more durable rival, *Punch*. At the time this cartoon appeared, O'Connell was awaiting sentence following his conviction for seditious conspiracy in February 1844. His arrest and trial followed a year of increasing political tension in Ireland, during which the growing rhetorical militancy of the repeal movement was matched by a build-up of government troops and artillery, as Peel's ministry prepared for the possibility of civil war. The boil of insurrection had been lanced in October 1843 when O'Connell

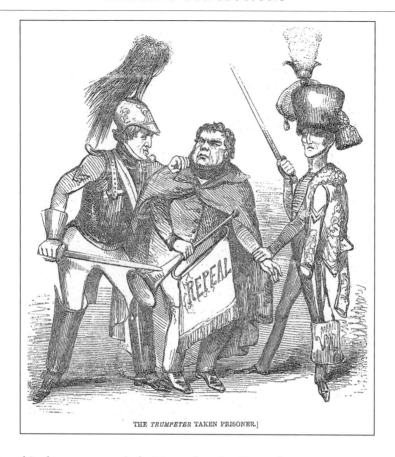

THE *TRUMPETER* TAKEN PRISONER.]

acquiesced in the government's decision to ban the Clontarf monster meeting. His subsequent arrest and conviction came as a devastating blow to a man whose whole political career was based upon a fastidious respect for the law of the land.

This cartoon ridicules O'Connell's claim that, because he eschews violence in his pursuit of repeal, he cannot therefore be held responsible for any acts of violence which might ensue. It shows the 'trumpeter' being taken prisoner by Peel (left) and another member of his government, probably Lord Lyndhurst, the lord chancellor. The Irish leader protests his innocence on the grounds that he is unarmed, but this fails to impress the soldiers, who make no distinction between incitement to violence and violent action. The clear implication is that O'Connell is a disingenuous and dangerous instigator of civil unrest in Ireland who must be held accountable for his actions.

On 30 May 1844, two weeks after this cartoon appeared, O'Connell was sentenced to a year's imprisonment and fined £2,000. He was freed on appeal in September on the grounds that his trial had been unfair.

"BROTHER, BROTHER, WE'RE BOTH IN THE WRONG!"

3.13 'Brother, Brother . . .', *Punch*, London, 15 June 1844

This cartoon comments on Anglo-Irish relations on the eve of the Famine from an oblique and somewhat unusual *Punch* perspective. It features Queen Victoria and Tsar Nicholas I of Russia in a moment of relaxed, intimate conversation, reflecting upon the roles their respective countries have played in the affairs of Ireland and Poland. Victoria openly admits Britain's culpability for Irish injustices and suggests that Nicholas is responsible for similar wrongs in Poland. The Vienna settlement of 1815 established a truncated Poland as a separate kingdom ruled by the Tsar of Russia. Poland, like Ireland, was a predominantly Catholic country with a long tradition of independence, and many Poles were deeply resentful of Russian domination. They staged an unsuccessful rising in 1830–31, after which Nicholas deprived them of the last vestiges of their autonomy. Though *Punch* could not have foreseen it, both Ireland and Poland were to recover independence in the immediate aftermath of the First World War, though many people in both countries considered that they had been denied territory which was rightfully theirs.

A DISTURBER OF THE PUBLIC PEACE.

PEEL.—'There's a Maynooth Grant for you! So you now be quiet, and move on!'

O'CONNELL.—'Grant, indeed! I never moves on under Repale! D'ye think I don't know the value of peace and quietness!'

3.14 'A Disturber of the Public Peace', Leech, *Punch*, London, 26 April 1845

This John Leech cartoon continues the theme of O'Connell's disruptive influence on Anglo-Irish affairs. Here he is cast as an itinerant street musician whose strident agitation annoys the respectable Peel, but this time the government response is shown to be conciliatory rather than coercive. Peel's instrument of pacification is the annual grant to Maynooth Catholic seminary, which he increased from £9,000 to £26,000 in June 1845, with a further grant of £30,000 for capital expenditure. The Maynooth grant had a curious history. Until the 1790s, Irish Catholic priests were educated on the Continent. Then, in 1795, the Protestant Irish parliament agreed to subsidise a seminary at Maynooth in order to prevent young Irishmen going abroad, where they might be exposed to seditious French republican ideas. After the Union, the United Kingdom parliament assumed financial responsibility for the college, to which it gave an annual grant of £9,000.

While Peel's policy of Catholic appeasement caused deep divisions within his party, the increase was warmly welcomed by the Irish hierarchy and by O'Connell, who regarded it as a part of an overall package of 'justice for Ireland'. Repeal remained his ultimate objective, however, and it is his refusal to be satisfied with anything less that Leech satirises in this cartoon, underscoring O'Connell's insolence by mimicking his Kerry brogue in the tradition of the burlesque stage Irishman.

YOUNG IRELAND IN BUSINESS FOR HIMSELF.

3.15 'Young Ireland in Business for Himself', Leech, *Punch*, London, 22 August 1846

In July 1846 Young Ireland withdrew from O'Connell's Repeal Association, dismayed by the Irish leader's readiness to contemplate another parliamentary Whig alliance and impatient for a more radical solution to the Irish question. With the country in the throes of famine, revolutionaries like John Mitchel and James Fintan Lalor began to consider violent insurrection as the most effective means of bringing about Irish self-government. Leech's cartoon comprises a devastating satire on this emergent revolutionary force. The heavily armed simian figure represents the degenerate, irreconcilable nature of Young Ireland, while the cartoonist's loathing for the arms–dealer is so intense as to cause him to dehumanise him to an unrecognisable degree. His spindly arms, disproportionate torso and unformed face are the embodiment of British abhorrence of the rebellious Irish. Such racist stereotyping was extremely pernicious and is comparable in some ways with the later Nazi portrayal of Jews as subhuman. There is, moreover, a curious similarity between the arms dealer's cap and the one worn by O'Connell in other *Punch* cartoons of the 1840s (for examples, see cartoons 3.14 and 3.16), a snide insinuation, perhaps, that O'Connell's constitutionalism is a dangerous deception. Leech's savage caricature is completed by the background array of pistols which seems to illuminate the seditious scene like a lethal sun.

FAMILY JARS AT CONCILIATION HALL.

3.16 'Family Jars at Conciliation Hall', Leech, *Punch*, London, 19 September 1846

In January 1847 William Smith O'Brien became leader of the Irish Confederation, a group made up of those who had seceded from the Repeal Association and were dedicated to the establishment of an Irish parliament within the Union by constitutional agitation. This cartoon anticipates the conflict between the O'Connellites and the Confederates by show-ing a feminised O'Connell blocking Smith O'Brien's entry to Conciliation Hall, the head-quarters of the Repeal Association in Dublin. The cartoon is particularly unfair, however, in its portrayal of Smith O'Brien as a fiery supporter of physical force, since he remained committed to the 'force of opinion' up to the spring of 1848. Indeed, it was not until July 1848, after the government had banned the confederation and suspended habeas corpus, that Smith O'Brien finally recognised that the moment for insurrectionary action had come. The real revolutionary firebrand at the time the cartoon appeared was John Mitchel, whose republican extremism was opposed by the moderate Smith O'Brien, leading to a division within the confederation in late 1847.

THE BRITISH LION AND THE IRISH MONKEY.

Monkey (Mr. Mitchell). "One of us MUST be 'Put Down.'"

3.17 'The British Lion and the Irish Monkey', Leech, *Punch*, London, 8 April 1848

This Leech cartoon is an arresting allegory of Anglo-Irish relations in the spring of 1848, by which time the British government was seriously concerned about the extremist rhetoric emanating from famine-striken Ireland. The source of much of this extremism was John Mitchel who, together with Smith O'Brien and T.F. Meagher, was arraigned on charges of sedition in March. While jury divisions allowed the latter two to walk free, Mitchel was successfully prosecuted under the new Treason Felony Act and sentenced to fourteen years' transportation to Van Diemen's Land (Tasmania) in May. The ferocity of Leech's depiction of Mitchel indicates the contempt in which his vociferous militancy was held in government circles. Not only is he fully simianised, his cap suggests he is also a presumptuous fool to challenge the imperious British lion. Thus, we are left in no doubt about which creature must be 'put down'.

4

THE GREAT FAMINE
1845–1851

The Great Famine of the 1840s was the greatest human catastrophe in Irish history. Chief among the many factors which caused it was the system of land tenure in nineteenth-century Ireland. This whole system required radical restructuring, but no British government of the time could have taken on the landlords and interfered with the sacred rights of private property, even if it had wished to do so. During the early part of the century competition for land became intense among a rapidly expanding population, which had grown to over eight million by 1841. This land hunger encouraged the practice of multiple subdivision, whereby small holdings were parcelled into increasingly smaller plots which were sub-let in turn to the poorest families. The result was a social pyramid of (often absentee) landlord, tenant farmer, cottier and landless agricultural labourer.

Those at the base of this inherently unbalanced structure maintained a precarious level of subsistence. Rents were high, few owned the land they worked and security of tenure was rare, except in parts of the north where a system prevailed known as the 'Ulster custom', which entitled an evicted tenant to compensation for improvements during his tenancy. Landlords, who were mostly alien in religion and language, commonly saw their tenants in the narrowest economic terms. To make matters worse, by the 1840s some three million Irish peasants were overwhelmingly dependent on a single crop for sustenance: the potato. Cheap, convenient and nutritious, a sufficient quantity of potatoes could be grown on an acre of ground to feed a family of five for six months. The health of the vegetable could not be relied upon, however, and many died as a result of potato shortages in the years 1816–19, 1822, 1826 and 1831.

What was unprecedented about the 1840s, however, was the prolonged nature of the crop failure and the persistence of the new potato blight, *Phytophthora infestans*. Initially, it was hoped that the outbreak of the disease in the autumn of 1845 would prove to be an ecological aberration, but such hopes had evaporated within the year, as the 1846 crop failed completely. There was a partial failure in 1847, followed by another total collapse in 1848. The blight continued until 1851, leaving behind a dreadful legacy of human misery, social devastation and political recrimination. Precise figures are difficult to calculate, but most historians accept that around one million people died of starvation and the diseases which accompanied it, while over another million emigrated between 1846 and 1852. Inevitably, mortality rates were highest among the poorest inhabitants of the poorest regions. Large areas of Connacht and Munster suffered the greatest population loss, and though the north and east escaped the worst ravages of the disaster, thousands perished in the fetid slums of Dublin and Belfast, which were swollen by hordes of rural destitutes.

A measure of the depopulation from famine, disease and emigration can be seen by comparing the census returns of 1841 and 1851. In 1841 the population of Ireland was over eight million; in 1851 it had dropped to six and a half million, a decline of almost 20 per cent. The decline was over 25 per cent in every county in the province of Connacht and even exceeded 30 per cent in County Roscommon.

Initial responsibility for dealing with the 1845 crisis fell to Conservative Prime Minister Sir Robert Peel (1788–1850). He reacted swiftly to alleviate suffering by issuing grants to local relief committees, instituting public relief works, setting up food depots to store and distribute imported Indian meal and repealing the Corn Laws in 1846. The latter measure, which was prompted partly by fears that famine would affect the British working classes, led to the collapse of the Peel administration and a damaging split in the Tory Party. In the summer of 1846 a new Whig government came to power under the leadership of Lord John Russell (1792–1878) and initiated a significant shift in famine relief policy which proved to be tragic for Ireland.

The key figures in providing relief were Charles Wood, the new chancellor of the Exchequer, and Charles Trevelyan, permanent secretary at the Treasury. Both were firm believers in the economic doctrine of *laissez faire* which dictated that the state should not normally interfere in trade or private enterprise, but allow market forces to operate freely. In a pre-welfare state era it was considered the proper role of government to promote self-sufficiency and discourage state dependency. Thus, the concept of minimum state intervention became the guiding principle of Russell's Irish famine policy. Food depots were closed and the provision of food to the destitute was entrusted to private enterprise. The state did establish a public works scheme, but this was to be paid for by Irish taxpayers, especially the negligent landlords, in the belief that 'Irish property should pay for Irish poverty'. Similarly, much of the £7 million total spent on famine relief by the government was advanced in the form of loans, repayable with interest from the local rates. What the Russell administration failed to appreciate, however, was that Ireland simply did not have the financial resources to deal with a calamity of such horrific proportions. In particular, Trevelyan's argument for the transfer of responsibility for relief to the Irish Poor Law in 1847 ignored the complete inadequacy of this system in Ireland.

As the crisis worsened, increasing numbers of starving families became dependent upon the relief works. By the spring of 1847 almost three-quarters of a million people, approximately one in three adult males, were employed in such tasks as road-building and hill-levelling. The physically demanding nature of the work meant that the weakest and most needy could not participate directly and so were unable to benefit. They, like many others, were often left to suffer a slow, wretched death.

Government concern about the accumulating cost of the public works schemes resulted in Trevelyan ordering their closure in the summer of 1846, but a public outcry led to them continuing until 1847, when they were replaced by a direct relief programme. Temporary soup kitchens were then set up to distribute free food to the hungry, the number of which stood at an appalling three million by this time. In September the soup kitchen scheme was replaced by an outdoor relief system which meant that the poor could receive cooked food without having to be admitted to the already desperately overcrowded workhouses. The receipt of relief was dependent on the fulfilment of certain preconditions, however. These included a labour test, whereby the poor were required to break stones for up to ten hours a day before they were fed, and the 'quarter-acre clause', which rendered tenants who occupied more than a quarter-acre of land ineligible for free rations. Despite these deterrents, the outdoor relief scheme had become the main source of food for an incredible 800,000 people by June 1848, with as many again clamouring for rations within the workhouse walls.

The winter of 1846–47, the severest in living memory, heaped misery upon misery. Contagious diseases had reached epidemic proportions and though several hundred temporary fever hospitals were opened, thousands succumbed to typhus, cholera, relapsing fever and scurvy. Mass burials were common, frequently by means of the re-usable trap coffin. Tragically, many doctors, priests and relief workers died from fever as a direct result of their selfless efforts to ease the suffering of the sick and dying. Children were among the most numerous and pathetic famine victims. Thousands were orphaned, abandoned in workhouses or simply deserted by desperate parents, who preferred to take their chances on the emigrant ship rather than await certain death at home. Several charit-able and religious groups generously devoted their limited resources to voluntary famine relief, especially the Quakers, who made prodigious efforts to counteract mass starvation by distributing free rice and establishing soup kitchens in many areas of the country. Others behaved less honourably, notably a minority of proselytising Church of Ireland zealots who, in exchange for free food, sought to win converts to Protestantism from among the starving Catholic peasantry, a practice which earned the emotive epithet 'souperism'.

In the summer of 1847 Russell's government declared the Famine officially over, though hundreds continued to perish daily. The purpose of this declaration was to transfer the responsibility for relief to the Irish taxpayer. The government's insistence on the collection of rates greatly increased the financial burden on Irish landlords and caused many to fall into debt as the crisis escalated. This had serious consequences for their tenants, as indebted landlords started to evict destitute tenants who were unable to pay rent, let alone rates, to make way for wealthier ones. This led to the mass clearances of smallholders, especially in the west of Ireland, which witnessed many harrowing scenes of sick and dying families being forcibly evicted. The Encumbered Estates (Ireland) Act of 1849, under which bankrupt landlords could sell their debt-ridden estates, precipitated a further wave of evictions, as the new landowners, many of them middle-class Catholic Irishmen, set about clearing their lands of the poorest families and consolidating their holdings.

For the dispossessed multitudes, emigration became the only alternative to death. One quarter of a million people left Ireland in 1847, with another million following over the next five years, mainly to Britain, North America and Australia. Thousands of trans-atlantic famine refugees died in transit amidst the appalling squalor of the notorious coffin ships. Of those who survived, few were ever to return, though many harboured a deep-seated anglophobic resentment and a determination to play a role in ending British rule in Ireland.

The Famine had a profound impact upon Ireland's demographic, social and economic structures. It established a pattern of population decline, underpinned by high emigration and low marriage and birth rates, which became unique in Europe and was not finally reversed until the 1960s. In post-Famine Ireland emigration became an accepted, even ex-pected, fact of life for generations of Irish men and women. It also led to the virtual disap-pearance of the cottier class and the elimination of very small holdings. Farms were no longer divided at inheritance between sons, but usually went to the eldest male, a practice which encouraged delayed marriages and low birth rates. This led in turn to a deterioration of the position of women in society. Faced with the prospect of a narrowly restricted life in rural Ireland, many young single women opted to leave, making this type of emigration a unique feature of the Irish experience. The Famine also delivered a major blow to the already weakening position of the Irish language and compounded the association of the language with poverty and failure. Many of those who died or emigrated were Irish-speaking peasants, with the result that by 1851 the number of Gaelic speakers had fallen to fewer than two million.

But while the Famine has undoubtedly left deep scars upon the Irish psyche and society, its legacy has not been entirely debilitating. The remarkably generous response of the Irish public to recent famines in the developing world is perhaps one indication of how the national memory of past sufferings has inspired a genuine concern for the present priva-tions of Africa and Asia. This is certainly a view endorsed by former President Mary Robinson, who has suggested that Ireland's past gives its people 'a moral viewpoint and an historically informed compassion on some of the events happening now'. Her own high profile visits to famine-striken African countries during her term of office epitomised this compassion, and in her new role as United Nations Commissioner for Human Rights she remains committed to the relief of suffering in developing countries.

For many in Ireland, the British government's response to the Famine made a mockery of the Act of Union. They argued that Ireland had not been treated as an equal partner within the United Kingdom, but rather as a marginal inferior which was expected to cope alone with an appalling catastrophe. For them the Famine highlighted Ireland's essential separateness from Britain and exposed the underlying colonial nature of the relationship between the two countries. Unprecedented levels of human suffering had occurred at the centre of the richest empire in the world, yet through its doctrinaire policies the Whig government had allowed fiscal and ideological orthodoxies to take precedence over a more generous and humane response. The question posed by Dublin's *Freeman's Journal* cut to the heart of the matter: 'Is there justice or humanity in the world that such things could *be*, in the middle of the nineteenth century and within twelve hours' reach of the opulence, grandeur and power of a court and capital the first upon the earth?'

Others took a more malign view, seeing genocidal intent in Britain's famine policies. Such an interpretation was not confined to extreme nationalists like John Mitchel; even the lord lieutenant, Lord Clarendon, writing to Russell in 1849, urged him to desist from his 'policy of extermination'. Among the most enduring and bitter Irish Famine memories was that of cattle, grain and other foodstuffs being exported by Irish merchants while people starved. Most of these exports went to England to alleviate food shortages. Retro-spective nationalist revulsion was also directed at the callous non-interventionism of Trevelyan, who was wont to regard the Famine as a punishment from God to teach the indolent, unreasonable, rebellious Irish a lesson, and crudely recommended that the country be left to 'the operation of natural causes'.

Traditionally, most Irish historians steered clear of research and writing on the Famine. Over the last forty years the tendency of revisionist historians has been to play down the significance of the event and to minimise the inadequacy of the British government's re-sponse. More recently, post-revisionist historians have begun to highlight the suffering of the Irish people and criticise the failures and blind spots in British policy. Accusations of British culpability for the Famine have troubled the Anglo-Irish relationship even in the contemporary era. The continuing sensitivity of this issue was highlighted at a major Famine commemoration event held in Cork in the summer of 1997. The gathering prompted the new British prime minister, Tony Blair, to seek to heal this festering wound by formally acknowledging Britain's inadequate response to the Famine. In a remarkable message to the Irish people he stated:

That one million people should have died in what was then part of the richest and most powerful nation in the world is something that still causes pain as we reflect on it today. Those who governed in London at the time failed their people through standing by while a crop failure turned into a massive human tragedy. We must not forget such a dreadful event.

While some were critical of the practice of a contemporary government effectively apologising for the deficiencies of its distant predecessor, the Irish government and most Irish people warmly welcomed Blair's comments, seeing them as a helpful contribution to Anglo-Irish understanding in the 1990s.

IRISH AFFAIRS

THE ABSENTEE *Scene Naples: Enter the Ghosts of starv'd Irish Peasantry!!!*

4.1 'The Absentee', Seymour, *Looking Glass*, London, August 1830

The massive scale and devastating impact of the Great Famine has tended to overshadow the fact that intermittent crop failures and food shortages were an integral part of Irish and European life in the preceding centuries. In 1740–41 Ireland was racked by a famine of such severity that some historians have estimated that more lives were lost in relative terms in these two years than during the 1840s. Less acute subsistence crises occurred in 1800–1, 1816–19, 1821–22 and 1830–31. Deaths from starvation and disease resulted during each of these periods, though mortality rates were kept at a relatively low level as a result of a combination of government aid and private charity.

'The Absentee' is a rare example of a British cartoon which testifies to the occurence of famine conditions in pre-Famine Ireland. Its publication in the *Looking Glass*, a monthly magazine of the 1830s which contained many cartoons of a radical flavour, coincided with the beginning of a food shortage which was greatest in the western counties of Mayo, Galway and Clare, though the cartoon itself makes no explicit reference to this crisis. Instead it approaches the theme of famine distress obliquely, by focusing on the figure of an absentee Irish landlord who is shown indulging himself in the culinary and carnal delights of Naples. His pleasure is rudely interrupted by the appearance of the skeletal ghosts of the 'starv'd Irish Peasentry' who evoke in him feelings of such horror as to suggest his manifest culpability for their terrible plight. Although many Irish landlords were absentees in the pre-Famine period, preferring to spend the money brought in by their rents in London or the Continent rather than in Ireland, the scale of absenteeism was not as great as some nationalist historians once claimed.

"RINT" *v.* POTATOES.—THE IRISH JEREMY DIDDLER.

'You haven't got such a thing as Twelve-pence about you?—A Farthing a week—a Penny a month—a Shilling a year?'

4.2 ' "Rint" *v.* Potatoes . . .', Leech, *Punch*, London, 15 November 1845

By the time the Irish Famine took hold, *Punch* had established itself as an influential shaper of British public opinion, not least about Ireland. The journal's initial attitude to the Famine was one of sympathy for the starving peasantry, tempered by a continuing antipathy towards O'Connell and the repeal movement. Two early Famine cartoons (4.2 and 4.3) comprise a coruscating personal attack on O'Connell, laying particular emphasis on

THE REAL POTATO BLIGHT OF IRELAND.

4.3 'The Real Potato Blight of Ireland', Leech, *Punch*, London, 13 December 1845

his decision to continue to collect repeal rent from the starving populace. The first depicts him as a 'Jeremy Diddler', a colloquial term for a swindler, brusquely demanding money from a destitute family. O'Connell's avarice is ruthlessly accentuated by the stark juxtaposition of his imposing corpulence with the peasantry's desperate emaciation. The second cartoon carries even greater graphic force, as Leech transforms the Irish leader into a grotesquely misshapen potato, seated above a repeal collection plate. The inference that the blame for Ireland's distress lay with O'Connell, and not *Phytophthora infestans* or government policy or even Providence, was absurd.

4.4 'Mr Trottman en Irlande', Cham, *Le Charivari*, Paris, 11 December 1845

The cartoon opposite is one of a series of illustrations which appeared in the French daily satirical journal *Le Charivari*, launched in 1830. 'Cham' was the pseudonym of Amédée de Noé (1818–79), one of the most prolific French caricaturists of his generation. His creation, 'Mr Trottman', visited various European countries and, half-factually, half-satirically, recorded his impressions. These drawings appeared at the beginning of the Famine and give a fair impression of the utter destitution which prevailed in Ireland even before the horrors of the late 1840s set in. They suggest a degree of poverty worse than that existing in any other country the artist visited.

The first scene, 'View taken anywhere – in Ireland', evokes the material destitution of a peasant family, with only their pigs between them and starvation. The pig – 'the gintleman that pays the rint' – was of such great economic importance to peasant families that it was frequently kept in the family home to ensure its safety and health. The next two scenes, 'Dining in a farm of the better off' and 'After which the family lies down to sleep', continue the grim narrative, while the fourth, 'Collection for O'Connell, the protector', suggests a poignant peasant faith in the efficacy of parliamentary agitation to alleviate their distress. Perhaps the most notable feature of this French sketch is its empathetic realism, especially when one compares it with the unsympathetic portrayal of the destitute Irish displayed in some contemporary *Punch* cartoons.

JUSTICE TO IRELAND.

" She gave them some Broth without any Bread,
Then whipp'd them all Round, and sent them to Bed."

4.5 'Justice to Ireland', Leech, *Punch*, London, 18 April 1846

This 1846 cartoon is about as close as *Punch* ever got during the Famine period to suggesting that responsibility for the catastrophe lay in part at the door of the British ruling classes. Yet even here one feels that it was the periodical's general *furor politicus* against the Conservative government which prompted its critique, rather than any great empathy for the Irish peasantry. The cartoon casts Peel as 'the Old Woman who lived in a shoe' of nursery-rhyme fame. As his government was unable to provide adequate food for its Irish 'children', it offered them a Coercion Bill instead, designed to give the Irish executive extraordinary powers to combat the wave of agrarian crime which inevitably accompanied mass starvation. The sketch perpetuates the tradition of depicting the sullen Irish male peasants as apelike creatures with intelligences to match. Though *Punch* disagreed with the particular measures the 'Old Woman' was taking in this instance, it did not dissent from the view that the Irish were irrational, choleric children who required firm parenting.

4.6 'Union is Strength', Doyle, *Punch*, London, 17 October 1846

Punch was a strong opponent of the Corn Laws, and when Peel at last brought about their repeal in 1846 its attitude towards him changed dramatically. In Britain this measure was of immense benefit to the industrial working class, but it had little impact upon the impoverished Irish peasantry, a fact which was not well understood in Britain. In this cartoon,

UNION IS STRENGTH.

John Bull. "HERE ARE A FEW THINGS TO GO ON WITH, BROTHER, AND I'LL SOON PUT YOU IN A WAY TO EARN YOUR OWN LIVING."

published shortly after the laws were repealed, a healthy and prosperous John Bull proffers bread and a spade to poverty-stricken Pat, believing that this will relieve his distress. The suggestion that his 'brother' should be grateful to the kindly alms-giver smacks of colonial condescension, as does the implication that charity coupled with more productive agricultural methods will solve the famine problem. The underlying political philosophy is that with a little help from Britain, Ireland could and should become more self-reliant, a view which was popular among the British middle classes in 1846–47. Irish wealth was there to be created if only the people had the intelligence and industry to realise it. The cartoonist, Richard (Dicky) Doyle (1824–83), was a second-generation Irish Catholic who later left *Punch* in protest over the magazine's anti-Catholic views.

4.7 'Height of Impudence', Leech, *Punch*, London, 12 December 1846

This Leech cartoon reflects the hardening of *Punch*'s attitude towards Ireland as agrarian agitation increased and the revolutionary rhetoric of Young Ireland grew more strident. Not only have the impossible Irish shown utter ingratitude towards British 'generosity' as portrayed in 'Union is Strength' (see above), they have added insult to injury by contriving to bite the hand that tries to feed. Hence, an affronted John Bull looks askance that simian Paddy's deferential request is not for alms, but for money to buy arms. The message

HEIGHT OF IMPUDENCE.

Irishman to John Bull.—'Spare a thrifle, yer Honour, for a poor Irish lad to buy a bit of—a
blunderbuss with.'

appears to be that since the Irish will misuse any concession which Britain might bestow
upon them, John Bull should eschew even charity and leave them to their miserable fate.

It is clear from this cartoon that *Punch*'s thematic emphasis had by now firmly shifted
from Irish suffering and starvation to Irish ingratitude and sedition, with all the political
and emotional ramifications that that entails. The fact that thousands of destitute Irish immigrants had begun to pour into British cities by this date, straining resources and engen-
dering much anti-Irish feeling, doubtless spurred Leech and others to make their acerbic
ethnic stereotypes even bolder and more offensive.

4.8 'Deaths by Starvation', 1847, BM 1868-8-8-13081

The scathing cartoon opposite by an unidentified artist is a late example of the type of one-
off print which was popular in the late eighteenth and early nineteenth centuries. It represents a view of the Famine which contrasts sharply with that of *Punch*. Far from attacking
the Irish peasantry for their alleged indigence and contumacy, it highlights the moral culpability of Irish landlords for the 'deaths by starvation' of thousands of their tenants during
the desperate hardships of 1847. It shows a large group of landlords, surrounded by figures
symbolising the pleasures of the wealthy, gorging themselves before the god Mammon,
who is blasphemously quoting the commandment: 'Thou shall have none other God but
me'. Since the landlords have assembled to render 'an account of their stewardship' during

DEATHS BY STARVATION

the Famine, the figures inscribed on the backs of their chairs presumably signify the number of deaths for which they are considered responsible. The diabolical nature of their stewardship is clearly suggested by the gloating presence of Satan, who presides over the obscene feast on an Irish bull, holding a pig, a lamb and a loaf of bread, and the waiter with a demonic tail who carries more decanters of port to the banquet. The ghoulish portrait is completed by the grotesque carpet of emaciated peasant cadavers beneath the diners' feet, creating a dramatic contrast to the selfish, sybaritic indulgence of the landlords.

4.9 'The English Labourer's Burden', *Punch*, London, 24 February 1849

From the autumn of 1847, responsibility for Irish famine relief rested almost entirely on the wholly inadequate Irish Poor Law system. Though thousands were starving to death weekly, Russell's government trusted to Trevelyan's chilling policy of leaving the country to 'the operation of natural causes'. By 1848 the government had declared the Famine to be officially over, a declaration which helped to justify their policy of minimum intervention and facilitate a further reduction in Treasury contributions to famine relief.

Such measures were welcomed by many sections of the British press, including *Punch*. Praise turned to condemnation, however, when the Whig government was persuaded to allocate a £50,000 parliamentary grant to the most distressed Irish Poor Law unions in 1849. *Punch* was outraged by this concession, and resorted to this highly emotive cartoon,

THE ENGLISH LABOURER'S BURDEN;

Or, THE IRISH OLD MAN OF THE MOUNTAIN.

based on the legend of the Old Man of the Sea, to register its anger. This image of the simian Irish peasant as a parasitical burden upon the decent, industrious English labourer tells us nothing about Irish famine realities and everything about the parochial, anti-Irish prejudices of the magazine. Not only are the reasons for the Irishman's distress ignored, so too is the question why the Englishman should be in such a parlous condition. This cartoon, like many others in this chapter, is a graphic testament to the callous and dogmatic moralism which characterised many contemporary British interpretations of the Famine.

PEEL'S PANACEA FOR IRELAND.

Russell. "Oh! this dreadful Irish Toothache!"
Peel. "Well, here is something that will cure you in an instant."

4.10 'Peel's Panacea for Ireland', Leech, *Punch*, London, 14 April 1849

In 1849 Peel, then in opposition, proposed a number of measures intended to expedite the socio-economic transformation of Ireland desired by many British ministers and officials. One initiative which attracted cross-party parliamentary support was his recommendation that indebted landlords be allowed to sell their estates without having to clear their debts first. The result was the Encumbered Estates (Ireland) Act of July 1849, the subject of this cartoon. Peel is pictured proffering Prime Minister Russell the Act as a cure for his 'dreadful Irish toothache', the suggestion being that this will bring instant relief to him, though not necessarily to Ireland. A similar measure had recently been passed for England, with apparently beneficial results for landlords and tenants alike. In Ireland the effect was very different. The Act, which led to the sale of three thousand estates over the next decade, the majority to Catholic entrepreneurs, proved to be a bitter pill for the Irish peasantry, thousands of whom were evicted by the new estate owners to make way for grazing. This is a striking example of the very common misconception that methods which had worked in England would also work in Ireland.

— Pitié, sir John Bull! nous mourons de faim.
— Patience, patience... Nous soulagerons plus facilement les survivants.

4.11 'Pitié, sir John Bull . . .', Draner, *Le Charivari*, Paris, 31 January 1882

Cartoons about the Famine did not end in 1851, partly because famine did not end then either. There were many minor famines in late-nineteenth-century Ireland, including that of 1879–80, brought on by the failure of the potato crop in many western counties. In all, over 500,000 people were in need of state aid, and though few died, government relief continued until 1886. The famine-induced suffering of these years was a contributory factor in impelling many tenant farmers to join the newly formed Land League in order to agitate for reform of the land tenure system.

Viewed in this context, this 1882 French cartoon on the theme of Ireland's plight in the 1840s carries a potent emotional charge. It depicts a ragged, starving Irishman beseeching a decidedly paunchy and menacing John Bull for alms. The latter's sinister reply – 'Patience, patience . . . we will be able to relieve the survivors more easily' – echoes the ultra-nationalist interpretation of the Famine as deliberate genocide, advanced by John Mitchel and others in the post-Famine period. While there was no evidence to support this interpretation, it proved attractive in some quarters, especially in France and among Irish-American émigrés.

The evocation of Famine memories in the *Weekly Freeman* cartoon opposite is equally

PAINFUL
MEMORY
OF
2,500,000
IRISHMEN and IRISHWOMEN
WHO DIED OF HUNGER AND STARVATION
3,197,419 DRIVEN INTO EXILE

A ST. PATRICK'S DAY REFLECTION

4.12 'A St Patrick's Day Reflection', *Weekly Freeman*, Dublin, 17 March 1888

polemical. A sorrowful Erin stands before a Celtic cross commemorating the millions of dead and exiled Famine victims, while an emigrant ship sets sail in the distance. An accompanying text implicitly blamed Britain for the Famine and cites it as an irrefutable argument in favour of Irish self-government. The dramatic fall in the Irish population was witnessed in the contrast between the 1841 census, which returned a record figure of 8.1 million, and the 1881 total of 5.2 million. This population loss continued, so that by 1901 the total had fallen to 4.1 million.

5

THE POLITICS OF NATIONALISM
1852–1878

The 1850s and 1860s were decades of slow recovery from the ravages of the Famine. Agricultural production and profits rose gradually during this period, bringing relative prosperity to many small farmers. The fundamental injustice of the land system remained, however, ensuring that agrarian reform would become one of the central issues of Irish politics in the late nineteenth century. Indeed, agitation for what were to become the key demands of Irish tenants – the 'three Fs', fair rent, fixity of tenure and free sale – was already being expressed in the early 1850s by the Tenant League Association. Fair rent signified rent fixed by an independent body; fixity of tenure meant that a tenant who paid his rent and adhered to other tenurial covenants could not be evicted; free sale implied that when a tenant left his holding, the value of any improvements made should revert to him, not the landlord.

The league was founded in 1850 and consisted mostly of prosperous grain farmers who were primarily concerned with protecting their incomes during a short-term agricultural depression. Although it never managed to transcend its sectoral origins, it was instrumental in the creation of the Independent Irish Party at Westminster, following the 1852 general election. League MPs formed an alliance with Irish members of a religious pressure group, the Catholic Defence Association, to extract agrarian and religious concessions from the British government through a policy of 'independent opposition'. The effectiveness of this alliance was soon destroyed, however, by sectarian divisions and the defection to government offices of two of its MPs. By the end of the decade this brief experiment in parliamentary agitation had withered away and in its place a reinvigorated revolutionary nationalist movement was taking shape.

On Saint Patrick's Day 1858 a secret revolutionary organisation, as yet unnamed, was established in Dublin and New York by veterans of the 1848 rising. James Stephens, fresh from a nationwide tour of the country to gauge the revolutionary mood, organised the movement in Ireland, while John O'Mahony and Michael Doheny were the American co-ordinators. It was O'Mahony who named the organisation the Fenian Brotherhood in honour of a warrior troop of ancient Irish legend, though the movement also became known as the Irish Republican Brotherhood (IRB). The Fenians' objective can be simply stated: the establishment of an independent, non-sectarian Irish republic by revolutionary means. As such, they invoked the historical memory of the 1798 rebellion and anticipated the rising of 1916. Within Ireland, they attracted support from among the working classes of town and country – shop assistants, small farmers, agricultural labourers – and also re-cruited many disaffected British soldiers to their ranks. Abroad, they drew from the well of post-Famine anglophobia that flourished among immigrant Irish communities in America and Britain.

The Fenians made their first, striking impact on Irish political life in November 1861 when they organised the funeral of Terence Bellew McManus, another 1848 veteran, who died in poverty in San Francisco. McManus's remains were transported across America to New York, from where they were shipped to Cork and on to Dublin for burial. This marathon procession attracted large crowds at every stage and rekindled a nationalist fervour which had lain dormant for thirteen years. It also drew the wrath of the Irish Catholic Church in the formidable person of Archbishop, later Cardinal, Paul Cullen, who vehemently opposed Fenianism because it did not promote the Catholic interest. Yet even the vociferous opposition of the most influential Irish clergyman of the age did not prevent the movement gaining many clerical sympathisers.

By 1865, the promised 'year of action', Stephens estimated that the Fenian movement had grown to over eighty thousand members in Ireland, but they were crucially lacking in the arms and money vital to the success of an insurrection. Whereas earlier rebels had looked to France for military support, Stephens looked to America, his hopes boosted by news of the willingness of many of the several thousand Irishmen who had enlisted on each side in the American Civil War to fight for Ireland's freedom. Though some soldiers did travel to Ireland after the war ended, sufficient American support failed to materialise.

Stephens's revolutionary plans received a further setback when he and other Fenian leaders were arrested by the authorities in the autumn of 1865. His subsequent prison escape and flight to America resulted in little more than a revised, rhetorical resolution to strike in 1866. Eventually, in December of that year, the vacillating Stephens was deposed as head of the IRB and replaced by an Irish-American colonel, Thomas Kelly.

Kelly travelled to London in early 1867 to co-ordinate plans for a rising scheduled for 11 February. The military plan was for arms and ammunition to be seized from Chester Castle in England and shipped to Ireland for immediate use by Fenian units in the east and south-west. However, news that a government informer had infiltrated the movement led to the last minute cancellation of the ambitious raid and a postponement of the rising to 5 March. Fenian fortunes fared little better on that occasion, as inadequate arms, ineffective leadership, informers and inclement weather conspired to confine the rising to a handful of isolated skirmishes in Kerry, Cork, Tipperary and Dublin. Kelly fled back to England, where he remained undetected until his arrest in Manchester on 11 September, along with another Irish-American conspirator, Timothy Deasy. A week later, a Fenian unit ambushed the prison van in which they were travelling and rescued them, fatally wounding a policeman in the process.

The 'smashing of the van' was the first significant act of Irish revolutionary violence on British soil and was followed within weeks by the first Fenian bomb explosion in Clerkenwell prison in London which killed several people. In October, amid widespread anti-Irish feeling, three men, William Allen, Michael Larkin and Michael O'Brien, were sentenced to death for the policeman's murder. Despite appeals for clemency, they were publicly hanged in Salford prison on 23 November. Their deaths gave the Fenians that priceless political commodity: popular martyrs. As thousands mourned their deaths at home and abroad, the Manchester Martyrs were assumed into the republican pantheon alongside Emmet and Tone.

The abortive 1867 Fenian revolt was more than a mere reaffirmation of the separatist republican faith. It refocused the minds of British politicians on Ireland's unresolved grievances to an unprecedented degree and prompted Liberal leader William Gladstone (1809–98) to pledge himself to the pacification of Ireland, following his general election victory of 1868. Gladstone's objective was to restore the faith of Catholic Ireland in the existing institutions of the Union by redressing Catholic and peasant grievances and undermining support for the militant separatism of the Fenians. He moved first to disestablish the Church of Ireland, which by now represented a mere fifth of the Irish population. The 1869 Irish Church Act specified that the Church of Ireland should become a voluntary body from 1871 and disendowed it of its holdings and property. The state grant to the Catholic seminary at Maynooth and the Presbyterian *regium donum* were also abolished. Although all three Churches received capital sums in compensation, no amount of money could alleviate the deep sense of betrayal felt by conservative Irish Anglicans, for whom disestablishment represented the first breach of the Union and a portent of the eclipse of Protestant ascendancy in Ireland by the advancing tide of Catholic nationalism.

Gladstone turned next to the thornier issue of Irish land reform. His 1870 Land Act sought to improve landlord–tenant relations by regularising the 'Ulster custom'. This was the first time the government had actively intervened on behalf of Irish tenants and showed Gladstone's willingness to change part of the machinery of Union in order to maintain the overall structure. Though radical in theory, in so far as it implicitly acknowledged the Irish tenant's moral, if not legal, right to his property, the Act had little practical impact on the lives of the peasantry. Indeed, if anything, it increased their impatience for more substantial reforms. The third aspect of Gladstone's positive Irish policy, and the one that proved least effective, was his attempt to redress Irish educational grievances. In 1873 he introduced an Irish Universities Bill, which sought to establish a new, national, non-sectarian University of Dublin, but the proposal was defeated in the Commons with the help of Irish Liberal MPs, a defeat which contributed to Gladstone's resignation and eventual replacement by Benjamin Disraeli's Conservative ministry in 1874.

If Fenianism delivered a significant stimulus to the 'greening' of Gladstonian Liberalism, it was also influential in revitalising Irish constitutional nationalism. In May 1870 Isaac Butt (1813–79) formed the Home Government Association in Dublin to agitate for a limited measure of Irish self-government. Butt, a Donegal-born Protestant barrister, began his political career as a Tory unionist but developed a respect for the political integrity, though not the violent methods, of revolutionary nationalists as a result of his experiences as defence counsel to accused Young Irelanders in the 1840s and Fenians in the late 1860s. He saw a constitutional home rule movement as the most effective means of curbing Fenian militancy and protecting his class interests against radical political and social change. As such, Butt's association, which was transformed into the Home Rule League in 1873, was essentially conservative in character, a point underlined by the fact that his proposed federalist arrangement of an Irish parliament, subject to Westminster, but with control over domestic affairs, was far less radical than O'Connell's earlier demand for the repeal of the Union. Butt's movement also lacked the mass appeal of O'Connell's campaign and never gained the wholehearted support of Protestant unionists or Catholic nationalists.

Despite this, home rulers scored a number of by-election victories in the early 1870s and won a surprising fifty-nine seats in the 1874 general election. While the result indicated the emerging trend of Irish political opinion, these delegates did not as yet constitute a cohesive parliamentary grouping, as their commitment to the home rule issue was complicated by their support for other causes. The parliamentary disparateness of the Irish MPs was exacerbated by Butt's ineffectual leadership, which soon alienated the more radically minded nationalists within the movement. In 1877 two disaffected MPs, Joseph Biggar, a Belfast Fenian, and Charles Stewart Parnell (1846–91), a Protestant Wicklow landlord, defied their leader and embarked upon a systematic campaign of parliamentary obstruction.

This involved delaying the passage of legislation by prolonging debates and proposing numerous amendments and adjournments, all of which was intended to exasperate Westminster politicians into confronting the issue of Irish home rule. Though this combative tactic appalled Butt, a sincere respecter of parliamentary manners, it won Parnell widespread popular support and led to his election as president of the Home Rule Confederation of Great Britain in 1877. It was in such circumstances that the man who was to become the greatest leader of nationalist Ireland since O'Connell arrived on the political stage.

THE FENIAN-PEST.

HIBERNIA. "O MY DEAR SISTER, WHAT *ARE* WE TO DO WITH THESE TROUBLESOME PEOPLE?"
BRITANNIA. "TRY ISOLATION FIRST, MY DEAR, AND THEN———"

5.1 'The Fenian-Pest', Tenniel, *Punch*, London, 3 March 1866

As a result of the artistic persistence of John Leech and other cartoonists, the caricatured figure of the apelike Irishman had become fixed in the minds of many middle-class readers of English comic weeklies by 1860. After this date, the stereotypical Irishman assumed a more thoroughly simian and unhuman appearance in many cartoons, especially those of John Tenniel (1820–1914), who became chief *Punch* cartoonist on the death of Leech in 1864, and drew the principal weekly cartoon until his retirement in 1901. Tenniel, who was also famous as the original illustrator of *Alice in Wonderland*, did not just simianise Irish republican revolutionaries, he turned them into grotesque, man-eating monsters. This was no mere personal whim on his part; rather, it represented a direct response to the armed threat to British authority in Ireland posed by the Fenian campaign for independence in the mid–1860s.

This 1866 cartoon is a classic example of its kind. Drawn at a time when Fenian activity was causing the Dublin authorities real concern, it shows the martial figure of Britannia advising her distraught sister Hibernia on how to deal with the irascible Fenian monster. The clue to the advice is in the cartoon title, a play on rinderpest, a disease which was widely prevalent among livestock in the mid–1860s and attracted much public attention. In the case of diseased cattle, the recommended treatment would have been 'isolation' followed by slaughter.

As in so many Tenniel cartoons, Irish male bestiality is contrasted with exemplary, if anguished, Irish femininity, a symbolic attempt to draw a distinction between the decent, loyal Irish majority and the degenerate, disaffected minority. Implicit also is the imperial message that defenceless Hibernia is in need of Britannia's 'protection'. Over a century later, *Fortnight* cartoonist Blotski wittily parodied this *Punch* cartoon in an ironic comment upon the contemporary Anglo-Irish relationship (see cartoon 14.18, p. 292).

ST. GEORGE AND THE DRAGON.

5.2 'St George and the Dragon', Proctor, *Judy*, London, 9 October 1867

5.3 'St Dragon and the George', Morgan, *Tomahawk*, London, 12 October 1867

Judy was a Conservative comic weekly which began publication in 1867 and continued until 1907. As its name implies, it was established as a rival to *Punch*, and closely modelled its style and format on that of its competitor. It took a similar view of revolutionary Ireland also, as the cartoon opposite vividly shows. It appeared at a time of widespread anti-Irish feeling in Britain, prompted by the bold rescue of two Fenian prisoners in Manchester in which a policeman was killed. As if no single image was adequate to express his utter revulsion for Irish separatism, John Proctor (1836–98), *Judy*'s principal artist until 1880, demonised Fenianism as a bizarre hybrid of human, ape, reptile and winged monster. The heroic Saint George, the embodiment of British law and order, is nevertheless shown to have the upper hand, suggesting that the cartoon was meant to reassure readers at the same time as it terrified them.

Three days after the *Judy* sketch appeared, an arresting counter-cartoon was published in the *Tomahawk*, a short-lived satirical magazine edited by Matt Morgan (1839–90). In a striking reversal of Proctor's image of British good triumphing over Irish evil, Morgan shows a murderous, scaly man-monster named 'Fenianism' about to slay England's fallen protector, thus conveying a less sanguine view of the prospects of defeating this dragon.

THE FRUITS OF FENIANISM—JOHN BULL FEELING THE STRAIN.

5.4 'The Fruits of Fenianism . . .', *Weekly News*, Dublin, 12 October 1867

The Dublin *Weekly News* was founded in 1860 by A.M. Sullivan (1830–84), a journalist who later became a nationalist MP. Although he opposed Fenian militancy, Sullivan was nevertheless highly critical of the harsh treatment of Irish prisoners following the Manchester and Clerkenwell outrages. His *Weekly News* was one of the few Irish newspapers which carried cartoons that were critical of the British government's handling of the Fenian threat. This drawing shows a sturdy Fenian revolutionary tying a frightened John Bull to a tree by a stream. The political commentary is provided by four figures on the opposite bank, representing the opinions of America, France, Prussia and Russia. Britain and France had long been European rivals. Prussia, recently victorious in its war with Austria, was now playing the 'game' of extending its hegemony over the other German states. The Russian game was to appropriate parts of the ailing Turkish empire, particularly in the Balkan region. All optimistically regard Fenianism as having succeeded in paralysing the government and delight in John Bull's reversal of fortune: 'He was always telling our subjects to rebel, and now he has rebellion at home. How the fellow roars.'

"IT IS DONE!"

MANCHESTER, NOVEMBER 23, 1867.

5.5 'It Is Done!', O'Hea, *Weekly News*, Dublin, 30 November 1867

This cartoon is an early drawing by John F. O'Hea (1850–1922), who went on to become one of the most accomplished Irish cartoonists of his generation. It is a stark and striking evocation of the execution of the Manchester Martyrs, Allen, Larkin and O'Brien, who were hanged for murder in Salford on 23 November 1867. By casting Britannia as a fierce and merciless murderess, who has slain the three men and left Erin weeping in her wake, O'Hea graphically conveys the sense of sorrow and anger felt by many nationalists at Britain's actions. The following year Sullivan himself was sentenced to six months in prison for a *Weekly News* article in which he protested against their execution.

AFTER THE ROBBERY.

5.6 'After the Robbery', Boucher, *Judy*, London, 11 August 1869

In marked contrast to *Punch*, the Conservative *Judy* was appalled at the disestablishment and disendowment of the Irish Church. This cartoon by William Boucher (1837–1906), *Judy*'s leading cartoonist between 1868 and 1887, views the 1869 legislation as an act of gross embezzlement. It depicts Gladstone and John Bright toasting their successful plunder of Irish Protestantism and sharing the spoils of victory with their arch co-conspirator, the Pope. Here is another appeal to the anti-Catholicism which was still popular among the British electorate in the 1860s.

A SOP FOR CERBERUS.

5.7 'A Sop for Cerberus', Boucher, *Judy*, London, 2 March 1870

The 1870 Land Act was Gladstone's first attempt to improve the rights and conditions of the Irish tenantry. Though it brought about little socio-economic change, *Judy* was nevertheless deeply critical of its putative radicalism, as this cartoon demonstrates. It pictures a gladatorial but frightened Gladstone casting his 1870 Bill to Cerberus, the three-headed hound which guards the entrance to Hades in Greek legend. Two of the three heads are simianised, signifying that this beast is a Fenian progeny, while the third resembles Cardinal Paul Cullen. Thus, violence and religion are depicted as inextricably linked elements of the Irish problem. Nearby, a land agent bearing a summons for rent arrears lies dead. The implication is that Gladstone is conceding not to justice but to intimidation, and is thereby undermining the authority of the landlord, and perhaps even condoning murder. The phrase 'a sop to Cerberus' means a propitiatory gesture.

THE IRISH "TEMPEST."

CALIBAN (RORY OF THE HILLS). "THIS ISLAND'S MINE, BY SYCORAX MY MOTHER, WHICH ,THOU TAK'ST FROM ME."—*Shakspeare*.

5.8 'The Irish "Tempest"', Tenniel, *Punch*, London, 19 March 1870

This Tenniel cartoon recasts the Anglo-Irish relationship in 1870 as a scene from Shakespeare's *The Tempest*, a play about power, exploitation and colonisation. In the play, Prospero, the civilised magician–prince, governs Caliban, whose island he has usurped and whom he regards as a savage and obdurate slave. Prospero seeks to civilise Caliban, but in the process gives him a new weapon, language, which he uses to curse, threaten and ultimately rebel against Prospero. In Tenniel's allegory Caliban is transformed into a composite monster called 'Rory of the Hills', the mythical fomenter of Irish rebellion 'who always warns before he kills'. This Irish Caliban is an amalgam of the evil forces labelled on his tunic: 'Ribandism', 'Orangeism', 'Fenianism' and 'Ultramontanism' (the acceptance of supreme papal authority). It is striking that Orangeism, which was staunchly Protestant, is considered to be as threatening as the three Catholic forces. Gladstone (Prospero) regards Caliban sternly, armed with his Land Bill staff and holding Hibernia (Miranda) in a protective embrace. Once again, the Irish male symbolises all that is degenerate and anarchic, the Irish female, all that is pure, cultured and in need of protection. The cartoon, like the play, warns that the coloniser must be constantly alert to the treachery of the colonised.

HOME-(RULE)-OPATHY.

IRELAND. 'Ah, sure, thin, it's cruel bad I am, intirely; and it's the dacent Gentleman here knows the stuff to do me good!'
DR. BULL. 'No, no, Friend Butt!—None of your nostrums! We saw her well through the 'Repeal' Fever,—and she'll come out of this all right yet!'

5.9 'Home-(Rule)-Opathy', Tenniel, *Punch*, London, 11 July 1874

The 1874 general election witnessed a dramatic breakthrough for Irish home rulers, who won 59 of the 103 Irish seats at Westminster. This new parliamentary 'third force' neglected to capitalise on its electoral mandate, however, and the issue of home rule remained of marginal concern to the vast majority of the British electorate and their elected representatives. The leader of the home rulers, Isaac Butt, failed to win support either from Disraeli's Conservative government or from the Liberal opposition. In this Tenniel cartoon Butt is cast as a practitioner of homeopathy, an alternative form of medicine which was attracting considerable public attention at the time. Homeopathy prescribes that a substance which produces symptoms of a disease in a healthy person can be used to cure that disease in a sufferer. Thus, Butt advocates home rule as a homeopathic remedy for Ireland's ills, but is contradicted by Dr Bull, who claims that the orthodox treatment which cured Ireland's 'repeal' fever in the 1840s will prove equally effective in the 1870s. The cartoon's politics are firmly pro-Union and show little sympathy for Butt's constitutional proposals.

JOHN BULL GOING HALF WAY IN THE HOME RULE QUESTION.

ISAAC BUTT (to John Bull)—You see, My Dear Sir, our Request is very moderate. Our Demand is expressed in these few words . . . 'Integrity of the Empire and a Local Irish Parliament.' That's the Whole of our Desire. Our Loyalty to Her Majesty's Throne, quite as much as our patriotism, impels us . . . the Conservative class . . . to make this Demand. Grant our Request, and you'll Beat off the Revolutionists!

JOHN BULL—No, no; I can't Grant your whole demand. But I'll go Half Way . . . You can have 'Integrity of the Empire.' You have always stickled for this; and I am sure you will, as a 'loyal' man, appreciate the concession.

5.10 'John Bull Going Half Way . . .', *Irish World*, New York, 12 December 1874

The *Irish World* was a radical New York newspaper founded in 1870 by Patrick Ford, a Galway-born immigrant. Ford was a strong supporter of Fenianism and his newspaper quickly established itself as the influential voice of nationalist Irish-America. From an early stage cartoons played a central role in conveying the newspaper's political message, and this 1874 sketch is indicative of Ford's trenchant critique of the politics of Irish constitutional nationalism in the 1870s. Isaac Butt is mocked for the moderate, almost apologetic nature of his home rule demand, which he carefully qualifies by stressing his imperial loyalty, class conservatism and commitment to constitutionalism. His impotence is made to seem all the greater by the duplicitous nature of John Bull's response, as he disingenuously agrees to a partial concession to Butt by granting 'Integrity of the Empire', which, of course, amounts to an effective rejection of Irish self-government. An accompanying verse underscored the ineffectualness of Irish constitutional agitation:

> You ask for 'Home Rule' and you kneel
> Before the throne, the scorn of men;
> The Saxon spurns you with his heel,
> And sends you howling to your den . . .

JOHN BULL— '... I tell you I *must* get into the House, I've got a lot of Bills to push on to-night.'

MR. BIGGAR— '... You made a rule yourself that no work should be done in the House after half-past twelve at night—if anyone made an objection. 'Twas always your way to keep the Irish business late, and you thought this little plan of yours would shut it out altogether. Well, now it's half-past twelve, and *you've* got *your* work to do, and I say you shan't do it to-night.'

JOHN BULL—'... Come, now, you're only joking. The business of the Empire must.'—

MR. PARNELL—'The Empire must wait, unless Ireland gets fair play ... It's half-past twelve. Go, John, and get on your nightcap. There's not a bit of use in your waiting here.'

5.11 'Caught in His Own Trap', *Weekly News*, Dublin, 24 February 1877

In the late 1870s a minority of Irish MPs began to adopt obstructionist tactics at Westminster to disrupt parliamentary business and frequently brought it to a standstill. The underlying purpose of obstructionism was to inconvenience the House of Commons to such an extent that it would eventually see the sense of granting a separate legislature to Ireland. This cartoon shows the two leading obstructionists, Charles Stewart Parnell and Joseph Biggar, symbolically blocking John Bull's entry into the Commons. They point out that it is 12.30 a.m., the time set by the government after which parliamentary business could not proceed. John Bull is indignant that the 'business of the Empire' should be sabo- taged in this manner, but Parnell succinctly states the nationalist maxim: 'The Empire must wait, unless Ireland gets fair play'. On one famous occasion in 1875 Biggar spoke for almost four hours in order to delay the passage of a Coercion Bill for Ireland. Butt opposed the tactic, however, as did the British press, which lambasted the Irish obstructionists for their temerity.

Punch was among the sternest critics of obstructionism, as the Tenniel cartoon overleaf

SPARING THE ROD.

Dr. Northcote. "TAKE DOWN THEIR——WORDS!"
Mr. Punch. "'WORDS'! NONSENSE! BETTER TAKE DOWN SOMETHING ELSE, WHEN YOU *ARE* ABOUT IT!"

5.12 'Sparing the Rod', Tenniel. *Punch*, London, 11 August 1877

reveals. It shows four recalcitrant Irish MPs, all wearing dunces' caps, being arraigned before the headmaster, Sir Stafford Northcote. When Disraeli became Earl of Beaconsfield in 1876, Northcote became leader of the House of Commons, as well as chancellor of the Exchequer, which explains his role in this cartoon. Three of the obstructionists are identified by their Irish constituencies: Frank Hugh O'Donnell (Dungarvan), Parnell (Meath) and Biggar (Cavan). Northcote is prepared to 'take down the words' of the miscreants, but to Mr Punch's disgust, appears reluctant to beat them with the birch of 'suspension', that is, to suspend them from the Commons.

Though the effectiveness of obstructionism was reduced by formal changes to the procedural rules of the House in 1881, the tactic yielded significant political dividends for Parnell. It increased his prestige among radical Irish nationalists everywhere, especially in America, where it played an important part in facilitating his acceptance as the leader of this new form of nationalist agitation by the more militant Irish-American republicans.

6

THE LAND WAR
1879–1882

In the late 1870s an agricultural depression hit Ireland. Wet weather caused the failure of the potato crop in 1877 and 1879, with an inadequate recovery in the intervening year. The worst affected province was Connacht, which experienced another disastrous potato harvest in 1880. Near-famine conditions prevailed in some parts of the west, notably in County Mayo, where the potato failure had a serious impact upon the rural economy as a whole. The crisis was exacerbated by the fact that Britain was also experiencing an agricultural slump at this time, thus depriving many Connachtmen of their main supplementary source of income as migratory labourers in the harvest fields of England and Scotland.

Unable to pay rent, many smallholders were faced with eviction. The number of evictions trebled between 1877 and 1879, each one evoking grim memories of the Famine. Unlike their predecessors in the 1840s, however, the western peasants were in no mood to capitulate before an impending agricultural catastrophe. Nor were they prepared to relinquish their hard-won post-Famine gains. Organised tenant resistance grew in response to rising evictions, occasionally erupting into violent clashes with landlords, one of which resulted in the murder of Lord Leitrim, a wealthy Donegal landlord, in 1878. As this land agitation gathered momentum, it attracted the involvement of many Fenian activists and sympathisers, one of whom sought to translate this localised agrarian radicalism into a national political movement. His name was Michael Davitt (1846–1906).

Davitt was born to poor Mayo parents who were forced to emigrate to Lancashire in 1851 following their eviction during the Famine. He joined the Fenians while still in his teens and was sentenced to fifteen years' penal servitude for arms smuggling in 1870. Following his early release in 1877, he met with Parnell to discuss the prospect of political collaboration. Davitt then travelled to America, where he worked closely with John Devoy (1842–1928), the leader of the revolutionary republican organisation Clan na Gael, on a plan to unite the divergent strands of Fenianism, constitutional nationalism and agrarian agitation. The result was the so-called New Departure, whereby Devoy offered Parnell American Fenian support, including financial aid, on condition that he commit himself and the Irish Parliamentary Party to the pursuit of the twin goals of Irish self-government and peasant proprietorship. Though never formally accepted by the Fenian leadership or Parnell, the tacit coalition of Irish agrarian and nationalist interests had a powerful galvanising impact on the inchoate expressions of tenant discontent occurring in the west of Ireland in the spring of 1879.

In April of that year a protest meeting of tenant farmers held in the Mayo village of Irishtown succeeded in forcing a local landlord to reduce his rents and the land war began. Though absent from the Irishtown meeting, Davitt quickly placed himself at the head of this popular agitation by helping to found the Land League of Mayo in August. In October the Irish National Land League was established with Parnell as president and

Davitt as secretary. Parnell had an ambivalent attitude towards the league in so far as he was wary of the large Fenian element in its membership, yet attracted by the possibility of moulding its mass militant support to his own political ends. As for the league itself, its pithy slogan, 'the land for the people', was sufficiently vague to encompass a mixture of moderate and radical aims, some of which were mutually inconsistent: the reduction of rents, the protection of tenants, the abolition of landlordism, the achievement of the three Fs, and, ultimately, the establishment of peasant ownership. Some Land Leaguers contemplated even more fundamental agrarian reforms such as the proposal for the collection of land values by the state, a solution much favoured by the radical Davitt.

Land League agitation spread rapidly through southern parts of the country and even attracted the sympathy of Protestant farmers in Ulster, though it later came to be perceived by them as a nationalist front. Membership was not confined to impoverished small-holders; large tenant farmers also became actively involved, as did landless labourers, though it had little to offer them in real terms. Nor was the league's base exclusively rural; many shopkeepers and publicans supported tenant resistance, not least because of their economic dependence on the prosperity of farmers. The movement also enjoyed the moral support of the Catholic clergy and won substantial financial backing from Irish-American Fenians.

While the league was officially committed to non-violent, constitutional methods, in practice local activists perpetrated various forms of coercive violence on landlords and their agents, ranging from threatening letters and intimidation to physical assault and murder. The league's most celebrated weapon was the social ostracism of those who took over evicted farms. This tactic was originally christened 'moral Coventry' by Parnell, but a new and more enduring epithet was coined from the surname of the English-born Mayo land agent against whom it was successfully used in the autumn of 1880, Captain Charles Boycott. The co-existence of legal and illegal methods worried Parnell, who was continually faced with the problem of having to decide how far to endorse, ignore or repudiate the activities of league supporters.

As the frequency of evictions increased, so too did the levels of retaliatory violence. Gladstone's new Liberal government responded by passing coercion legislation and imprisoning Davitt in February 1881. Legislation of a more conciliatory kind followed in August in the form of Gladstone's second Land Act. This affirmed the principle of dual ownership by landlord and tenant, granted tenants the right of free sale and introduced arbitration courts to adjudicate in cases of disputed rent increases. In effect, the three Fs were conceded. The Act had only limited success, however, since it made no provision for the thousands of tenants who were in arrears with their rent, or for leaseholders.

Rural unrest continued and in October Parnell, who was now the leader of the Irish Parliamentary Party, was arrested and imprisoned along with other league leaders in Dublin's Kilmainham jail. In an unprecedented expression of Irish female politicisation, the Ladies' Land League, led by Parnell's sister Anna (1852–1911), assumed direction of the campaign in the absence of the male leaders. Anna, who espoused a more radical policy than her brother, was in favour of more extreme forms of civil disobedience, including an all-out rent strike. However, the apathetic rural response to this proposal, coupled with her brother's curt dismissal of her and her pioneering organisation on his release from prison, left her rightly sceptical about the true revolutionary potential of the league, which she later derided as 'a great sham'.

Meanwhile, the war escalated during the winter of 1881–82. Parnell, as a temporary tactic, issued a fruitless 'no-rent' manifesto from prison, directing tenants to begin a rent strike. The government responded by banning the league and intensifying its coercive measures, which in turn provoked further agrarian outrages. With rural anarchy looming, Gladstone and Parnell came to a mutual recognition of the need for compromise. The result was the Kilmainham 'Treaty' negotiated in April 1882. Gladstone agreed to amend the terms of the 1881 Land Act to include tenants in arrears and leaseholders, in return for which he received assurances from Parnell that he would use his influence to bring about an end to rural lawlessness and support Liberal reforms. Though the murder of Lord Frederick Cavendish, the new Irish chief secretary, and his under-secretary, Thomas Burke, in Dublin's Phoenix Park on 6 May overshadowed the announcement of the agreement, the Kilmainham accord effectively brought the land war to an end. Although agrarian agitation continued on a sporadic basis throughout the following two decades, tenant disaffection was never again so massively or so effectively mobilised.

The effects of the land war were numerous and far-reaching. It brought about a major change in the Irish landholding system by beginning the process of peasant ownership, which was continued by further Land Acts over the next twenty years, culminating in the Wyndham Act of 1903 (amended in 1909). By 1914, two-thirds of Irish farmers owned their land. Over the following fifty years, this massive transfer of land led to a great reduction in the number of traditional landlords, while, at the same time, other changes would lead to the virtual disappearance of the class of landless farm labourers. Yet 'the fall of feudalism', as Davitt famously termed it, did not alter the *nature* of landholding in Ireland, since land was consolidated in the hands of the owners as a result of the land war, not redistributed. This meant that the main beneficiaries of the crisis were the propertied classes, especially the strong farmers, a fact which underlines the socially conservative nature of the tenurial reforms. Nor did the land war bring about the desired Irish agricultural miracle, since the Land Acts were political in their ends, not economic. Thus, Irish farming remained as inefficient and uncompetitive after the land reforms as before.

The land war established Parnell as the dominant figure on the Irish political landscape. His skilful manipulation of the potentially destructive forces unleashed by the war gave him a popular appeal of regal proportions, as reflected in his metaphorical enthronment as 'the uncrowned king of Ireland', a title which had formerly been applied to O'Connell. He had adroitly walked the tightrope between the poles of constitutional and revolutionary agitation and managed to keep his political balance. Not only this, but his successful conjunction of nationalist and agrarian issues revitalised the home rule movement and gave it a crucially important social base among the Irish tenantry. Yet, as rural agitation abated and Catholic Ireland contemplated the significance of his – and its – victory in the summer of 1882, Parnell's ultimate political goal of Irish home rule lay as far away as ever. It was to the pursuit of this goal that he now turned, vigorously reasserting the primacy of constitutional agitation over agrarian activism.

6.1 'The New Patent Tenant-Crushing Machine', *Weekly News*, Dublin,
15 December 1877

This Irish cartoon is of particular interest because it appeared a year and a half before the
outbreak of the land war in 1879. It highlights the fact that the agricultural crisis which
precipitated the war had its origins in the economic conditions of the previous years and
indicates that the 1870 Land Act had failed to ameliorate the insecurity of Irish tenant
farmers. The wet summer and consequent poor harvest of 1877 left many tenants in arrears
with their rent and under threat of eviction. Landlords, many of them absentees, and their
agents showed little sympathy for the plight of their tenants, often using 'notices to quit' as
a threat to extract increased rent. The ruthlessness of such methods are savagely satirised in
this *Weekly News* cartoon, which presents us with a view of 'a new tenant-crushing and
rent-extracting machine' being operated by a rapacious land bailiff. The accompanying
prose satire adopts a Swiftian tone and perspective: 'The several landlords who have tried
it speak highly of its smooth and effective working; and the manufacturer expects to make
a fortune by the invention, believing that no well-managed Irish estate will be left long
without one of those useful articles.'

6.2 ' "Doing" Ireland', *Weekly Freeman*, Dublin, 4 October 1879

By the late 1870s, most Dublin newspapers had begun to publish weekly cartoons, many of which expressed much-needed Irish perspectives on political events. *Weekly Freeman* cartoons were among the most graphic and polemical of these. They devoted much attention to the grievances of Irish tenant farmers rather than those of landless agricultural labourers or urban industrial workers and, like most other periodicals of the time, tacitly assumed that the interests of Irish women were identical with those of Irish men. Furthermore, the farmers chosen for attention were relatively prosperous tenants of the south and east rather than the poor western smallholders, thus indicating the readership at which the paper was aimed.

   This cartoon satirises the duplicity of Irish landlords at the start of the land war. It depicts Sir Stafford Northcote, chancellor of the Exchequer in Disraeli's ministry, in conversation with two landlords, who have presented him with their report. The report gives a completely distorted picture of conditions in rural Ireland and conceals the reality of flooded fields and ruined harvests from Northcote. His request to see the situation for himself meets with an indignant response from the landlords, one of whom says: 'If you insist on doing so un-English an act as using your own eyes to view Irish interests, you will have the goodness to put on my spectacles, the glasses of which are of an agreeable rose tint, which prevents the landscape looking so confoundedly blue.'

RAISING THE—OLD MISCHIEF.

6.3 'Raising the Old Mischief', Boucher, *Judy*, London, 15 October 1879

The Irish land war operated at two levels. At a grassroots level, it comprised a struggle between landowners and peasants; at a political level, it involved a campaign to produce legislation which would ameliorate peasants' economic condition. The outbreak of the war in the late spring of 1879 prompted many London artists to revive traditional cartoon icons to deplore the bestial nature and irascible behaviour of the Irish. Cartoons 6.3 and 6.4 appeared at the start of this new wave of anti-Irish caricature, a few days before the National Land League of Ireland was established with Parnell as its president. Both denounce Parnell's involvement in the land movement, though with varying degrees of intensity.

Boucher's is the more condemnatory cartoon, showing 'Parnell's political petroleum' fanning the flames of 'disaffection' and 'ignorance' from which the spectre of murder emerges. *Judy* deplored the fact that a good deal of peasant violence was already taking place against landlords and their agents, as suggested by the top-hatted establishment figure who is shown fleeing from the fire. The gullible figure of Pat advances towards it, however, transfixed by the beckoning apparition. The restraining influence of the clergyman appears to be of little avail. The cartoon is notable for its far-fetched imputation of communistic motives to the Land League, an accusation which reveals more about the scaremongering tactics of *Judy* than the league's actual demand for the three Fs.

THE WRONG CARD.
Parnell's bad Lead at "*Beggar my Neighbour*."

6.4 'The Wrong Card', Sambourne, *Punch*, London, 18 October 1879

Punch's response to Parnell's Land League involvement is considerably less inflammatory, politically and metaphorically. Linley Sambourne (1844–1910) criticises Parnell's political judgement by suggesting that he has mistakenly chosen to play the knave of spades – drawn as the stereotypical Irish peasant, complete with whiskey, pistol and pig – rather than the queen of hearts – Victoria and the order and equanimity she represents. *Punch* would subject Parnell to much greater graphic indignities in the years ahead.

6.5 'The Land Thief's Claim', *Irish World*, New York, 17 January 1880

In the late 1870s the *Irish World*, which by now had a weekly circulation of almost twenty thousand in Ireland, came out strongly in favour of the Land League. Its editor, Patrick Ford, was involved in organising and fundraising activities for the league's American branches, and the newspaper itself featured much pro-league propaganda. The cartoon overleaf expresses the rationale behind the League's activities. It features a confrontation between a John Bull-ish landlord and a sturdy, decent-looking Irish tenant farmer, the antithesis of the simian caricatures of *Punch*. The landlord is cast as a land thief who has no rightful claim to Irish land or Irish rents. The spirit of natural justice points up the message that the only just title to Irish land can come from God, not man, least of all an *English*

THE LAND THIEF'S CLAIM.

man. This polemical point was reinforced in a lengthy prose dialogue between the two protagonists which accompanied the cartoon, in which the farmer refutes the legitimacy of the landlord's title to Irish land on the grounds that it was unjustly appropriated from the native Irish during the Cromwellian period.

6.6 'The Irish Grievance Grinder . . .', Thomson, *Fun,* London, 6 October 1880

Fun was a London-based *Punch* rival which began publication in 1861. It was hostile to the aims of the Land League and frequently employed simian imagery to denigrate the actions of its members. The cartoon opposite satirises what it sees as the duplicitous nature of Parnell's involvement with Irish agrarian politics. It appeared shortly after he publicly endorsed the social and commercial ostracism of the enemies of the league at a speech in Ennis, County Clare. It ridicules his overt advocacy of non-violent, constitutional methods by insinuating that he is covertly inciting and controlling the underground violence of the league. J.G. Thomson's metaphor is both witty and memorable. Parnell is cast as an organ-grinder, a type of busking street musician commonly found in many late-

THE IRISH GRIEVANCE GRINDER
AND HIS MONKEY.

Victorian British cities, frequently accompanied by a performing monkey. Thomson found in this monkey a ready-made simian metaphor for the violent activities of the Fenian-infiltrated league, which the organ-grinder has harnessed for his own political ends. Significantly, however, here as in other cartoons, the cartoonist stops short of simianising Parnell himself.

The cartoon greatly simplifies the complexity and delicacy of Parnell's political position at this time. As the recently elected leader of the Irish Parliamentary Party at Westminster and president of the Land League in Ireland, he was trying to keep two very different groups working together – a relatively moderate constitutional movement and an increasingly violent agrarian movement with links to Fenianism. It required all his skill to achieve and maintain this difficult balancing act during the 1880s, and in the process avoid alienating possible British support for his political goals of immediate land reform and eventual home rule.

6.7 'Shutting Them Up', Thomson, *Fun*, London, 15 December 1880

6.8 'The Irish Question . . .', Thomson, *Fun*, London, 19 January 1881

As agrarian agitation reached its climax in the winter of 1880–81, Gladstone, prime minister since April 1880, came under increasing pressure to take tough action to curb rural lawlessness in Ireland. His chief secretary for Ireland, W.E. Forster, was a strong advocate of coercion as the best means of curtailing the activities of the Land League. He recommended

SHUTTING THEM UP.

Mr. Bull:—'LET YOU ATTEND TO YOUR PARLIAMENTARY
DUTIES? NO, THANK YOU; I'LL JUST HAND YOU OVER AS A
CHRISTMAS PRESENT TO JUSTICE.'

THE IRISH QUESTION.—ADVICE GRATIS.

'HANG THEM ALL; LET THEM ALONE; SIT ON THEM; GIVE
THEM ALL THEY WANT,' &c., &c.

that the league leaders be prosecuted for conspiring to pervert the course of law in Ireland and inciting unrest. That *Fun* endorsed such measures is clear from the first Thomson cartoon, which shows a powerful John Bull vigorously cramming a protesting Parnell into a chest, having earlier disarmed him. As Parnell correctly prophesied, agrarian violence would recur on a greater scale without his controlling influence.

The second sketch welcomed Gladstone's announcement of his government's intention to introduce a Coercion Bill and a Land Bill in the queen's speech of January 1881. It depicts the prime minister besieged by advisors, all offering contradictory advice. The most prominent of these are Forster and John Morley, an influential Liberal journalist who later became an important Liberal politician and who was sympathetic to Irish grievances. Gladstone is silent, regarding them all with an imperious stare, yet concealing behind his back a Coercion Bill for use if necessary.

6.9 'Which will he give her?', O'Hea, *Pat*, Dublin, 19 March 1881

In the 1870s a number of Dublin-based comic weekly and monthly magazines emerged which were aimed at an educated, urban middle-class readership. Though most proved short-lived and none emulated the success of London's *Punch*, they nevertheless brought to the fore a number of talented Irish cartoonists who produced work high in artistic quality and political wit. *Pat* (1879–83) was one such magazine and John O'Hea was one such artist, one of whose early cartoons has already been seen in chapter five (see p.71, 5.5).

The O'Hea cartoon opposite appeared two weeks after Gladstone's 1881 Coercion Act became law and shortly before an Arms Act banned the possession of weapons in proclaimed districts of Ireland. At the same time, a more conciliatory response to agrarian

WHICH WILL HE GIVE HER?

agitation was being prepared in the form of the Land Bill, which came before parliament on 7 April. The cartoon shows Erin gagged and bound to the stake of coercion against a landscape of rural eviction, while Gladstone considers which shamrock he will give her. His choice is a stark one between the three Fs, which were the Land League demands, and the 'sham' three Fs of force, famine and failure, which *Pat* suggests have been the traditional misguided responses of British governments to Irish land agitation. Five months later, in August 1881, *Pat*'s hope that Gladstone would choose the better shamrock was realised when his Land Act effectively granted the rights of fair rent, free sale and fixity of tenure to the Irish tenantry.

PUTTING TO THE TEST.

Mr. GLADSTONE.—Well, Mr. Pat, I have brought the Bill to you at last, in order that
you may have an opportunity of examining it during the vacation. It cost me a deal of
trouble, and I hope it will satisfy you.

PAT—Yes, William, I *will* examine it most carefully. I have lately studied a little political
chemistry, and as most things which I have got from across the water have been largely
adulterated with selfishness and injustice, I intend to put the Bill to the severest tests,
which you see I have at hand.

6.10 'Putting to the Test', *Pat*, Dublin, 2 April 1881

This *Pat* cartoon appeared five days before Gladstone introduced his Land Bill in parliament. It shows a sweating prime minister delivering his new Bill to a dapper Irish tenant
farmer for his consideration. Pat promises to subject the Bill to various political 'tests' in
order to determine whether it meets the demands of the Irish tenantry. Later that same
year, after the Bill became law in August, Gladstone's handiwork was put to a much more
rigorous legal 'test' by Irish farmers at Parnell's behest. The *Weekly Freeman* cartoon
opposite, almost certainly by the same unknown artist, refers to Gladstone's admission
when introducing his Land Bill on 7 April that he had drafted it under 'powerful influ-
ences'. The cartoon suggests that Land League militancy was the most compelling of these,
by showing a truculent tenant farmer threatening an anxious prime minister with league

THE GENIUS OF THE BILL.

6.11 'The Genius of the Bill', *Weekly Freeman*, Dublin, 16 April 1881

violence as he drafts the Bill in honeyed ink. Seven months earlier, in a speech in County Clare, Parnell told his peasant audience that 'the land question must be settled, and settled in a way that is satisfying to you' if they persist in their activism, energy and determination to resist government coercion. The wastepaper basket contains discarded copies of Gladstone's previous failed attempts to resolve the Irish land problem.

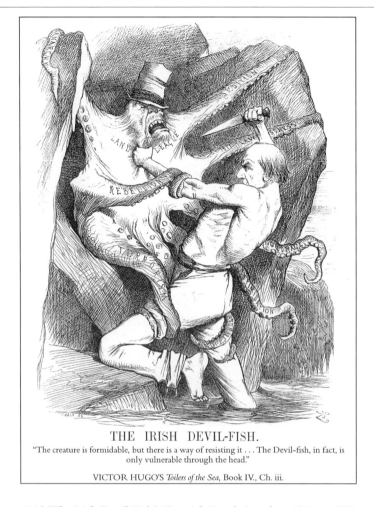

THE IRISH DEVIL-FISH.
"The creature is formidable, but there is a way of resisting it . . . The Devil-fish, in fact, is
only vulnerable through the head."

VICTOR HUGO'S *Toilers of the Sea*, Book IV., Ch. iii.

6.12 'The Irish Devil-Fish', Tenniel, *Punch*, London, 18 June 1881

This is another Tenniel variation on the theme of the revolutionary Irish beast. Here the
Land League becomes a demonic octopus, complete with simian head, whose tentacles en-
wrap a tenacious Gladstone. The accompanying Hugo quote suggests that the monster
will only be destroyed if the leadership is removed. Four months later Parnell and other
league leaders were arrested and the league outlawed.

6.13 'The Most Recently Discovered Wild Beast', Boucher, *Judy*, London, 3 August 1881

Opinion was divided within the Land League over how to respond to Gladstone's second
Irish Land Bill. Parnell criticised it for its inadequacy, though he recognised that it con-
ceded the three Fs, while falling short of granting peasant proprietorship. Radicals such as
Davitt rejected it more thoroughly, as did the influential Irish–American wing of the land
movement, many of whom called for a 'no-rent' campaign. Meanwhile, more extreme
American Fenians were lending their support to the militant tactic of 'skirmishing', their

THE MOST RECENTLY DISCOVERED WILD BEAST.

term for random guerrilla attacks in Britain. Between January and June 1881 several bombs exploded in British cities, causing damage to buildings but no loss of life. Much of the money and materials for this campaign came from Irish-Americans, and it is this which prompted Boucher to produce this arresting cartoon.

It features the caged 'Irish-American Dynamite Skunk', the Fenian bomber in bestial form, which policeman John Bull has put on public display. The cartoon's setting is derived from the fact that late-nineteenth-century European explorers discovered many hitherto unknown species of animals in Africa and Asia, some of which were paraded before an eager British public in cages and zoos. Here, a feminised Gladstone holds up an infant Irish Land Bill to feed this 'recently discovered' beast a biscuit entitled 'concession to violence'. This alludes to the Conservative criticism of Gladstone's Bill as a capitulation to agrarian terrorism, a charge which *Judy* echoed. Meanwhile, the demonic creature is reviled by Irish peasants, one of whom tears up a copy of the *Irish World*, which came out in favour of the dynamite campaign. The relatively unsimianised appearance of these peasants marks them out as loyal, law-abiding subjects who deplore the violence perpetrated in their name by their sub-human American cousin.

"AVAUNT AND QUIT MY SIGHT."

SPIRIT OF ASSASSINATION.—Try *This*.

ERIN.—Away fiend, I will never use such an abominable weapon as that.
Let me perish first. My cause is just, and with the arms of justice and virtue,
and with them alone, will I advance it.

6.14 'Avaunt and Quit My Sight', *Pat*, Dublin, 6 August 1881

This cartoon represents the disapproving attitude of the majority of Irish nationalists towards the Fenian bombing campaign in Britain in the first half of 1881. The campaign was
organised by three maverick American-based Fenians, Jeremiah O'Donovan Rossa,
Thomas Gallagher and William Lomasney, and involved the use of comparatively
recently invented dynamite to attack military barracks and significant public buildings.
Both the IRB and Clan na Gael opposed the dynamiters, whose tactics were aimed at
striking terror into the government. *Pat* displays its abhorrence of such militancy by
depicting the dynamiters as a skeletal 'Spirit of Assassination' who proffers Erin the tools
of terror. She steadfastly refuses this 'abominable weapon' and reaffirms her commitment
to the force of moral argument rather than the argument of physical force. In the background a mass of protestors files past, a reminder that the majority of Irish people support
'legitimate agitation' as the most effective means of nationalist resistance.

Further dynamiting took place in 1884, when Lomasney was killed trying to blow up
London Bridge, and 1885, when a bomb caused extensive damage to the chamber of the
House of Commons. Over one hundred years later, in February 1991, the IRA sought to
emulate their Fenian ancestors in an audacious mortar bomb attack on 10 Downing Street.

A CLEAN SWEEP.

6.15 'A Clean Sweep', Thomson, *Fun*, London, 26 October 1881

The passage of the Irish Land Act in August 1881 did not end Irish agrarian disturbance. Parnell advised his parliamentary followers to abstain from voting in the critical parliamentary division on the Bill. The following month he persuaded the Land League to 'test the Act' by taking cases to the land courts, confidently predicting that these test cases would expose the hollowness of Gladstone's legislation. He was also under political pressure to be seen to be upholding the fight against the British authorities in Ireland. The vehemence of his public opposition to the Act prompted the government to arrest him on 13 October and incarcerate him in Kilmainham jail, where he was later joined by five other leading agitators. One week later the league was suppressed. This resolute government action was the inspiration for this *Fun* cartoon, which shows Gladstone and Forster forcefully sweeping away the refuse of the league. In reality, Irish unrest was not so easily disposed of, as the leaders' arrests resulted in increased agrarian violence.

A BE LEAGUERED POSITION

BOTHERED BRITISH MINISTER—Well, I shall never understand this country. No sooner have I with the
greatest trouble bound one League that others immediately start up at my feet. These surely are the most League-al
people in the universe; they will certainly drive me into a lunatic asylum or the House of Lords.

6.16 'A Be Leaguered Position', *Pat*, Dublin, 19 November 1881

Following the imprisonment of the leaders and suppression of the Land League in October
1881, the Ladies' Land League assumed control of the land movement. This organisation
had been formally established in January of that year by Anna Parnell, at the instigation of
Michael Davitt. It brought together a remarkable group of radical female activists in what
was the first movement of its kind to emerge in Ireland. Initially, the ladies concentrated
their energies on providing moral and material support for evicted families, but after the
removal of the male leadership, Anna's tactics became more radical. The league's growing
activism and support for an all-out rent strike led to it being proscribed on 16 December,
but the women continued their resistance campaign, despite arrests and harassment by the
authorities. Meanwhile, the imprisoned Parnell was growing increasingly concerned about
the women's militancy and independence, and on his release in May 1882 he set about dismantling the Ladies' League, which was eventually dissolved in August.

This *Pat* cartoon portrays the Ladies' Land League as a powerful new force in Irish agrarian politics. As such, it contrasts with the disparaging reaction of many leading British and
Irish newspapers, which attacked female activists for contravening the Victorian codes of
feminine 'respectability'. The cartoon shows a confident representative of the Ladies'
League advancing towards an alarmed Gladstone. Behind her the ghost of an eighteenth-
century Volunteer, presumably Henry Grattan, carries the flag of home rule, suggesting
that if he were alive today he would support the Parnellite cause. The figures of Parnell
and another man, possibly Davitt, may be discerned in the shadows, both bound to a stake.
The implication is that British coercion of Ireland is destined to prove counter-productive
as long as underlying grievances remain unresolved.

7

THE HOME RULE CONTROVERSY
1882–1893

Parnell's shift from agrarian to political agitation was formally marked by the establishment of the Irish National League which replaced the Land League in October 1882. This organisation had as its primary objective the achievement of national self-government by constitutional means, with land law reform relegated to a list of subsidiary aims. Over the next three years the National League became a highly efficient political machine which Parnell used to transform his parliamentary following into the first modern Irish political party, and home rule into a national movement.

The third Reform Act of 1884 was an important contributory factor in this transformation. This Act increased the Irish electorate to around 740,000 by adding more than half a million men to the voting register. Many of these new voters, especially the small farmers and labourers, flocked to Parnell's party which by 1885 had come to embody the political aspirations of Catholic nationalist Ireland. Parnell himself gave eloquent expression to these aspirations in one of his most famous speeches, delivered in Cork in January 1885, when he proclaimed that

> no man has the right to fix the boundary to the march of a nation. No man has a right to say to his country, 'thus far shalt thou go and no further', and we have never attempted to fix the *ne plus ultra* to the progress of Ireland's nationhood, and we never shall.

At Westminster Parnell maintained an independent opposition to both major parties, while simultaneously remaining open to the possibility of a tactical alliance with any faction which might further his cause of Irish legislative independence. Such an opportunity presented itself in June 1885 when Parnellites combined with Conservatives to defeat Gladstone's Liberal government in a Commons budget vote, after which Lord Salisbury (1830–1903) formed a caretaker administration, pending a December general election. Attempts to extract a pre-election commitment to Irish home rule from either Salisbury or Gladstone proved fruitless, however, as both leaders maintained a studied vagueness on the issue. In the end Parnell came out in favour of the Tories, encouraged by their recent conciliatory Irish policies, and with memories of Liberal coercion still fresh in his mind.

The result of the 1885 election could hardly have been more momentous for nationalist Ireland. In what was essentially a referendum on home rule, Parnellites won an astonishing eighty-six seats (including one in Liverpool), Irish Liberal representation disappeared completely, and Irish Conservatives were reduced to a rump of sixteen pro-Union MPs overwhelmingly concentrated in the north-eastern part of Ulster. Home rulers now held the balance of power at Westminster between the Liberals with 335 seats and Conservatives with 249. With British political minds focused intensely on the Irish question, the Liberal leader's son, Herbert, suddenly announced on 17 December that his father had been 'converted' to the principle of home rule for Ireland. While there was obviously an element of political calculation in Gladstone's decision, it also contained a strong measure of that moral conviction which had shown itself in his 1869 Church Act. But to seek to refine the machinery of Union was one thing; to suggest that the whole structure might be dismantled, quite another.

Gladstone's political conversion precipitated a dramatic and durable realignment of forces within the Anglo-Irish political nexus. Whereas Parnellites gratefully embraced the Liberals and secured Gladstone's appointment as prime minister for a third time in February 1886, Conservatives reaffirmed their commitment to maintaining the integrity of the Union. In an age of empire, Ireland became an issue upon which they could unite, as Salisbury's succinct statement confirmed: 'Ireland must be kept, like India, at all hazards; by persuasion, if possible; if not, by force.' Some English Tories adopted a more belligerent unionist stance, notably Lord Randolph Churchill (1849–95), an ambitious young Conservative with leadership aspirations. He saw in the developing crisis an opportunity for political self-advancement and decided that if Gladstone tried to introduce Irish home rule, 'the Orange card would be the one to play'.

Playing the Orange card meant tactically exploiting Ulster Protestant opposition to rule by a Dublin parliament dominated by Catholic nationalists. As the nationalist demand for legislative independence grew ever more vociferous in the 1880s, so too did resistance to home rule among Protestant Conservatives in Ulster, the only province where they were in a majority. Ulster Protestant attachment to the Union was rooted in a complex amalgam of factors. In the post-Union period Ulster Protestants' distinct sense of cultural identity was overlaid by an emotional attachment to the trappings and traditions of the British crown, which they came to perceive as part of their common British inheritance.

This loyalism was further underpinned by an economic faith in the material benefits of the empire. By the late nineteenth century north-east Ulster had developed into the most prosperous part of Ireland, its economy founded on the linen, shipbuilding and engineering industries of Belfast and its hinterland. This industrial wealth, which was concentrated in Protestant hands, was highly dependent upon Britain and the empire for its raw materials and markets. Hence, many Ulster businessmen and workers feared that home rule would jeopardise their economic prosperity and imagined a bleak future where, as Arthur Balfour prophesied in 1893, 'the wealthy, the orderly, the industrious, the enterprising portion of Ireland' would be dominated by the 'less orderly, less industrious, less enterprising and less law-abiding' portion.

Deep-seated religious anxieties also played a part in Ulster's opposition to home rule. Undimmed historical memories of the Protestant massacres of 1641 and 1798 meant that the fear of popery was never far from the Ulster Protestant mind. More recently, the widespread Protestant unease generated by the disestablishment of the Church of Ireland in 1869 was deepened by the unmistakably Catholic character of agrarian and Parnellite agitation, all of which led many Ulster Protestants to conclude that home rule would mean Rome rule. Whereas class, regional and denominational divisions had conspired to divide Ulster Protestants heretofore, the gravity of the situation in the mid-1880s forced the disparate groups to cohere into a united anti-home-rule movement, which formed the basis for the formal political organisation known as Ulster unionism.

In January 1886 Belfast Conservatives formed the Ulster Loyalist Anti-Repeal Union to co-ordinate a campaign of resistance to home rule. They were joined in protest by members of the Orange Order which underwent a popular revival in the early 1880s and received an influx of members from all social classes. What was once an almost exclusively working-class body was now transformed into an organisation to which lords, labourers and landed gentry belonged. A key figure in both organisations was Edward Saunderson (1837–1906), Tory MP for North Armagh, who arranged a series of public meetings in early 1886 to stir popular Protestant opposition. The meetings culminated in a massive gathering in Belfast's Ulster Hall on 22 February at which Churchill pledged that 'Ulster at the proper moment will resort to the supreme arbitrament of force', and gave unionism its enduring rallying cry: 'Ulster will fight and Ulster will be right.'

Such inflammatory sentiments inevitably heightened sectarian tension in the city and contributed to the eruption of rioting in June. In the longer term, Churchill's intervention laid the foundation for an alliance between unionists in Britain and Ulster which was to have far-reaching implications for future Anglo-Irish relations. His militant theme was quickly taken up by Saunderson, who was instrumental in moulding Ulster Conservative MPs at Westminster into a distinct parliamentary grouping which vehemently opposed Gladstone's first Home Rule Bill, introduced in the Commons on 8 April 1886.

The Bill proposed the establishment of a two-tier Dublin parliament which would have responsibility for a limited range of domestic Irish affairs, with the imperial parliament retaining control over such matters as foreign policy, trade and defence. Irish representation at Westminster would cease, though the country would continue to contribute to imperial expenditure. British Conservatives joined Ulster unionists in opposing the Bill, while Parnell and his party welcomed it as a modest devolutionary measure which could be extended at a later date. But the most decisive opposition originated from within Gladstone's own party.

Liberal dissent came from two main factions, one led by the Whig Lord Hartington (1833–1908), the other by the radical Joseph Chamberlain (1836–1914). Both men saw in Irish home rule the seeds of separatism and the disintegration of the empire. When, on 8 June, a vote was taken, ninety-three Liberals voted against the government and the Bill was defeated by thirty votes. A historic opportunity to resolve the Irish question had been squandered and Gladstone's prophetic words went unheeded: 'Ireland stands at your bar expectant, hopeful, almost suppliant . . . Think, I beseech you, think well, think wisely, think, not for the moment, but for the years that are to come, before you reject this bill.'

He immediately called an election in which Irish home rule was the central issue. His devolutionary plans were comprehensively rejected by the English electorate, however, though Wales and Scotland returned home rule majorities. The Conservatives returned to power, supported by the dissident Liberals, now reconstituted as the Liberal Unionist Party. Salisbury's government remained in office until 1892, during which time Irish home rule languished with the Liberal–Parnellite alliance on the opposition benches.

The events of 1885–86 had a lasting significance for politics in Ireland, north and south. Not only did these years witness the birth of modern Irish political parties, they also established the basic framework within which the territorial and constitutional conflicts which culminated in the partition of the island in 1920 were played out. The new geographic and demographic contours of Irish democracy were revealed, as the clear emergence of two distinct, mutually antagonistic movements, nationalism and unionism, polarised Irish politics along religious grounds. From now on denominational affiliation became the key determinant of political allegiance, obscuring social, class and regional differences. With very few exceptions, to be Catholic in Ireland was to be nationalist, to be Protestant, unionist. This correlation between religion and politics was particularly intense in Ulster because of the evenly divided nature of the Protestant/unionist Catholic/nationalist divide there, which became visible in the mid-1880s and changed little in the following two decades. Thus, the roots of the Ulster problem are deeply embedded in the political developments of 1885–86.

The late 1880s was a time of mixed political and personal fortunes for Parnell. With home rule postponed indefinitely, nationalist attention in Ireland reverted to the issue of land reform. Agrarian agitation was renewed in the autumn of 1886 in the form of the Plan of Campaign, whereby tenants on various estates organised a series of co-ordinated rent strikes. Though the campaign was spearheaded by two of his acolytes, Parnell himself disapproved of it, seeing it as a distraction from the larger political objective of self-government. Meanwhile, a series of articles appeared in *The Times* in the spring of 1887 accusing Parnell of Fenian conspiracy and purporting to show that he had condoned the Phoenix Park murders of 1882. The judicial commission which was set up to inquire into the affair eventually exonerated him and exposed the allegations as false in a report published in February 1890. Parnell had little time to savour this public vindication of his political integrity, however, as a much graver crisis was already upon him.

In December 1889 Captain William O'Shea filed a petition for divorce from his wife, Katharine, naming Parnell as co-respondent. The couple had been lovers since 1880 and had lived together, with O'Shea's knowledge, since 1886. When the case came to court in November 1890 Parnell did not contest the divorce because he wanted to marry Katharine. Consequently, the evidence submitted about his private life went unchallenged. Victorian society on both sides of the Irish Sea was scandalised by the lurid revelations which emerged, and Parnell's reputation was seriously damaged.

Moral outrage was especially strong among English non-conformists, who comprised the bedrock of Liberal support in Britain. A dismayed Gladstone realised that if Parnell did not resign, his own leadership would become untenable and home rule would be jeopardised. However, his request that Parnell relinquish his party leadership, even temporarily, in order to save the Liberal alliance met with an intransigent response. The Irish leader's stubbornness led in turn to an acrimonious split within his own parliamentary party, the majority of whom rejected him in order to preserve the alliance.

Parnell responded by appealing to the people who had once acclaimed him as their king. He spent much of 1891 in Ireland, campaigning intensively on behalf of Parnellite candidates in three by-elections, all of whom were defeated. Exhausted and in ill health, he returned to Brighton where he died unexpectedly on 6 October 1891, aged forty-five, with Katharine, his wife of four months, at his side. Five days later, over two hundred thousand mourners lined the streets of Dublin to honour the man who had embodied their dream of political autonomy and dignified the quest to realise it. In the nation as a whole a collective sense of guilt seemed to prevail, as people came to terms with the premature death of Ireland's uncrowned king.

Parnell's influence on Irish nationalism was both divisive and unifying. His immediate legacy was a bitterly divided Irish Parliamentary Party which remained fragmented until 1900 when it was reunited under John Redmond (1856–1918). At a more fundamental level, however, Parnell forged a powerful sense of Irish nationhood and bequeathed a potent legacy of expectation to the next generation of Irish nationalists, the great majority of whom carried on the tradition of parliamentary agitation for home rule which he so brilliantly revitalised.

The Irish Parliamentary Party, as we shall see, eventually recovered from the traumas of the 1890s, and by 1914 had succeeded in placing home rule on the statute book, only to have its implementation deferred by the outbreak of the First World War. In the ensuing hiatus, the Parnellite legacy was spectacularly and unexpectedly eclipsed by the minority Fenian tradition of non-constitutional, revolutionary nationalism, which achieved its apotheosis in the 1916 rising. By then Parnell's fate had assumed legendary proportions in the Irish historical consciousness, his memory lionised by writers like W.B. Yeats and James Joyce, who saw in his demise a tragedy of epic dimensions and mythologised him as a prophet betrayed by craven minds.

It was also Parnell's achievement to establish the issue of Irish home rule at the centre of *British* politics, and its importance did not end with his death. Gladstone was returned to power in 1892 with home rule high on his legislative agenda, despite the fact that the Irish Parliamentary Party was now hopelessly split between anti-Parnellites, who were in the great majority, and Parnellites. A second Home Rule Bill was introduced early in 1893 with somewhat different provisions from its predecessor. It received a small Commons majority in September but was overwhelmingly rejected by the large unionist majority in the Lords a week later. In March 1894 Gladstone, aged eighty-four, resigned as prime minister and was succeeded by the imperialist Lord Rosebery (1847–1929). When Rosebery's ministry was replaced by a Conservative-dominated government in 1895, a decade of Tory rule began, during which time home rule was, in Salisbury's words, left to sleep 'the sleep of the unjust'.

7.1 'The Irish National Platform', *Weekly News*, Dublin, 21 October 1882

The Irish National League was founded by Parnell on 17 October 1882 to replace the suppressed Land League. Its formation signalled Parnell's decision to prioritise constitutional nationalism over semi-revolutionary agrarianism and the emergence of home rule as the Irish Parliamentary Party's principal demand. One of the most important functions of this new organisation was to provide the Irish party with a strong constituency structure, an essential prerequisite for the Parnellite electoral success of 1885, by which time the National League had over 1,200 branches. The nationalist *Weekly News* welcomed news of the league's inauguration with cartoon 7.1. It depicts leading members of the Irish Parliamentary Party busily involved in the construction of this new 'national platform' under the adroit supervision of Parnell. He himself symbolically stands on the central plank of 'self government', while his co-workers nail the supporting beams into position. Among the workmen are William O'Brien, John Dillon, Tim Healy and Michael Davitt. The whole edifice is supported by trestles marked 'justice' and 'right', clearly indicating the fundamental principles underpinning Irish nationalist demands.

7.2 'Up Hill Work!', *Weekly Irish Times*, Dublin, 12 January 1884

Throughout 1882 and 1883 Parnell concentrated his energies on building the National League into a disciplined political organisation, capable of mobilising mass support behind his home rule campaign. His efforts received a timely boost in 1884 when the third Reform Act was passed, greatly extending the Irish male electorate from about 230,000 to approximately 740,000. The rather snobbish cartoon (7.2) from the *Weekly Irish Times*, a newspaper with unionist sympathies, adapts the Sisyphus image to represent Gladstone's struggle to secure the passage of the Act. Gladstone, one of whose favourite physical recreations was wood-chopping, is weighed down by a bundle of chips on his shoulder, an oblique reference perhaps to the factionalism which then existed within his Liberal Party. Ahead of him, the face of Lord Hartington, one of the more Whiggish of his Liberal followers, blocks the path of his franchise reforms, while behind him lies the abyss of 'dissolution' into which the Liberal government is in danger of falling if he fails. Curiously, an affluent-looking tenant farmer Pat refuses to co-operate because he fears the effect the increased enfranchisement of the English working class, represented by four stereotypical figures, might have upon the electoral fortunes of Irish home rule.

GIVING HIM A "CROPPER."

Man in the Gap.—'I told you that if you attempted to take that jump I
would trip you up—And there you are!!'

7.3 'Giving him a "Cropper" ', *Weekly Freeman*, Dublin, 20 June 1885

In May 1885 Gladstone decided that coercion was again necessary in Ireland. This naturally provoked the resentment of the Irish Parliamentary Party, which resolved to bring down the government in the hope that a Conservative administration might prove more amenable to their wishes. On 8 June the Parnellites voted with the Tories over an amendment to the budget and the government fell. This turn of events was the occasion for the Irish cartoon 7.3, which shows Gladstone being knocked from his horse by a piqued Parnell. The bars of the fence refer to the two issues on which the Parnellites opposed the Liberals, coercion in Ireland and the budget proposal to increase the duty on spirits. Though the first issue was obviously of paramount importance, it should be remembered that distillers and publicans constituted an important element of Irish Parliamentary Party support in Ireland.

7.4 'The Serenade', *Weekly Freeman*, Dublin, 26 September 1885

An immediate general election was not possible in June 1885 because the new voting registers necessitated by the 1884 electoral reforms were not yet compiled. Thus, the Tories, under Lord Salisbury, formed a minority government with Irish Parliamentary Party support. During the summer months, Parnell held secret, inconclusive talks with government ministers Lord Carnarvon, the lord lieutenant, and Lord Randolph Churchill on the issue of Tory support for a home rule settlement. The Liberals were equally keen to win Irish Parliamentary Party support and Gladstone indicated that he was willing to grant a limited form of Irish self-government if returned to power in December.

The wooing of the Irish vote in the build-up to the election is the subject of cartoon 7.4. Gladstone and Sir Michael Hicks Beach, chancellor of the Exchequer, are cast as a pair of itinerant ballad-singers, raucously competing for Erin's affections with songs from their respective manifestos. Both are shown to be striking discordant notes, however, and drowning out the dulcet tones of a handsome Parnell, Erin's true love. Having listened to the Liberal and Conservative repertoire, Parnell eventually decided he liked the latter better, and issued a call on 21 November for the Irish in Britain to vote for Conservative candidates.

THE IRISH "VAMPIRE."

7.5 'The Irish "Vampire"', Tenniel, *Punch*, London, 24 October 1885

The next two striking cartoons constitute a classic example of the Anglo-Irish propaganda war which was occasionally fought out in the pages of the London and Dublin comic weeklies. Tenniel's depiction (7.5) of the National League vampire, bearing the features of Parnell, about to attack a defenceless Hibernia received a swift riposte from the cartoonist of the *Pilot*, a short-lived Dublin comic magazine. The unknown Irish artist casts

THE ENGLISH VAMPIRE

7.6 'The English Vampire', *Pilot*, Dublin, 7 November 1885

Hibernia (7.6) in a much more defiant pose, ready to slay the startled vampire of 'British Rule' with the shield and sword of the National League, an image which reflects the widespread faith in Parnell and his party to further the aspirations of nationalist Ireland in the forthcoming election.

7.7 'The Political Graveyard', *Weekly News*, Dublin, 12 December 1885

The December 1885 general election, the first to be held since the franchise reforms of the previous year, transformed the Irish political landscape. The Irish Parliamentary Party's massive total of eighty-six seats was gained at the expense of the Liberals, who were wiped out completely in Ireland, and the Conservatives, whose Irish representation shrank to sixteen MPs, almost all of whom were returned for Ulster constituencies. The *Weekly News* cartoon opposite celebrates the Parnellite victory by gleefully depicting the burial of the enemies of Irish nationalism. The first gravestone marks the death of the Irish Loyal and Patriotic Union which was founded in May 1885 to co-ordinate resistance to home rule. It failed to attract widespread popular support, however, and took only one seat (Trinity College, Dublin) in the election. The second grave commemorates the death of Liberalism in Ulster, an event of which John Morley later said that 'the whole of the Liberal candidates in Ulster fell down as dead men'. The third grave contains the remains of the

THE POLITICAL GRAVEYARD.

'nominal home rulers', that is, those former Liberals who had espoused the cause of home rule in order to ensure their political survival in Ireland. The only mourner who is clearly identified is the *Express* newspaper, whose unionist sympathies were anathema to the nationalist *Weekly News*.

The *Weekly Freeman* welcomed the Irish Parliamentary Party's election success with commensurate glee. Cartoon 7.8 refers to the fact that Parnell now held the balance of power between the two major British parties at Westminster. It shows Salisbury and Gladstone approaching 'Boxkeeper' Parnell for 'tickets for Treasury Seats', that is, for government. Whereas it is not clear what Salisbury is willing to pay, Gladstone is only prepared to offer the meagre amount of 'local self-government', as recently proposed by Joseph Chamberlain, rather than the separate parliament which Parnell was demanding.

Salisbury and G.O.M. together.—Give me a Ticket for Treasury Seats. What's to pay?
Boxkeeper.—Legislative Independence of Ireland is the price.
Both.—Bless me, you have raised the price enormously—I thought a much smaller sum would secure a place.
Boxkeeper.—No, gents, nothing short of that sum will do—You see we have added to our company many new members, and our price has gone up accordingly.

WHICH WILL PAY!!!

7.8 'How We Three . . .', *Weekly Freeman,* Dublin, 12 December 1885

To the consternation of both, however, the ticket-master insists on full legislative independence for Ireland as the price of Parnellite support. The question, 'which will pay?', received a dramatic answer five days after this cartoon appeared, when Gladstone's son Herbert unexpectedly announced his father's conversion to home rule.

7.9 'Mr Parnell . . .', *Weekly News,* Dublin, 30 January 1886

Gladstone's public conversion to home rule in December 1885 provoked a reflex reaction in the Conservative Party, which immediately saw the advantages of uniting in opposition to that cause. Salisbury reaffirmed his caretaker government's commitment to the Union in the queen's speech on 21 January 1886 and five days later he announced his intention to introduce coercion legislation to suppress the National League. Liberals and Parnellites were already conspiring to bring down the government, however, and they succeeded in a vote on an issue unrelated to Ireland in the queen's speech in the early hours of 27 January. Salisbury's ministry resigned and Gladstone became prime minister again with the support of the Parnellites. The cartoon opposite shows Parnell wielding his new-found

MR. PARNELL. (To Lord Salisbury).—"You put down your foot upon Home Rule, did you? Well, my fine fellow, you'll have to take it up again very much faster than you put it down."

parliamentary power, in the form of the eighty-six Irish nationalist MPs, over Salisbury, who had attempted to crush the home rule movement four days earlier. At the time, the Irish leader's parliamentary influence was at its height; subsequent events determined that he would never again enjoy such a commanding position in British politics.

7.10 'Lord Randolph Churchill . . .', *Weekly News*, Dublin, 27 February 1886

As the prospects of a Home Rule Bill increased following Gladstone's *démarche*, the fears of Protestant Ireland grew. Political tension was particularly acute in Ulster, the most Protestant of the Irish provinces. Unionist resistance coalesced around the renascent Orange Order and the Ulster Loyalist Anti-Repeal Union, formed in January 1886. In Britain, the thrusting young Tory radical Lord Randolph Churchill saw in this Ulster opposition an opportunity to damage the new Liberal government, defeat home rule and so preserve the integrity of empire. He therefore set about forging an alliance between English conservatism and Ulster unionism, despite the fact that he had only recently written disparagingly of the 'foul Ulster Tories who have always ruined our party'. In February he travelled to Belfast and made a militant speech to a packed Ulster Hall, in which he fanned the embers of sectarian animosity and conjured up the spectre of civil war.

WEEKLY NEWS.

Lord Randolph Churchill leads on the Demon of religious strife to do the work of Hell in the North of Ireland.

This *Weekly News* cartoon graphically conveys the inflammatory nature of Churchill's intervention in Irish politics by showing him directing the devil to incite bigotry and sectarian hatred throughout Ulster. The cartoonist's fears were borne out later that year when Belfast experienced some of the worst sectarian violence in Ireland that century, which left fifty people dead and several hundred injured. Churchill, father of Sir Winston, went on to become chancellor of the Exchequer in the new Conservative government in 1886, but resigned his post in December following a dispute with Salisbury. His determination to play 'the Orange card' in 1885 was an important factor in bringing about the defeat of home rule later that year and exacerbating tensions which have plagued British and Irish politicians ever since.

7.11 'Much Too Tempting . . .', Boucher, *Judy*, London, 3 March 1886

Gladstone's detractors – of whom *Judy* was one of the most virulent – were quick to accuse him of opportunistically conceding home rule in order to secure a third term in office in 1886, with Irish Parliamentary Party support. Hence this unflattering depiction of the Liberal leader as a greedy rodent unable to resist the bait of office in the home rule trap set by a gloating Parnell. The suggestion that the 'Grand Old Man' had made a Faustian pact

MUCH TOO TEMPTING A BAIT FOR THE G.O.M.

with Parnell was an unduly harsh judgement, however, as there seems little doubt that Gladstone had become genuinely convinced of the merit of Irish home rule and was prepared to devote the remainder of his political career, and the political fortune of the party which he had largely created, to the attainment of this goal. In so doing, he was pitching himself against enormously powerful opponents in the British establishment, all of whom united around the 'patriotic' issue of the integrity of the empire.

7.12 'The Conspirators' Chorus . . .', Reigh, *United Ireland*, Dublin, 22 May 1886

Gladstone introduced his Home Rule Bill to a packed Commons on 8 April 1886. The following day, the radical Liberal MP Joseph Chamberlain resigned from the cabinet in protest, citing his concern for 'the honour and influence and integrity of the Empire' as his reason. Chamberlain's resignation precipitated a split in the Liberal Party over the home rule issue which proved to be the decisive factor in the Commons vote in June, when ninety-three disaffected Liberals – later known as Liberal Unionists – voted with the Tories and the Ulster unionists to defeat the Bill.

Not surprisingly, the opponents of Gladstone's Bill were vilified in the Irish nationalist press. Special animus was directed against the dissenting Liberals, or the 'Chamberlain Invincibles' as they are labelled in this graphic cartoon by J.D. Reigh which appeared in *United Ireland*, the newspaper founded by Parnell in 1881. It shows the chief anti-home-rule 'conspirators' about to take a blood-oath to destroy Gladstone and his party. Their name is a direct reference to the Irish revolutionary group which stabbed to death Cavendish and

Burke in the Phoenix Park in 1882. In addition to Chamberlain himself, the other prominent plotters are Sir George Trevelyan, Sir Henry James, George Goschen, Lord Hartington and the diminutive Randolph Churchill, the leading Tory unionist. Trevelyan eventually returned to the Gladstonian camp; the other Liberals did not.

7.13 'The Loyal Minority', *Weekly News*, Dublin, 19 June 1886

The defeat of the first Home Rule Bill on 8 June 1886 led to the outbreak of serious sectarian rioting in Belfast. Protestant and Catholics fought each other over several days, and police intervention resulted in the deaths of seven people and the wounding of several others. Many Catholic workers were driven from the shipyards and linen mills and there was widespread looting and house burnings. Sporadic rioting continued during the summer months and by the time it subsided in September, over fifty people had been killed and hundreds wounded.

The Irish cartoon opposite reflects the way in which this violence was perceived by the three British politicians who had done most to defeat Gladstone's home rule proposals. Tory leader Salisbury and his minister Churchill delight at the sight of the 'loyal'

WEEKLY NEWS.

IRELAND

THE LOYAL MINORITY.

MARQUIS OF SALISBURY.—'Churchill, your Ulster Chivalry are behaving splendidly. The loyal manner in which they are beating the police, murdering Catholics, burning houses, and plundering whiskey shops, is magnificent.'

CHURCHILL.—'Yes, I knew they would act on the hints and suggestions I gave them. This will be a great help to us at the coming elections.'

CHAMBERLAIN.—'England can never be ungrateful to those noble fellows. They have made it quite clear that I was right in saying Ulster ought to have a parliament of her own.'

Protestant minority's violent actions, from which they expect to make political capital in the forthcoming general election. Joseph Chamberlain takes an equally sanguine view of the rioting, seeing it as a vindication of his proposal during the home rule debate that Ulster be given a separate legislature. The cartoon's satire reflects the dismayed reaction of nationalist Ireland to the defeat of Gladstone's Bill and the prevailing view that Ireland had been shown to be a mere pawn in the game of domestic and imperial British politics. It also conveys nationalists' resentment that so-called Ulster loyalists can indulge in open acts of violence and destruction under the benign gaze of British Conservatives and Liberal dissidents.

7.14 'Kündigung', *Kladderadatsch*, Berlin, 20 June 1886

British politics, and particularly the fate of Ireland, occasionally attracted the attention of continental cartoonists in the late nineteenth century. This cartoon, 'Notice', which comes from the Berlin weekly satirical magazine *Kladderadatsch*, represents a German perspective on the fate of Gladstone's Home Rule Bill. It shows a tenant of the 'lower House' of the British parliament protesting to Gladstone, the landlord, that home rule was 'not in the contract' – in other words, that there was no clear Liberal commitment to home rule at the general election of December 1885. Gladstone, holding a note marked 'dissolution', tells the tenant that he can go, with effect from the end of June, implying that the prime minister will seek a new tenant as a result of the election. The underlying assumption that Gladstone would remain as prime minister proved to be unfounded.

THE BIRMINGHAM CAT'S PAW.

7.15 'The Birmingham Cat's Paw', Reigh, *United Ireland*, Dublin, 10 July 1886

The general election of July 1886 did not give any party a clear overall majority, but the Liberal Unionists were prepared to give a measure of external support to the Conservatives, who were thus able to form a government. This Irish cartoon cleverly comments on this outcome through Aesop's fable of the cat's paw. Salisbury, the monkey, is shown using the paw of Chamberlain, the cat, to retrieve the hot coal of power from the fire, while an alarmed British bulldog looks on. Chamberlain, whose political power base was in Birmingham, had hoped to return to the Liberal ranks, and is therefore clearly uneasy about his manipulation by his new political master. In fact, he never did rejoin his erstwhile colleagues and went on to become a minister in a later Conservative administration.

— Ils disé tous que l'Ile Sœur n'être pas attachée à moà... Infâme calomnie!

7.16 'Ils disé tous...', Draner, *Le Charivari*, Paris, 4 April 1887

Much French opinion in this period was bitterly hostile to Britain, and the plight of Ireland attracted considerable public sympathy. In this cartoon from the leading Parisian satirical journal, a sadistic Britannia seeks to repudiate the 'infamous calumny' that her 'sister island' is 'not attached to me'. As Draner vividly shows, England's sovereignty over Ireland is not only absolute, but also despotic. The curious spelling of some of the French words seems to be the cartoonist's way of representing an English accent.

DISMEMBERMENT—A MIDSUMMER DAY'S DREAM.

7.17 'Dismemberment . . .', Boucher, *Judy*, London, 27 July 1887

This *Judy* cartoon helps to explain the determination with which many Britons resisted home rule, even though Ireland was a considerable expense and a political embarrassment to the British government. A sleeping Gladstone is visited in a dream by representatives of three parts of the United Kingdom, namely, a demure Welshwoman, a kilted Scotsman and an Irish pig, each wearing the crown of national independence. Their presence is a source of pain and anguish to a severely disabled John Bull, who has lost three of his limbs. Boucher conveys the apprehension felt by many in Britain that Irish home rule would trigger a political chain reaction in other parts of the United Kingdom, leading the Scots and Welsh to demand their own parliaments also. Indeed some observers feared that conceding home rule to Ireland might encourage British colonies overseas to agitate for self-government, thus heralding the dismemberment of empire and the eclipse of Britain as a world power.

STRANGE BEDFELLOWS.

"Fortune makes us acquainted with strange bedfellows."

7.18 'Strange Bedfellows', Lex, *Union*, Dublin, 11 February 1888

Fears that the granting of home rule to Ireland would threaten the integrity of the United Kingdom and of the British empire were felt by unionists in Ireland as well as in Britain. Such fears were frequently the subject of cartoons in the *Union*, a short-lived Dublin magazine of the late 1880s which, as its title suggests, espoused a staunchly anti-home-rule line. Most of its cartoons were drawn by 'Lex', the pseudonym of Richard Moynan (1856–1906). This Moynan sketch from 1888 depicts a morose Gladstone in bed with the two *bêtes noires* of Irish unionism, a simian Fenian separatist and a sombre Catholic bishop. The latter represents the embodiment of the unionist fear that home rule would mean Rome rule, as does the cat of disestablishment above the Liberal leader's head. Thus the cartoon conjures up a unionist vision of a home rule Ireland, where power would be in the hands of bishops and bombers. The cartoon's sub-title misquotes Shakespeare's *The Tempest*: 'Misery acquaints a man with strange bedfellows.'

PENANCE!

"HIS HONOUR ROOTED IN DISHONOUR STOOD,
AND FAITH UNFAITHFUL MADE HIM FALSELY TRUE."—TENNYSON.

7.19 'Penance!', Tenniel, *Punch*, London, 9 March 1889

In March and April of 1887 the London *Times* published a series of articles entitled 'Parnellism and Crime' which accused Parnell and members of his party of having conspired in agrarian crime during the land war, including the Phoenix Park murders. The newspaper's trump card was a letter purporting to prove that Parnell himself approved of the killing of Cavendish and Burke in May 1882. The intention was to discredit the integrity of the Irish leader and the cause he stood for, and so wreck the alliance between the Liberals and the Irish Parliamentary Party. Parnell refuted the allegations and called for the establishment of a select Commons committee to clear his name. Instead, the Tory government set up a special judicial commission to investigate and, Salisbury hoped, prove Parnell's guilt. Such hopes were dashed in February 1889 when the commission exposed a Dublin journalist named Richard Pigott as the forger of the incriminating letters. Both *The Times* and the government, whose attorney-general acted as prosecutor in the case, were humiliated, whereas Parnell emerged with his reputation enhanced.

This *Punch* cartoon reflects the ignominy suffered by *The Times* as a result of its attempt to discredit the Irish leader. The newspaper appears embarrassed and crestfallen, holding a candle of apology which lights up news of Pigott's confession. The whole affair seriously damaged the paper's reputation for accuracy and impartiality and led to a drop in circulation. Further 'penance' came in February 1890, when it was forced to pay £5,000 and costs as a result of the libel action brought against it by Parnell. The quotation from Tennyson, the much-read poet laureate of the time, alludes to Sir Lancelot's affair with Queen Guinevere, to whom he was 'falsely true'. This adultery led to the ruin of King Arthur's court and its high ideals. Is it possible that Tenniel had some inkling of Parnell's adultery, and could he have guessed that it would soon spell ruin for the Irish leader and his cause?

UNDER WHICH FLAG?

7.20 'Under Which Flag?', *United Ireland*, Dublin, 6 December 1890

Within months of Parnell's exoneration by *The Times* commission, the personal crisis which was to destroy his political career began. On 24 December 1889 Captain William O'Shea initiated divorce proceedings against his wife Katharine, Parnell's mistress of nine years. His motive was mainly financial; Katharine's wealthy aunt had recently died, leaving her a vast inheritance, to which O'Shea felt partially entitled. Parnell did not contest the adultery charges when the case came to court in November 1890, and the verdict went against him. Despite calls for his resignation from members of his own party and the Liberals, he was re-elected chairman of the Irish Parliamentary Party on 25 November. The following day, Gladstone, mindful of the damaging impact the adulterous revelations would have on the Liberal vote and therefore on the home rule cause, publicly called for him to stand down. Parnell denounced Gladstone in turn, thus jettisoning the Liberal alliance. This sent shock waves through the Irish Parliamentary Party, which assembled to debate the issue in Committee Room 15 of the House of Commons on 1 December.

HAIL TO THE CHIEF!

7.21 'Hail to the Chief!', Reigh, *United Ireland*, Dublin, 13 December 1890

Over the next five days seventy-three of the MPs tried in vain to reach a compromise. The split eventually occurred on 6 December, when forty-five walked out of the meeting, leaving Parnell with just twenty-seven parliamentary supporters.

Cartoons 7.20 and 7.21, which appeared within a week of each other in Parnell's *United Ireland*, are graphic testaments to the deep divisions which the dramatic developments in Committee Room 15 precipitated within both the Irish Parliamentary Party and the nation. The first appeared on the day the party split and shows a group of anti-Parnellites, including Tim Healy, Thomas Sexton and Justin MacCarthy, standing at 'the parting of the ways' with a despondent Erin. They point her in the direction of liberty, while a solitary Parnell encourages her to follow him in the opposite direction of 'dissension'. She has already decided to follow the former course, however, and has turned her back on him. The cartoon's criticism of Parnell's obstinacy was echoed in an article in the same edition written by the deputy editor Matthew Bodkin.

Four days later, on 10 December, an enraged Parnell led an attack on the Dublin offices of *United Ireland* and regained control of the paper. The second cartoon appeared three days after this event, and is predictably pro-Parnell. It is drawn by J.D. Reigh, the regular *United Ireland* cartoonist, who casts Parnell as a latter-day Saint Patrick. He is shown symbolically proclaiming his faith in his party's independence and Irish public opinion, while trampling underfoot the snakes of 'Whig treachery', 'sham home rule' and 'Liberal intrigue'. Taken together, these drawings highlight the frontline role of cartoonists in the propaganda war which was played out in the bitter aftermath of the Parnellite split.

THE TWO PARNELLS; OR, THE MAN BESIDE HIMSELF.
PARNELL THE PATRIOT AND PARNELL THE TRAITOR.

7.22 'The Two Parnells . . .', Thomson, *Fun*, London, 10 December 1890

London's *Fun* chose this striking conceit to represent the Parnellite split. The divisive impact of the Irish leader's stance is conveyed in an image of the patriotic Parnell confronting his traitorous, quasi-demonic *Dopplegänger*, who places his own self-interest above Irish self-government.

7.23 'Barred out at Kilkenny', *Irish World*, New York, 27 December 1890

Very soon after the Parnell scandal broke, a by-election was held in the constituency of North Kilkenny, which had long returned a nationalist MP. The campaign was one of the most acrimonious in living memory, as Parnellites and anti-Parnellites indulged in coruscating verbal attacks on each other, which sometimes spilled over into violence. On one occasion Parnell had lime thrown in his eyes by mineworkers, an incident which showed just how bitter the political and moral divisions had by now become. Parnellites insisted that loyalty to their leader took precedence over the dictates of British politicians and public opinion; anti-Parnellites, supported by the Catholic hierarchy, condemned him as a

BARRED OUT AT KILKENNY.

moral outcast who was unfit to be leader. The latter faction felt vindicated by the by-election result, which saw the anti-Parnellite candidate returned with a majority of over 1,100 votes.

This *Irish World* cartoon represents Parnell's by-election defeat in vivid terms. It shows the disconsolate leader walking away from his broken battering ram, which bears the name of Vincent Scully, Parnell's candidate, while an angry Erin rebukes him from the battlements of Kilkenny Castle. Parnell is accompanied by the diminutive, weeping figure of John Redmond, one of his staunchest supporters, whose ballad sheet is entitled 'Men of the Hillsides'. This is a reference to Parnell's by-election appeal to the revolutionary Fenians, 'the hillside men', as a possible alternative means of securing legislative independence if constitutionalism were to fail.

After the Kilkenny defeat, Parnell resolved to fight on, energetically launching himself into another by-election campaign in North Sligo. This also ended in defeat for the Parnellite candidate, as did a third contest in Carlow in July. In June he married his beloved Katharine, and spent the summer months commuting weekly between their Brighton home and Ireland. The marriage provoked intense condemnation from the Catholic hierarchy and the Dublin media, most of whom had now deserted him. On 6 October Parnell died unexpectedly in Brighton, aged forty-five. The internecine war within the Irish Parliamentary Party nevertheless continued until 1900, when Redmond reunited the party under his leadership and reinvigorated the parliamentary home rule campaign.

THE ULSTER GHOST—THE SAME OLD BOGIE!

Wullie.—" IS THIS A GENERAL RISIN' THE NOO OR ARE YE JUST HAVIN' A WEE BIT DAUNDER BY YERSEL'?"
—*After* DEAN RAMSAY.

7.24 'The Ulster Ghost . . .', Thomson, *Fun*, London, 18 May 1892

Gladstone's promise to introduce a second Home Rule Bill if returned to power in the 1892 general election renewed Ulster unionists' fears of forcible absorption into a nationalist Irish parliament. In the spring of 1892 the Ulster Loyalist Anti-Repeal Union began to mobilise opinion, culminating in an 'Ulster Unionist Convention' in Belfast on 17 June, at which twelve thousand delegates pledged their opposition to home rule. British Conservative politicians supported this unionist opposition, thus reviving the Tory–unionist alliance forged in 1885. *Fun*, which was at this time in a Liberal phase, makes light of Ulster unionist agitation and satirises Tory attempts to exploit it. It shows Salisbury manipulating the Ulster 'bogie' in the hope of intimidating Gladstone, who reacts with mild amusement to the spectre. An 'Ulster' was the name for a long loose overcoat of the kind shown here.

Ten months later, the Conservative *Judy* regarded developments with growing unease. The July 1892 election resulted in a victory for the Liberals. In Ireland, eighty-one home rulers were elected, only nine of whom were Parnellites. On 13 February 1893 Gladstone introduced his second Home Rule Bill in the Commons. It met with concerted unionist opposition in Ulster, where further mass demonstrations were held. In scenes reminiscent of 1885, several English politicians travelled to Belfast to encourage unionists in their

BUTCHERED.

BUTCHERED TO MAKE THE GRAND OLD MAN'S MAJORITY.

7.25 'Butchered', Parkinson, *Judy*, London, 8 March 1893

opposition, including Salisbury, Chamberlain and Arthur Balfour. Parkinson's cartoon reflects this prevailing sense of unionist doom. It portrays Ulster as an innocent martyr about to be sacrificed to the Liberal–Irish Parliamentary Party tiger at the stake of home rule. Emperor Gladstone gleefully anticipates the imminent slaughter, as do the jubilant icons of mercy and justice. As the Bill passed through the Commons during the summer months of 1893, the Conservatives continually stressed the problems of Protestant Ulster in the hope of destroying home rule for all of Ireland, while many Liberals glossed over unionist apprehensions. Neither side as yet contemplated the possibility that the solution to the Irish question might lie in some form of partition of the island.

"OUT YOU GO!"

7.26 'Out You Go!', Parkinson, *Judy*, London, 20 September 1893

Gladstone's second Home Rule Bill eventually passed the Commons on 1 September 1893 by a majority of thirty-four, but was crushed by the massive unionist majority in the Lords seven days later. The Liberal leader resigned as prime minister six months later, finally accepting that he had failed in his mission to 'pacify Ireland'. *Judy* welcomed the Lords' rejection of the Bill with this cartoon of Salisbury contemptuously kicking the tattered Bill down the steps of the Lords, to the delight of a smiling John Bull. This action by the Lords greatly angered the Liberals and disposed them to favour 'mending or ending' the powers of the upper House. Sixteen years later, the Lords' right of veto precipitated a major constitutional crisis which had profound implications for Ireland. Not only did the defeat of the 1893 Bill herald the end of Gladstone's long political career, it also brought to a close one of the most eventful decades in the history of Anglo-Irish relations.

8

THE NATIONALIST REVIVAL
1894–1912

Gladstone's retirement in 1894 marked the end of an era in Anglo-Irish politics. Without his energy and enthusiasm, the alliance between the Liberal and Irish parties began to disintegrate. The Liberals, increasingly beset by internal splits and schisms, lost much of their commitment to the Irish cause, while the Irish Parliamentary Party ended the century in a weak and fragmented state. The responsibility for solving the Irish problem now passed to the Conservatives, who were in power from 1895 to 1905. For much of this period the Tories adopted a conciliatory approach towards Ireland known as 'constructive unionism' or, more revealingly, 'killing home rule with kindness'. As this phrase suggests, the government hoped to undermine nationalist support for home rule by ameliorating some of the country's most pressing social and economic ills. Constructive unionism also represented a final attempt by the defenders of the Irish propertied classes to devise a settlement which would preserve something of their power and privilege. Its eventual failure sealed the fate of the Anglo-Irish ascendancy class as a political force in Irish life, leaving them, like their big houses, vulnerably isolated in a changing social and political landscape.

The first exponent of constructive unionism was Arthur Balfour (1848–1930), Irish chief secretary from 1887 to 1891. Whereas Gladstone saw legislative independence as the panacea for Irish unrest, Balfour proposed a dual policy of resolute government and radical reform, declaring: 'I shall be as ruthless as Cromwell in enforcing obedience to the law, but at the same time I shall be as radical as any reformer in redressing grievances and especially in removing every cause of complaint in regard to the land.' The first fruits of his pledge were the Irish Land Acts of 1887, 1888 and 1891, all of which he successfully piloted through parliament. In 1891 he also established the Congested Districts Board to ameliorate the economic problems of the west and south through the promotion of such measures as farm modernisation and local cottage industry.

Gerald Balfour, chief secretary of Ireland from 1895 to 1900, continued his brother's progressive economic policies by increasing the amount of money available for land purchase and overseeing the Local Government Act of 1898. The democratic reforms carried out under this Act brought about such a dramatic transfer of power from unionists to nationalists at a district council level that the result was a form of local home rule. Five years later, the policy of constructive unionism culminated in the Wyndham Land Act, which effectively completed the process of creating a peasant proprietorship and abolishing landlordism with the tacit consent of the beleaguered landowning class.

Though it brought about several far-reaching social and economic changes, constructive unionism ultimately failed to silence the nationalist demand for home rule. Whatever their material benefits, land purchase schemes and local government reforms were no substitute for legislative autonomy, the desire for which had, if anything, grown more intense during ten years of Tory rule. The nationalist revival of this period came, not from the faction-ridden home rulers, but from extra-parliamentary quarters. The late nineteenth and early twentieth centuries witnessed the burgeoning of a vibrant Irish cultural nationalism and the revitalisation of a moribund revolutionary separatism, both of which challenged the hegemony of constitutional nationalism, the former implicitly, the latter explicitly. The dividing line between cultural and political activism faded as intellectuals and revolutionaries came together in a plethora of literary and cultural societies, all seeking to forge a new spirit of Irishness and engender a popular reawakening of national consciousness. The result was a potent, mutually reinforcing bond between culture and politics, the nature of which was succinctly encapsulated in the advice given to the young W.B. Yeats (1865–1939) by the veteran Fenian John O'Leary: 'There is no great literature without nationality, no great nationality without literature.'

Irish cultural nationalism had its roots in the 1880s. One of the first and most popular manifestations of this phenomenon was the Gaelic Athletic Association, a national sporting organisation founded in 1884 with the aim of promoting native Irish sports such as hurling and Gaelic football. The GAA was an essentially rural movement with a distinctly anti-English sporting bias which made it attractive to more politically minded Irish separatists in the Fenian movement. The association consequently became a recruiting ground for militant nationalists, two thousand of whom formed a guard of honour at Parnell's funeral, bearing hurling sticks. This fusion of cultural and political nationalism was also a feature of the Gaelic League, in many ways the urban counterpart of the GAA. The league was founded by Douglas Hyde (1860–1949) and Eoin MacNeill (1867–1945) in 1893 for the specific purpose of reviving Irish as a national spoken language. Hyde, a Protestant scholar who became the first Irish president in 1938, saw language revival as the first step towards the 'de-anglicization' of the nation and the recovery of a distinct sense of Irish nationality.

Like the GAA, the league began as a non-political organisation, but quickly assumed a nationalist character and came under the formal political influence of the IRB in 1915, a move which prompted Hyde's resignation. Many Gaelic Leaguers went on to participate in the 1916 Easter Rising, including Patrick Pearse (1879–1916), whose vision of an Ireland 'not free merely, but Gaelic as well; not Gaelic merely, but free as well' was heavily influenced by the league's ethos.

Two events in the closing years of the century provided cultural and political separatists with a timely focus for the expression of their nationalist feeling: the centenary celebrations of the 1798 rising and the South African Boer War (1899–1902). IRB members and cultural activists were prominent in the establishment of 1798 commemorative committees, many of which also contained Irish MPs. Indeed, there was a rich irony in the spectacle of modern Irish constitutional nationalists commemorating the violent deeds of their militant republican ancestors. Those late-Victorian politicians might even have reflected that the government against which the 1798 rebels had taken arms was an Irish one with powers remarkably similar to those for which latter-day home rulers were clamouring.

The 1798 centenary was also celebrated thousands of miles away in Johannesburg by Irish soldiers, many of whom came to see in the Boer cause a reflection of their own anti-imperial struggle. Among those who organised the Johannesburg celebrations was Arthur Griffith (1871–1922), a young Dublin journalist and IRB member who, on his return to Ireland, recognised the need for a national organisation to co-ordinate the activities of the disparate nationalist groups, separatist and otherwise, then flourishing. The result was the Sinn Féin League established in 1907 and reconstituted as a national organisation in 1908 as Sinn Féin, meaning 'ourselves'.

Sinn Féin's central objective was the re-establishment, by non-violent means, of an independent Irish parliament in Dublin under the British crown. Griffith recommended that Irish nationalists withdraw from Westminster, constitute themselves as an Irish government and implement policies of economic protectionism to encourage industrial development. His policies failed to win popular support, however, and Sinn Féin remained a marginal force in Irish politics until its sudden resurgence after the 1916 rising. A key factor in its marginalisation was Griffith's failure to capture the middle ground between constitutional nationalism and militant republicanism, both of which were undergoing a revitalisation at this time. On the republican side, some of the more militant Sinn Féin members found Griffith's idea of a dual monarchy too conservative and looked instead to a revival of the dormant IRB. Inspired by the return to Ireland in 1907 of the veteran Fenian Tom Clarke, they set about recruiting energetic new members and renewing the revolutionary ethos of the organisation. Yet, for all its internal changes, the IRB remained a secret, underground movement which had little impact upon politics at a popular level at this time. Instead, it was to the reunited Irish Parliamentary Party at Westminster that the majority of Irish nationalists looked when the issue of home rule returned to the top of the Liberal agenda in 1910.

The 1906 general election returned the Liberals to power with a parliamentary majority so large that it made them independent of the Irish Parliamentary Party. However, the new Liberal prime minister, Sir Henry Campbell-Bannerman (1836–1908), was sympathetic to nationalists' demands and pledged himself to a gradualist devolutionary policy. Thus, the Tory approach of 'killing home rule with kindness' gave way to the Liberal policy of conceding 'home rule by instalments'. The first instalment came in 1907 when the government proposed the establishment of an Irish Council which would grant Dublin a measure of administrative, but not legislative, autonomy. However, this compromise solution proved wholly unacceptable to Irish nationalists and was rejected by Redmond and his party. Despite this setback, the Liberal alliance went on to achieve more modest reforms in the areas of Irish housing and education until 1909, when the House of Lords' rejection of the reforming budget drawn up by the chancellor, David Lloyd George (1863–1945), precipitated a constitutional crisis and led to two general elections in 1910.

The elections wiped out the Liberal majority, and left the Irish nationalists, with eighty-two MPs, holding the balance of power for the first time since 1885. Redmond's strategy was to trade Irish parliamentary support for a public commitment from the new Liberal leader, Herbert Asquith (1852–1928), that he would introduce a Home Rule Bill. Redmond's cause was boosted in 1911, when the continuing conflict between the Commons and the Lords culminated in the passing of the Parliament Act, which drastically reduced the power of the Lords to veto legislation to a maximum of two years. This landmark Act made the implementation of Irish home rule virtually inevitable, so long as the Liberals remained in government. This inevitability came a step closer in April 1912, when Asquith brought the third Home Rule Bill before the Commons. The Bill resembled Gladstone's 1893 proposals in its provision for a two-tier Irish legislature under the overall control of Westminster. Irish MPs would continue to attend Westminster, but their number would be reduced to forty-two. After years of desert wanderings, Irish nationalists seemed finally within sight of the promised land. But as the bright vista of self-government opened up before them, the daunting obstacle of Protestant Ulster suddenly loomed back into view, blocking the path to freedom.

While the home rule issue dominated Anglo-Irish politics during the late nineteenth and early twentieth centuries, this period also saw the emergence of other political forces, notably the labour and suffrage movements. The labour movement in Britain was spearheaded by James Keir Hardie, who formed the Independent Labour Party in 1893 and was elected chairman of the first parliamentary Labour Party in 1906. The first Irish socialist party was formed in Dublin in 1896 by James Connolly, whose vision of an independent Irish socialist republic led him to take part in the 1916 Easter Rising, after which he was executed.

One of the many democratising measures which Connolly supported was the extension of the franchise to women in Ireland and Britain. The two decades between the second and third Home Rule Bills witnessed the rise of militant women's suffrage movements in both countries. Prior to this, a small number of women's rights activists had campaigned for educational and political reforms with limited success. A new model presented itself in 1903 when Emmeline Pankhurst and her daughters established the Women's Social and Political Union in Manchester. This organisation introduced the concept of militant action into the English suffrage campaign and its influence soon spread to Ireland, where the Irish Women's Franchise League was founded by Hanna Sheehy-Skeffington (1877–1946) and Margaret Cousins in 1908.

The league was a non-party association which aimed to obtain the parliamentary vote for Irish women on the same terms as men. Proclaiming 'suffrage first before all else!', it pressurised Irish Parliamentary Party MPs to insist on the inclusion of a women's suffrage clause in the 1912 Home Rule Bill. Redmond consistently opposed the suffragists' demands, however, as did Asquith, Edward Carson and Andrew Bonar Law. The activists' subsequent resort to militant tactics shocked many observers but failed to win concessions. This failure was compounded by the outbreak of war in 1914, which saw suffragist unity give way to divergent strands of political activity, as some women supported the war effort, others remained pacifist, while more committed themselves to the struggle for Irish independence.

A degree of solidarity between the various women's groups was restored in the aftermath of the 1916 rising, which proclaimed the equal citizenship of Irish men and women. Less than two years later, in February 1918, the Representation of the People Act granted the vote to women over thirty years of age, despite continuing opposition from the Irish Parliamentary Party and Ulster Unionists at Westminster, both of whom feared the effect a new female electorate would have on their political fortunes. In the 1918 general election Sinn Féin's Constance Markievicz (1868–1927) became the first female MP elected to the British parliament, but did not take up her seat. Instead she was appointed minister for labour in the first Dáil Éireann in January 1919. Three years later, following a heated debate which revealed a formidable degree of chauvinism among Irish male politicians, the Irish Free State constitution of 1922 granted the right to vote to all men and women over the age of twenty-one. Women in Northern Ireland and Britain had to wait until 1928 to be similarly enfranchised.

BRIMSTONE AND TREACLE, OR KILLING WITH KINDNESS.
BALFOUR THE SECOND. "Open your mouth and shut your eyes, and take what the Tories send you."

8.1 'Brimstone and Treacle . . .', Fitzpatrick, *Weekly Freeman*, Dublin, 26 October 1895

The defeat of the Liberals in the general election of July 1895 ushered in ten years of Tory government. Though the Irish Parliamentary Party returned eighty-two MPs, they no longer held the balance of power and were in any case a divided force. Home rule sank to the bottom of the British political agenda, and the new government sought to remove it completely by reviving its policy of constructive unionism, first implemented by Arthur Balfour in the late 1880s. This was a broad-based initiative which embraced a range of remedial socio-economic measures, from land purchase schemes to local government reform. The new administrator of this policy from 1895 to 1900 was Arthur's brother Gerald, Irish chief secretary, who once tellingly described his government's corrective measures as 'killing home rule with kindness'.

This cartoon shows an agitated Gerald Balfour trying to administer his Tory policy to a knowing, scornful Pat. The Irishman has obviously recognised Balfour's medicine for what it is, a brimstone mixture sweetened with treacle to make it more palatable. Fitzpatrick was thus highlighting the ulterior motive behind the Tory's conciliatory policy, namely, to undermine support for nationalists' home rule demands and defuse the perennial land problem. Pat's suspicions were shared by many home rulers in the 1890s, though the actual reforms did have their nationalist and unionist adherents, notably Horace Plunkett MP, founder of the Irish agricultural co-operative movement. But while a number of reforms was introduced, the demand for home rule did not disappear.

"WHO FEARS TO SPEAK OF '98."

BRITANNIA—"Come and join in my jubilation."
ERIN—"No! My place is here."

8.2 'Who Fears to Speak of '98', Fitzpatrick, *Weekly Freeman*, Dublin, 26 June 1897

Queen Victoria's diamond jubilee in 1897 generated a mass outpouring of jingoism in Britain, culminating in a large imperial pageant in London on Jubilee Day, 22 June. While many parts of the empire, including Ireland, celebrated the royal anniversary, some advanced Irish nationalists organised anti-jubilee demonstrations to protest against Britain's refusal to grant Ireland independence. This Fitzpatrick cartoon captures this mood of nationalist dissent. Erin firmly refuses Britannia's invitation to join in her jubilee celebrations, cleaving instead to the memory of the United Irishmen, whose leaders' graves she tends.

Plans to commemorate the centenary of the 1798 rebellion were already well under way by this date, with '98 committees being established by IRB activists nationwide. The year itself began with torchlight processions in many towns and continued with further celebratory events at home and abroad. Irish periodicals contained many articles and cartoons marking the centenary and the Fitzpatrick drawing opposite reflects this universal upsurge of Irish patriotic feeling under the flag of nationalist idealism. However, the image conveniently glosses over the jockeying for control of the commemorative committees between

8.3 'United Irishmen Still', Fitzpatrick, *Weekly Freeman*, Dublin, 8 January 1898

the various shades of nationalist opinion, which at one point threatened to obscure the actual commemoration itself. This was especially so over the planned Wolfe Tone monument in Dublin, which never progressed beyond the plinth stage. Nor does the cartoon explain that while nationalists celebrated in 1898, northern unionists were hostile, since Tone's ideal of uniting Protestant, Catholic and Dissenter in an independent Irish republic was no longer one with which they could empathise. There was therefore a sad irony in the spectacle of the mainly Presbyterian and Catholic 1798 rising in Antrim and Down being honoured mostly by Catholics in 1898, while alienated Presbyterians stayed away.

THE IRISH " PLANCHETTE."

RIGHT HON. G-RGE W-NDH-M (*to* Mr. J-HN R-DM-ND *and* COLONEL S-ND-RS-N) 'LAND PURCHASE! HOW SINGULAR! NOW, WHAT *COULD* HAVE MADE IT WRITE *THAT?*'

8.4 'The Irish "Planchette" ', Partridge, *Punch*, London, 11 March 1903

In December 1902 a conference of representatives of Irish landlords and tenants was held in Dublin to negotiate what they hoped would be a final settlement of the land problem. The resultant report recommended that tenants be enabled to purchase their farms from landlords with the aid of government loans. This formed the basis of the Land Purchase Bill which was introduced in the Commons on 25 March 1903 by the Irish chief secretary, George Wyndham. The Bill became law in August and led to a massive transfer of land to the Irish tenantry.

This *Punch* cartoon seeks to dramatise the forces that impelled Wyndham to introduce his 1903 Bill. The cartoon's setting is derived from the cult of spiritualism which was attracting many adherents at this time, including W.B. Yeats. Some spiritualists practised automatic writing by means of a planchette, a small board fitted with castors and a pencil, through which messages from the spirits were supposedly received when one or more people laid their hands upon it. In this sketch Bernard Partridge (1861–1945) shows an astonished Wyndham watching his shamrock-shaped planchette spell the words 'land purchase'. This message has a political rather than spiritual source, however, as the manipulating presence of the nationalist Redmond (right) and unionist Saunderson (left) makes clear. The Land Bill was supported by both nationalist and unionist tenant farmers, both of whom stood to benefit from the new legislation.

IRELAND OVER ALL.

FREE TRADER AND PROTECTIONIST TO PAT—"Help! Help!!"
PAT—"I know who I'll help."

8.5 'Ireland Over All', Blake, *Weekly Freeman*, Dublin, 29 August 1903

In 1903 Joseph Chamberlain, by now a member of the Tory cabinet, started his tariff reform campaign to end free trade in order to regenerate British industry by reducing foreign competition. The Conservative Party split over the issue, prompting Chamberlain to resign his cabinet post and form the Tariff Reform League. There was a very real danger that the issue would have a divisive impact on the recently reunited Irish Parliamentary Party also, hence this polemical *Weekly Freeman* cartoon, designed to reinforce nationalist unity.

It depicts Erin's jailer, John Bull, divided against himself over tariff reform, with both sides appealing for help to a well-to-do Pat. He shows no desire to become embroiled in this British squabble and remains committed to the first principle of Irish constitutional nationalism: to unlock the Act of Union with the key of home rule. Blake's attempt to portray the dispute over Britain's trade policy as irrelevant to Ireland is unconvincing, however, since its outcome was of considerable economic significance to the country. But the *Freeman*, like other nationalist publications of the time, placed the national question high above social and economic issues.

8.6 'Mr W.B. Yeats...', Beerbohm, London, 1904

This cartoon is by the English satirist and drama critic Max Beerbohm (1872–1956), who throughout his life produced many celebrated caricatures of his literary friends and acquaintances. It features two leading figures of the Irish literary revival, the poet and dramatist W.B. Yeats and the novelist George Moore. A willowy Yeats is shown introducing Moore to 'the Queen of the Fairies', a mocking allusion to the former's lifelong interest in mysticism and visionary experiences, to which the titles on his bookshelf attest. Moore, however, had more of the realist than the spiritualist in him. The son of a wealthy Catholic landowning MP for Mayo, he exposed the unjust social conditions of women and the Irish tenantry in his early novels, before scrutinising Irish rural life with ground-breaking realism in *The Untilled Field* (1903). Dissatisfaction with Britain's war against the Boers prompted him to leave England for Ireland in 1901, where for a time he worked alongside Yeats in the Irish theatre movement and also became involved in the activities of the Gaelic League. Beerbohm hailed Moore as 'a true eccentric', while confessing his inability to find 'definite meanings in the faint and lovely things of Yeats'.

"WILL HE TACKLE IT!"

8.7 'Will He Tackle It!', Fitzpatrick, *Lepracaun*, Dublin, February 1906

Tory divisions over tariff reform were a major contributory factor in the Liberals' landslide victory in the January 1906 general election. They were returned to office under Henry Campbell-Bannerman with a record majority, large enough to make them independent of the Irish Parliamentary Party. Redmond nevertheless welcomed this Liberal victory after a decade of unionist rule, in the hope that it might bring about a revival of home rule fortunes. However, the Liberals had little appetite to resurrect an issue which had proved so divisive in the recent past, and which would in any case be rejected by the Lords. Indeed some Liberals urged that the party's Irish policy be abandoned completely. Campbell-Bannerman was more sympathetic, however, and while he ruled out the possibility of home rule for at least five years, he did pledge himself to a devolutionary approach, which acquired the label 'home rule by instalments'.

Cartoons 8.7 and 8.8 appeared in a Dublin satirical monthly, the *Lepracaun*, founded in 1905 by Cork-born cartoonist, Thomas Fitzpatrick (1860–1912), whose artistic career stretched back to *Pat* in the early 1880s. The first shows an elephantine Liberal Party, bearing the head of Campbell-Bannerman, and its mahout, Redmond, both looking equally uncertain about the other's intentions. Liberal objectives had become clearer by the time the second cartoon appeared eight months later. A devolutionary plan had by then been

IMPERIAL MEASURE.

JOHN REDMOND : "That is not a full measure. I'll take none of your half measures, so fill it up !"

BARMAN BRYCE : "It's Imperial Measure, sir. It's a bit fresh, and we're not long opened in this house."

8.8 'Imperial Measure', Fitzpatrick, *Lepracaun*, Dublin, October 1906

drawn up by the new chief secretary, James Bryce, and his under-secretary, Antony MacDonnell. It fell far short of self-government, however, and was given short shrift by Redmond and his party. Fitzpatrick shows an indignant Redmond spurning barman Bryce's 'imperial measure' – much of which is in any case froth – closely watched by the pub landlord, Campbell-Bannerman, and barman MacDonnell. 'The Crown' may be under new management, but it still had much to do to please its Irish nationalist patrons.

8.9 'Prosperity . . .', Morrow, *Republic*, Belfast, 24 January 1907

On 13 December 1906 a new weekly newspaper, the *Republic*, began publication in Belfast. It was edited by IRB member Bulmer Hobson and was the official organ of the Dungannon Clubs, the organisation he co-founded with Denis McCullough in March 1905 and named after the meeting place of the Irish Volunteers in 1778. This was a non-sectarian, separatist organisation committed to the Sinn Féin ideal of an independent Irish republic, the development of native industries and the cultivation of the Irish language and culture. Propagandist cartoons played a central part in the propagation of Hobson's republican message, and each issue featured a full-page drawing, one of which is reproduced here.

It takes as its theme the Sinn Féin policy of industrial development, which was based on a commitment to protective tariffs and the exclusive use of native materials. Norman Morrow illustrates the supposed damage done to Irish industry by its exposure to unregulated market forces, in particular British imports. The cartoon clearly suggests that only the power and energy of Sinn Féin can demolish the wall of 'anglicisation' and lead the nation to prosperity. Financial problems led to the demise of the *Republic* in May 1907.

THE WAKE.

WIDOW BIRRELL—"Oh! Johnny, darlin', why did you let me poor boy get bet? Shure, it was he that was goin' to do grand things entirely."
JOHN REDMOND—"But, mother, dear, he hadn't the ghost of a chance ag'in so many. I had to help in the killin' of him myself, to save me own skin, bedad I had!"

[Mr. Birrell's Irish Council Bill has been unanimously rejected by the National Convention held in the Round Room, Mansion House, Dublin, 21st May, 1907. Mr. John E. Redmond, M.P., presided.]

8.10 'The Wake', Fitzpatrick, *Lepracaun*, Dublin, June 1907

The Irish Council Bill, which was introduced in the Commons on 7 May 1907 by Chief Secretary Augustine Birrell, provided for the establishment of a 106-member council which would have control over 8 administrative areas, including education and local government. Redmond gave it a cautious welcome and convened a nationalist convention in Dublin on 21 May to discuss it. He quickly realised that he had badly misjudged the mood of his supporters, however, when the Bill was unanimously rejected by delegates. This left him with no option but to denounce the proposal, which led in turn to the government's withdrawal of the Bill on 3 June.

Fitzpatrick represents this turn of events with mordant wit. He shows a widowed chief secretary and her son, Redmond, mourning at the corpse of the deceased Bill. While the Irish leader openly admits to his own self-interested role in the Bill's murder, the portrait of Parnell serves as a pointed reminder of the Irish Parliamentary Party's abandonment of its

8.11 'Mr Birrell's Blunder', *Nomad's Weekly*, Belfast, 1 June 1907

leader at the behest of the Liberal leadership, which, the cartoonist suggests, resulted in the killing of the much more substantial prospects of Irish home rule seventeen years earlier.

Nomad's Weekly, an independent Belfast satirical journal which flourished between 1905 and 1914, views Birrell's 'blunder' from a different political angle. By introducing his Council Bill, the chief secretary is shown to have chosen to play the wrong gramophone record, resulting in a cacophony of Irish protest. He regrets not having picked 'Catholic University' instead, a reference to the attempt to establish a new Catholic university college in Dublin, which had recently been opposed by unionists and the board of Trinity College. This record would have provoked discord from another Irish quarter, therefore, as, of course, would his third possibility, 'Home Rule'. The cartoonist would appear to have some sympathy for Birrell's dilemma, therefore, and his desperate attempt to find a compromise position between the extremes of unionism and separatism.

Over a year later, in August 1908, the Irish Universities Act was passed. This replaced the Royal University of Ireland with the National University of Ireland, comprising the existing Queen's colleges in Galway and Cork and a new University College Dublin. Trinity College retained its autonomy and Queen's University Belfast was given its independence, thereby acknowledging the concept of partition in university education.

THE NEW "OLD MAN OF THE SEA."

"I am convinced that Parliamentary agitation, as now conducted, has spent its force,
and that nothing more can be gained by it on its present lines." . . . . . "I do not
believe that the English-speaking people will ever grant Home Rule or anything like it."
Letter from Sir Thomas Esmonde, M.P.—*Daily Papers*, July 22nd, 1907.

8.12 'The New "Old Man of the Sea"', Fitzpatrick, *Lepracaun*, Dublin, August 1907

On 21 April 1907 two nationalist organisations, the Dungannon Clubs and Cumann na
nGaedheal, amalgamated to form the Sinn Féin League under the direction of Arthur
Griffith and Bulmer Hobson. The primary political objective of this organisation, which
was renamed Sinn Féin in 1908, was the re-establishment of an independent Irish legislature, similar to Grattan's parliament of 1782. Inspired by the Austro-Hungarian *Ausgleich*
of 1867, which made Austria and Hungary autonomous states with a common sovereign,
Griffith proposed that Irish MPs withdraw from Westminster and constitute themselves as a
de facto Irish parliament under the British crown. Such radicalism was obviously at odds
with the policy of the Irish Parliamentary Party, whose support base was targeted by the
new movement.

This Fitzpatrick cartoon represents the potentially deadly threat posed to the Irish
Parliamentary Party by Sinn Féin. It is based on the figure of the Old Man of the Sea in

the Sinbad legend, who strangled unwary mariners by clinging tightly to their necks. This 'new' Old Man is perched on the shoulders of an anxious John Redmond, who appears stuck in the swamp of parliamentarianism. Although the cartoonist's vision was not borne out in the short term, as Sinn Féin's popular appeal proved to be very limited in the pre-war period, his striking sketch anticipates the movement's dramatic eclipse of the Irish Parliamentary Party in 1918 with uncanny piquancy.

8.13 'Under the British Lash', Fitzpatrick, *Lepracaun*, Dublin, June 1909

The genesis of the third Home Rule Bill can be traced to 29 April 1909, the date on which the chancellor of the Exchequer, David Lloyd George, introduced his 'people's budget' in the Commons. Faced with the need to raise money to finance social reforms and build more dreadnought battleships, he put forward a radical set of tax proposals. Additional duties on tobacco, spirits and liquor licences were augmented by new taxes on land and wealth. The budget provoked outrage in Ireland, especially among distillers, publicans and landowners, all of whom were key Irish Parliamentary Party supporters. British Conservatives denounced the measures also and resolved to use the Lords to block the chancellor's bold initiative.

This Fitzpatrick cartoon graphically illustrates the perceived oppressive impact of Lloyd George's budget on Ireland's commercial and industrial interests. The enslaved sectors are shown pulling the heavy budgetary yoke towards the imperial gates, driven on by a merciless chancellor and his prime ministerial protector, Asquith. The inscribed pillars proclaim Irish nationalists' anger at the fact that the money raised from these taxation increases will be spent on Britain's naval race with Germany and not on Ireland's needs. Criticism is also directed at Redmond, who, in spite of his lack of sympathy for Lloyd George's economic reforms, felt unable to oppose the budget lest this jeopardise the Liberal alliance. His nurse is T.P. O'Connor, MP for a Liverpool division from 1880 to 1929, and the only Irish Parliamentary Party member to sit for an English constituency.

THE IRONY OF CIRCUMSTANCE.

Mr. John Redmond. "WELL, IF I CAN'T RULE IN DUBLIN, I CAN HERE!"

8.14 'The Irony of Circumstance', Partridge, *Punch*, London, 2 February 1910

The Tory-dominated House of Lords' rejection of Lloyd George's radical budget in November 1909 brought to the boil the dispute between the upper and lower Houses of the British parliament which had simmered since 1893. The Lords' right to veto Commons legislation was at the heart of the matter, and it was this issue on which the general election of January 1910 was fought. The prospect of a close result enabled Redmond to extract a pre-election public commitment to home rule from the Liberals in return for Irish Parliamentary Party support. This acquired immediate significance when the two main British parties emerged from the election with an almost equal number of seats, leaving the balance of power with the eighty-two Irish nationalist MPs and forty Labour MPs.

The *Punch* cartoon opposite caricatures Redmond's sudden political empowerment at Westminster by showing him installed upon his new throne, a compound of the coronation chair and Big Ben, holding the orb of the British constitution and a shillelagh sceptre. His resolution to 'rule here' refers to his party's power to support the Liberal budget and so enable the government to curb the Lords' powers, which would in turn facilitate the enactment of home rule. Partridge is struck by the irony of the fact that Redmond had no Irish parliament in which to exercise power, but this was not the only paradoxical aspect of his political circumstance. The Irish Parliamentary Party had no enthusiasm for the budget, but decided to support it rather than bring about an anti-home-rule Conservative government. Secondly, Redmond was by no means completely master of his own house. Some of his Munster supporters were about to be wooed by William O'Brien's All-for-Ireland League, established in Cork in March, while militant nationalists sniped at him from another direction. If home rule was not delivered soon, his power might well be usurped.

8.15 'Backing the Double Event', Fitzpatrick, *Lepracaun*, Dublin, May 1910

UNDER PRESSURE

8.16 'Under Pressure', *Irish World*, New York, 4 March 1911

Asquith immediately set about introducing legislation to curb the power of the Lords after the January 1910 election. On 25 April the Commons passed his Parliament Bill, which Redmond supported in the expectation that once the Lords' veto was removed a Home Rule Bill would be passed soon afterwards. Fitzpatrick's cartoon (8.15) is decidedly sceptical about this strategy, however. It shows Redmond, encouraged by a lugubrious John Dillon, placing a double bet with 'bookie' Asquith on the prospect of the Lords' veto being removed and the Liberal budget being passed. Meanwhile, the Machiavellian Lloyd George tells Asquith to make whatever promise is necessary in order to secure the Irish Parliamentary Party vote, meaning, of course, the promise of home rule. The unmistakable suggestion is that the Irish gamblers are about to be swindled by the unscrupulous Liberal bookmakers, whose commitment to home rule is based on pragmatism rather than principle.

Ten months later, the prospects of the Parliament Bill becoming law were much brighter from a nationalist perspective. A second general election in 1910 left the state of the parties virtually unchanged, with Redmond again using his parliamentary strength to maintain the Liberals in office, and so keep up the pressure for the removal of the Lords' veto. This *Irish World* cartoon of an emblematic peer being squeezed in the Irish Parliamentary Party vice graphically illustrates the power which he now wielded. Faced with a government threat to create sufficient Liberal peers to secure the passage of its reforms, the Lords eventually capitulated and the Parliament Act was passed in August 1911. This removed the Lords' absolute power to defeat a Bill and replaced it with a suspensory veto of two years. The passage of the Home Rule Bill now appeared inevitable, as long as the Liberals remained in office.

THE TREE OF LIFE.

8.17 'The Tree of Life', *Sinn Féin*, Dublin, 13 March 1911

Founded and edited by Arthur Griffith, *Sinn Féin* first appeared on 5 May 1906. It replaced the *United Irishman*, which Griffith had edited since 1899, and became the main organ of the Sinn Féin movement until its suppression by the British authorities in December 1914. It regularly featured a front page cartoon by an artist called Molloy, who was almost certainly the author of this 1911 sketch representing the organic nature of Sinn Féin's political philosophy.

Firmly rooted in the soil of a national policy of agricultural development, the sturdy trunk sprouts two strong branches, one commercial, the other cultural. The first refers to the Sinn Féin policy document of 1908, which called for the protection of Irish industries and commerce from foreign competition in order to strengthen the country's manufacturing base. The afforestation of unproductive land was to be one element of this policy. The second branch alludes to the movement's commitment to the preservation of the Gaelic language and the creation of Irish art and literature, aims it shared with the Gaelic League and the cultural revivalists. Curiously, there is no explicit mention of the central Sinn Féin tenet: 'the re-establishment of the independence of Ireland'.

DRIVE HIM OFF THE STAGE.

WE have in the past driven the vulgar "stage Irishman" from the theatre. We will not tamely submit to our race being misrepresented by his still more disgusting successor "The Playboy of the Western World." A good beginning has been made. Let the work go on.

8.18 'Drive Him off the Stage', *Irish World*, New York, 9 December 1911

On 26 January 1907 *The Playboy of the Western World* by J.M. Synge opened at the Abbey theatre in Dublin, Ireland's national theatre. It tells the story of how a young man, Christy Mahon, is lionised by Mayo peasants when he boasts that he has killed his father, but who is later rejected by them when he is exposed as a liar. The play provoked riots among the Abbey's conservative nationalist audience, many of whom denounced Synge for his brutally frank portrayal of the Irish peasantry at a time when the nationalist aim was to project an image of a people capable of assuming the responsibilities of self-government. It was, said the *Freeman's Journal*, an 'unmitigated, protracted libel upon Irish peasant men and, worse still, upon Irish peasant girlhood'. The latter remark refers to Christy's use of the word 'shift', a loose-fitting woman's undergarment, which scandalised puritanical theatre-goers.

Almost five years later, in the autumn of 1911, the Abbey company undertook its first American tour. The announcement that the *Playboy* was to be performed provoked angry reactions from conservative Irish-American groups, one of which pledged 'to drive the vile thing from the stage'. Open rioting broke out during the play's performance in New

York in November, and the entire cast was arrested in Philadelphia in January 1912 and charged with presenting immoral and corrupting plays. Throughout the tour, the *Irish World* led a sustained attack on Synge's unsentimental Irish characters, which, it confidently asserted, simply did not exist. The cartoon opposite reflects the newspaper's hostile criticism. It shows an indignant Erin driving a 'decadent Irish playwright', presumably Synge, from the theatre. An accompanying commentary declares that moral Irish-Americans 'will not tamely submit to our race being misrepresented' by such writers, an objection which echoes those made by many Gaelic Leaguers during the original riotous demonstrations in Dublin.

"BOW=WOW=WOW."

ERIN—"John, what is that savage, discordant noise I hear?"
CHAUFFEUR JOHN—"It is only the barking of some vicious dogs; but as they are tied up they can't bite as they should like to do."

8.19 'Bow-Wow-Wow', Spex, *Lepracaun*, Dublin, May 1912

Tension mounted in Ulster in the months leading up to the introduction of the Home Rule Bill in April 1912. The year began with Orangemen and members of unionist clubs openly practising military drill, though as yet they were unarmed. Meanwhile, their political leaders pledged their vehement opposition to the government's Bill and prophesied

8.20 'The New Conspiracy', *Belfast Weekly News*, Belfast, 7 November 1912

bloody civil war if it became law. Edward Carson told unionists to prepare for 'the government of the Protestant Province of Ulster' if the Bill succeeded, and the new Tory leader, Andrew Bonar Law, committed his party to the defence of unionist Ulster by all means necessary.

Unionist protest culminated in a mass rally at Balmoral, near Belfast, on 9 April, at which Carson and Bonar Law addressed a crowd of over one hundred thousand loyalists beneath the largest Union Jack ever seen. Two days later, Asquith introduced his Bill in the Commons. It passed its first reading on 16 April and its second on 9 May. The nationalist *Lepracaun* greeted the Bill's progress with a cartoon (8.19) by 'Spex', the pseudonym of veteran cartoonist John F. O'Hea. It shows Redmond chauffeuring Erin towards the promised land of home rule, past three 'vicious' unionist dogs, Carson, Bonar Law and Lord Londonderry, president of the Ulster Unionist Council, chewing on the bones of 'hatred' and 'bigotry'. Redmond's reassurance that the chained dogs pose no threat to Erin is indicative of the prevailing nationalist view that loyalist belligerence was mere bluster or 'Ulsteria', as it was dismissively dubbed. This failure to comprehend the depth and intensity of unionist resistance to home rule remained a feature of much nationalist thinking about Ulster for many years to come.

The Protestant *Belfast Weekly News* cartoon opposite, on the other hand, vividly under-lines the precise nature and extent of unionist fears at this time. It shows the conspiratorial trio of Redmond, Asquith and Churchill preparing to detonate two kegs of home rule explosives which look set to destroy the very foundations of the empire and bring about social, economic and moral ruin. The labelled fuse trail highlights unionists' deep-seated antipathy towards what they perceived as the corrupt nature of home rule politics, which is characterised by bribery, tyranny and deception.

8.21 'The Angel of Freedom', EK, *Irish Citizen*, Dublin, 15 March 1913

Unionists were not the only group to denounce Asquith's Home Rule Bill. Irish suffra-gists, of whom there were an estimated three thousand in 1912, were deeply angered by its failure to extend the franchise to women and resorted to militant acts to register their

IF ONLY GOOD ST. PATRICK WERE ALIVE.

("Yus, he'd soon slipped it across them Suffragettes"—The Orfis Boy)

8.22 'If Only Good . . .', Greer, *Nomad's Weekly*, Belfast, 15 March 1913

protest. In June 1912 eight members of the Irish Women's Franchise League, including its leader, Hanna Sheehy-Skeffington, were arrested for breaking windows in government buildings in Dublin Castle. This was followed by the arrest and imprisonment of two English suffragettes for violent demonstration during Asquith's visit to Dublin in July. Suffrage militancy continued over the next two years, during which time several women were imprisoned, usually on charges of causing damage to government property.

Cartoon 8.21, taken from the Dublin-based *Irish Citizen*, the official organ of the Irish Women's Franchise League, satirises John Redmond's inconsistent attitude to national and female emancipation. This advocate of Irish self-government continually opposed Irish female enfranchisement right up to the Representation of the People Act in 1918. His concept of Irish 'liberty' is represented as being fundamentally flawed, therefore; it is certainly one for which 'no Irish woman need apply', as the bound corpse of a suffragist reveals. The 'new liberator' is actually an old enslaver. Cartoon 8.22 takes a more flippant view of militant suffragism. Casting off the shackles of historical credibility, Greer enlists the redoubtable Saint Patrick to chastise these hammer-wielding women, confident that Ireland's national saint would have thoroughly disapproved of such outrageous female behaviour!

9

ULSTER AND HOME RULE
1905–1914

For Ulster unionists the period between the second and third Home Rule Bills was a time of uneasy calm punctuated by moments of heightened tension. The Lords' rejection of Gladstone's 1893 Bill and the subsequent defeat of the Liberals in the 1895 election allayed immediate unionist anxieties, but left endemic Protestant fears intact. The home rule tiger was not dead but sleeping, so vigilance, fortitude and solidarity needed to be maintained. But whereas the minority southern unionist community began a slow, painful process of *rapprochement* with the emergent Catholic nationalist order as the 1900s unfolded, Ulster Protestants retreated into a robust insularity, fortified by their sense of cultural and religious separateness.

This psychological isolationism manifested itself politically in a continuing determination to maintain Protestant ascendancy in Ulster by all means necessary. The slogan of the 1880s still expressed the essence of unionist resistance to an independent Irish parliament: 'home rule is Rome rule'. The first crisis of the new century occurred in 1904–5 when some southern unionist landlords collaborated with Conservative government officials in the formulation of a devolutionary scheme for Ireland. The move alarmed Ulster unionists, who perceived the proposals as a disguised form of home rule. They responded by forming the defensive Ulster Unionist Council in March 1905, an umbrella organisation which embraced MPs, Orangemen, landowners and businessmen. But the real crisis lay some years in the future.

Unionist apprehensions resurfaced when the outcry caused by Lloyd George's 1909 budget enabled Irish nationalists to extract a commitment to home rule from Asquith. Memories of the 1880s were revived as Redmond tried to play Parnell's part by using his party's balance of power as a bargaining card in negotiations with the Liberals. When Asquith curbed the Lords' veto in 1911 and signalled his intention to introduce a third Home Rule Bill, unionist alarm reached fever pitch. The Ulster Unionist Council stepped up its campaign of resistance by organising unionist clubs in Ulster and mobilising anti-home-rule opinion in Ireland and Britain. Mass rallies were organised, at which the new hardline leaders of Ulster loyalism, Edward Carson (1854–1935), a Dublin-born lawyer who became leader of the Irish unionist MPs at Westminster in 1910, and James Craig (1871–1940), the son of a millionaire Ulster Presbyterian whiskey distiller, prophesied militant action if home rule was introduced.

Carson's fundamental political objective was to preserve the whole of Ireland from home rule. His leadership of the Ulster unionists was predicated on the belief that if home rule could be resisted by Ulster, then it could not be applied to the rest of Ireland. His eventual acceptance of a partitionist compromise was arrived at reluctantly, after he realised that all of Ireland could not be saved from what he regarded as 'the most nefarious conspiracy that has ever been hatched against a free people'. Craig's primary concern, on the other hand, was to preserve the position of Protestant Ulster within the Union; he had little concern for the rest of Ireland. He proved himself throughout to be an able defender of Ulster, and his organisational flair proved crucial to the success of the resistance campaign.

Both men had a powerful parliamentary ally in Andrew Bonar Law (1858–1923), leader of the Conservative Party since 1911, who was himself of Presbyterian Ulster stock. Bonar Law's natural affinity for the unionist cause was given added pungency by his desire for British electoral advantage. Like Randolph Churchill before him, he seized upon home rule as a weapon with which to beat the government and quickly aligned himself with Carson's campaign. In July 1912 Bonar Law publicly denounced the Liberal alliance which led to Asquith's Home Rule Bill as a 'corrupt parliamentary bargain' with the Irish Parliamentary Party which would jeopardise the integrity of the empire. This was followed by the dark assertion that 'there are things stronger than parliamentary majorities' and a tacit incitement to civil war: 'I can imagine no length of resistance to which Ulster can go in which I should not be prepared to support them and in which they would not be supported by the majority of the British people.' For the democratic leader of the parliamentary party traditionally associated with law and order to sanction the use of extra-parliamentary force as a means of jettisoning government legislation was a truly extraordinary intervention which could only inflame sectarian passions further.

Bonar Law's rhetorical extremism was matched by Carson's orchestration of mass loyalist solidarity. On 28 September 1912 over 471,000 Ulster men and women signed the Solemn League and Covenant and the Declaration, in which they pledged to resist home rule 'using all means which may be found necessary'. But while the signatories were committing themselves to the maintenance of the unionist integrity of Ireland as a whole, Carson was formulating a tactical amendment to exclude all nine Ulster counties from the Bill. This was defeated in January 1913, however, and the Bill passed its third Commons reading.

The same month saw the formation of the paramilitary Ulster Volunteer Force by Carson and Craig, both of whom were eager to assert their political control over militant loyalists, who quickly joined up in their thousands. Ulstermen now began drilling in public, openly expressing their resolve to resist the implementation of home rule by force. The political implications were ominously clear: unionist leaders, no longer able to defeat home rule in parliament, were moving politics on to the streets, where deeds might achieve more than words.

Such a display of militant defiance, even if technically legal, represented a serious challenge to the government's authority in Ulster. Asquith's inaction, therefore, betrayed a fatal weakness which was seen by loyalists as vindicating their actions. The prime minister's hesitancy also encouraged Irish nationalists to imitate the unionists' example by forming the Irish Volunteers in Dublin in November 1913. There were now two private armies in Ireland, whose ability to mount a serious military threat was hampered only by their lack of sufficient arms.

This situation changed in April 1914 when German-purchased arms and ammunition were landed at three Ulster ports and quickly distributed to Ulster Volunteer Force members throughout the province, while the authorities stood by. This daring move was calculated to raise the political stakes, but in so doing the Ulster militants reintroduced the gun into Irish politics. Restless nationalists followed suit in July, when arms, again from Germany, were landed at Howth harbour near Dublin. Government forces intervened on this occasion, however, and four people were killed when troops fired on an unarmed crowd. Angry nationalists drew an invidious comparison between this prompt response and the authorities' inaction at the time of the Ulster gun-running.

Meanwhile, Asquith's Bill was progressing fitfully through the parliamentary process. It passed the Commons again in July 1913 only to be rejected again by the Lords. This was the last occasion on which the Lords could block the Bill, however; home rule now seemed destined to become law in 1914. This prospect concentrated the minds of the leading antagonists, many of whom, including Carson and Bonar Law, were privately resigned to some form of compromise based on the exclusion of all or part of Ulster. The idea of partition had earlier been mooted by a backbench Liberal MP, T.C. Agar-Robartes, but his proposal that the four most Protestant counties be excluded from the Bill was decisively rejected in June 1912. The idea was now revived by Lloyd George and then by Asquith, who tried to persuade Carson and Redmond to accept a partitionist compromise.

In March 1914 Redmond, still harbouring the illusion that Ulster was bluffing, eventually agreed to support Asquith's proposal to allow individual Ulster counties to opt out of home rule for a six-year period. This nationalist concession was not enough to satisfy the Tories, however, or Carson, who rejected it as a 'sentence of death with a stay of execution for six years'. Subsequent fears that the government might coerce the unionists into home rule precipitated the 'Curragh mutiny', when British army officers stationed near Dublin indicated that they would resign rather than take part in offensive action against Ulster to impose a home rule settlement. The limits of the government's authority had again been exposed and the crisis deepened.

In an effort to prevent civil war, King George V convened an all-party conference at Buckingham Palace in July 1914. All the participants accepted the principle of partition; the problem lay in deciding the area of Ulster to be excluded and for how long. Agreement proved impossible, however, and the conference ended inconclusively after three days. Privately, Asquith expressed his exasperation at the now seemingly intractable nature of the Ulster question, angrily blaming 'that most damnable creation of the perverted ingenuity of man – the County of Tyrone' for its geographical obstinacy. Sadly, he would not be the last British politician whose failure to comprehend the intricacies of Irish political realities would end in impotent, imperial rage. Asquith, however, was luckier than many of his successors, in being rescued from the morass of Anglo-Irish politics by a greater European conflict, as the sudden outbreak of war in August 1914 swept Ireland's divisions up into a completely new political context.

9.1 'The Ulster Rebellion, 1905', *Nomad's Weekly*, Belfast, 3 June 1905

The relationship between the Conservative government and Ulster unionists in the early years of the twentieth century was, at times, a very strained one. British cabinet ministers were sometimes appalled at the parochialism, sectarianism and suspect loyalty of their Irish allies. Relations worsened in 1902 when the chief secretary, George Wyndham, appointed Sir Antony MacDonnell as his under-secretary, that is, the permanent head of the Irish administration. Mayo-born MacDonnell was the first Catholic to hold this post and, as well as having a brother in the Irish Parliamentary Party, was a well-known Liberal sympathiser.

Unionist fears were confirmed in autumn 1904 when it was revealed that MacDonnell was working with the Earl of Dunraven on a scheme for devolved government in Ireland

THE ULSTER REBELLION, 1905.

[The Ulster Unionist M.P.'s declared they would *never, never* support the Government while Sir Anthony MacDonnell was retained.
See how the brave rebels (ungrateful shades of their manly forefathers of 1798!) carry out their determination.]

CHAMBERLAIN : I know these Ulster M.P.'s Dogs have more spirit, and I find them much easier
to deal with than my Chinese slave.

LAMA LONDONDERRY : Oh! I have only to crack my whip to bring them cringing. They are
damnably poor stuff.

based on elected councils which would have some tax-raising powers. While this was
not home rule, it was certainly a step in that direction. Angry unionists called for
MacDonnell's dismissal and quickly formed the Ulster Unionist Council to co-ordinate a
resistance campaign. Since Wyndham had known the general thrust of the devolutionary
proposals, he was forced to repudiate them and eventually resign in March 1905 as a result
of the unionist outcry. MacDonnell, however, remained in his post and went on to help
the Liberals produce an alternative devolution plan in the Irish Council Bill of 1907.

This Belfast cartoon savagely lampoons this putative unionist 'rebellion' over devolution. It suggests that the Ulster MPs' victory was more apparent than real, since their *bête
noire*, MacDonnell, remained in office, despite unionists' threats to withdraw their support
for the government unless he was removed. The reality, of course, was that unionists
realised that the best means of defending the Union was to keep the Conservatives in
power, rather than risk a pro-home-rule Liberal administration. Hence this image of
Joseph Chamberlain and Lord Londonderry, two leading opponents of home rule, contemptuously coercing a group of submissive unionist MPs into marching behind a government banner of MacDonnell in the caricatured style of an Orange parade. The epigraph
underlines the MPs' complaisance by contrasting the *soi-disant* revolt of these latter-day
'rebels' with the genuinely rebellious spirit of their 'manly forefathers of 1798', whose
politics, of course, were of a radically different kind.

WHICH WILL IT BE ?

[It is now certain that a new form of government for Ireland will be laid bare within the next few months.]

Mr. Campbell-Bannerman conceals the pea in the old game of political thimble-rigging.

9.2 'Which Will It Be?', *Nomad's Weekly*, Belfast, 15 September 1906

The Liberals' sweeping victory in the 1906 general election was greeted with joy at first by the Irish Parliamentary Party, but they soon recognised that the sheer size of the government's parliamentary majority gave them little leverage on policy making. This was borne out by the Liberal leadership's adoption of a 'step-by-step' approach to home rule, the first fruits of which were seen in the 1907 Irish Council Bill. This was little more than a revised version of MacDonnell's earlier devolution scheme and as such was a poor substitute for home rule. Indeed Campbell-Bannerman acknowledged as much when he described it as a 'little, modest, shy, humble effort to give administrative powers to the Irish people'. Unsurprisingly, the Bill was summarily rejected by both nationalists and unionists, albeit for different reasons.

This cartoon casts Campbell-Bannerman as a political trickster who is attempting to mislead a puzzled Irishman about his plans for the future government of Ireland. Only he knows where the pea is hidden, but while his hand hovers over the devolution thimble, the implication is that if this or home rule is not introduced, revolution may follow. In the background stands a disgruntled Ulster unionist who regards the prime minister's antics with suspicion and who would prefer if this political trick were not being performed at all.

The Babes in the Woods, Belfast.

JOHNNIE REDMOND : You must lead Winnie. After all you're only our catspaw, you know.
WINSTON CHURCHILL : I feel awfully, awfully funky. Sydney Street when I had all the forces was easy, but Bedford Street is impossible. Why even my father's shades forbid me. Why did I ever leave home.

9.3 'The Babes in the Woods, Belfast', Greer, *Nomad's Weekly*, Belfast, 27 January 1912

Before 1912, Winston Churchill (1874–1965), like many Liberals, discounted as bombast Ulster unionists' threats to resist home rule by force. He soon experienced the ferocity of loyalist opposition at first hand, however, when he was invited by the Ulster Liberal Association to speak in Belfast's Ulster Hall on 8 February 1912. Unionist outrage was deepened by the fact that he was due to appear in the very hall where his father, Lord Randolph, had delivered a stirring anti-home-rule speech in 1886. Indeed, many noted the paradoxical fact that whereas the father had played 'the Orange card' with devastating effect to destroy Gladstone's 1886 Home Rule Bill, the son was now a key supporter of Asquith's 1912 Bill. The Ulster Unionist Council, supported by Carson and Bonar Law, vowed to prevent the meeting taking place, prompting the nervous authorities to move troops into the city. Churchill was eventually forced to hold the rally in Celtic Park football ground, near the Catholic Falls Road, where he addressed a crowd of fifty thousand people.

This cartoon ridicules the whole episode as a farcical political pantomime. A frightened Churchill is being prodded towards the Ulster Hall by Redmond, who hopes to derive maximum propaganda value from this pro-home-rule British minister. Among the opposition forces waiting to ambush him are Carson in his barrister's wig, a regal Craig and the shade of Lord Randolph, chanting his famous 1886 mantra. 'Sydney Street' alludes to an earlier siege in the East End of London when a group of anarchists were surrounded by police. Churchill, who was home secretary at the time, had made a dramatic appearance at the scene, but here finds Belfast's Bedford Street far more intimidating.

THE ORANGEMAN'S ATTITUDE

CATHOLIC EMANCIPATION BILL | IRISH DISESTABLISHMENT BILL | HOME RULE BILL

"If you give Catholic Emancipation we shall revolt!" (*But they didn't!*) | "It you disestablish the Irish Church we shall revolt!" (*But they didn't!*) | "If you give Ireland Home Rule we shall revolt!" (*But they won't!*)

9.4 'The Orangeman's Attitude', *Irish World*, New York, 25 May 1912

This Irish-American cartoon, drawn shortly after the third Home Rule Bill was published, reflects a widely held nationalist view of unionist resistance to a Dublin parliament. It juxtaposes Ulstermen's opposition to Irish self-government in 1912 with two earlier occasions when northern Protestants reacted angrily to constitutional reforms which benefited the Catholic nationalist majority. The first refers to the passing of Catholic emancipation in 1829, the second to the 1869 Irish Church Act. On both occasions, the threatened Protestant revolt failed to materialise, leading the cartoonist to infer that Carson's current predictions of unionist rebellion are equally bogus. However, such hubris later turned to anger and indignation when Ulster loyalists stubbornly refused to conform to this nationalist paradigm. The *Irish World*, like many of its nationalist counterparts in Ireland, failed to appreciate the fact that, unlike the earlier Acts, the 1912 Home Rule Bill threatened the very foundations of unionist hegemony in Ireland and was therefore bound to be met with unionist resistance by any means necessary.

9.5 'Dangerous Leading', FCG, *Westminster Gazette*, London, 4 September 1912

In November 1911 Andrew Bonar Law succeeded Balfour as Conservative leader. Born in Canada to immigrant Ulster parents, he had a strong personal commitment to Irish unionism and also recognised its political potential to unite the Tories and give them electoral victory following their loss of three successive general elections and the emasculation of the House of Lords. By committing his party to the defeat of home rule, therefore, he firmly aligned British unionists with their Ulster counterparts, while he himself joined Carson and Craig in a campaign of constitutional and unconstitutional resistance. Like them, Bonar Law aimed to use Ulster as a primary means of destroying home rule for all of Ireland. If this did not prove feasible, however, he, like them, was prepared to abandon the southern Irish unionists in order to maintain Protestant Ulster's position within the Union. Either way, he was willing to countenance the use of force, as he made clear in a number of radical speeches in 1912.

The Liberal *Westminster Gazette*, like its Conservative counterpart, the *Pall Mall Gazette*, was addressed to a small but influential London readership. This drawing is by the Liberal artist Francis Carruthers Gould (1844–1925), who became the first regular staff cartoonist on a daily newspaper in 1888 and went on to play a key part in establishing the role of the political cartoon in British dailies. It depicts the 'blind Unionist Party', represented by Bonar Law, being led to the very edge of a steep precipice by the pugnacious Ulster Orange dog, Carson, apparently unconcerned about the hazard that lies ahead. Gould is clearly warning British Conservatives of the dangers inherent in their alliance with the Ulstermen, and suggests that it could lead to the mutual destruction of the parties.

ULSTER WILL WRITE.

(General Carson. "THE PEN (FOR THE MOMENT) IS MIGHTIER THAN THE SWORD.
UP, NIBS, AND AT 'EM!"

9.6 'Ulster Will Write', Raven-Hill, *Punch*, London, 25 September 1912

Throughout 1912 Ulster unionists organised a sustained campaign of direct action against the Home Rule Bill, culminating in a huge display of loyalist solidarity on 28 September, Ulster Day. Led by Carson, Ulster-born British subjects signed the Declaration and the Solemn League and Covenant, with its deliberate allusion both to God's Old Testament covenant with the Jews and to the seventeenth-century Scottish Covenanters. Over 471,000 signatures were received from those who pledged themselves 'to stand by one another in defending ... our cherished position of equal citizenship in the United Kingdom, and in using all means which may be found necessary to defeat the present conspiracy to set up a Home Rule Parliament in Ireland'. As most unionists were opposed to female suffrage, women signed the separate Declaration. The whole event was a massive publicity coup which impressed many uncommitted British voters and raised the stakes in the political game being played on several stages.

ULSTER DOUBLY READY!
The Pen is mightier than the Sword—and Ulster can use both.

9.7 'Ulster Doubly Ready!', Greer, *Nomad's Weekly*, Belfast, 28 September 1912

The title of the *Punch* cartoon (9.6) by Leonard Raven-Hill (1867–1942), drawn a few days before the covenant was signed, is a punning allusion to the slogan used by Randolph Churchill in his famous Belfast speech of February 1886, 'Ulster will fight and Ulster will be right'. It shows Carson mounted on his charger in a pose reminiscent of paintings of King William of Orange at the Boyne in 1690, declaring his temporary faith in the power of peaceful mass protest to defeat Irish home rule. The implied threat, however, is that the sheathed sword by his side may yet be required if the pen fails. The *Nomad's Weekly* cartoon, which appeared on Ulster Day itself, is a variation on the same theme. A defiant Ulster, framed by the Union Jack and the loyalist red hand emblem, affirms the power of the pen over the sword by signing the Covenant. However, the epigraph unequivocally asserts unionists' readiness to resort to force to resist home rule if necessary.

"THE IRRECONCILABLE."

9.8 'The Irreconcilable', Spex, *Lepracaun*, Dublin, October 1912

Although Asquith had declared that 'Ireland is a nation, not two nations, but one nation', some Liberal MPs had already begun to consider special concessions for Ulster by 1912. The first such parliamentary suggestion was made in June of that year, when a Liberal member, Agar-Robartes, proposed the exclusion of the four most Protestant counties, Antrim, Down, Armagh and Londonderry, from the provisions of the Bill. Although his amendment was defeated in parliament, it indicated a growing belief in some Liberal and nationalist circles that Ulster may have to receive special treatment. On the other side of the political divide, Conservative and unionist propaganda was increasingly concerned to argue the claims of 'loyal Ulster' for exclusion from home rule, rather than to argue that home rule was contrary to the interests of the whole of Ireland. Carson, however, believed that a partitioned Ireland would not be viable economically, and that Ulster could still be used to kill off home rule.

In this nationalist *Lepracaun* cartoon Mother Ireland and her four happy sons are shown inviting a sullen and recalcitrant north-east Ulster to share their 'home, sweet, home, rule'. One of the children represents the south-west and south-east Ulster counties, three of which, Donegal, Cavan and Monaghan, had nationalist majorities, while the remaining two, Tyrone and Fermanagh, were almost equally divided between the two parties. His north-eastern brother remains stubbornly apart, however, clinging to his sash, drum and Boyne water, historic symbols of Ulster loyalism. While Spex is obviously critical of such sour loyalist obstinacy, he nevertheless implies that coaxing is preferable to coercion if Irish

ASQUITH SURPRISED!

Asquith (astonished)--"That's funny, extremely funny. He doesn't
seem to want to be killed."

9.9 'Asquith Surprised!', TES, *Belfast Weekly News*, Belfast, 17 October 1912

family discord is to be avoided. The cartoonist's underlying perception of northern resistance is typically nationalist in so far as he suggests that unionists would come to appreciate the benefits of home rule if only they would give it a chance.

The staunchly unionist *Belfast Weekly News* views the matter from a dialectically different perspective. Far from seeing home rule as a benign overture to unionists to participate in a new self-governing Ireland, it depicts it as a lethal threat to Ulster's distinctive political identity. So while butchers Redmond and Asquith might be surprised at the Ulster cock's reluctance to submit to their sharp knives, its evasiveness is not only understandable but indeed imperative from a unionist perspective.

9.10 'Who's Afraid?', Raven-Hill, *Punch*, London, 15 January 1913

Under the terms of the 1911 Parliament Act, the Lords could reject a Bill twice, but if the Commons passed it a third time, it would automatically receive the royal assent. This reduction of the Lords' powers of veto meant that the Home Rule Bill which had been introduced in the Commons in April 1912 was due to become law in 1914. It was this

WHO'S AFRAID?

inability to prevent home rule by parliamentary means which eventually led frustrated Ulster unionists and some British Conservatives to consider resorting to the use of force to stop it.

On 16 January 1913 the Bill passed its first stage in the Commons, but was defeated in the Lords two weeks later. *Punch* anticipated this parliamentary battle with this suitably martial image of the simianised Bill heading towards the Lords behind the shield of the Parliament Act, on the boss of which is a gagged Minerva, goddess of wisdom. The cartoonist, Raven-Hill, who was himself a strong critic of the Liberal government, opposed the reform of the Lords, partly because it would bring about an Irish home rule parliament. This may explain his revival of the crude simian stereotype of the Victorian era to denigrate the Liberal alliance in 1913. Other *Punch* cartoonists of the period adopted a less harsh attitude to the home rule question.

9.11 'Will England Sully . . .', Greer, *Nomad's Weekly*, Belfast, 28 June 1913

In signing the Covenant, Ulster men and women pledged themselves to refuse to recognise the authority of any home rule Irish parliament. This left the Liberal government facing the daunting prospect of having to enforce such legislation against the wishes of a defiant

Will England Sully Her Boasted Honour?

DEFIANT ULSTER—" Will you permit your Army at the order
of rebels to fire on your own flag? Weigh heavily what it
means to so bring about proud England's sad dishonour?"

unionist minority, which in turn raised the question of whether all cabinet members were prepared to sanction the use of force against British citizens who proclaimed their loyalty to the crown. This provocative cartoon penetrates to the heart of these crucial matters. It depicts a British army firing squad taking aim at a defiant Ulster, whose only protection is a flowing Union Jack. The soldiers await the order to fire from commander John Redmond, an image which underlines the unionist conviction that Irish nationalist 'rebels' were behind Liberal moves to coerce Ulster. Two years later, the government's ability to rely upon the army to enforce its authority was seriously damaged as a result of the 'Curragh mutiny'.

9.12 'True Proportions . . .', SHY, *Lepracaun*, Dublin, October 1913

After the signing of the Covenant, the Ulster Unionist Council continued to prepare for the provisional government of Ulster, if required, and to recruit Ulster Volunteer Force members. By the end of 1913 this paramilitary body boasted a membership of ninety thousand, though the absence of weapons obliged the men to drill with dummy rifles. Since unionists were a small and traditionally law-abiding minority in Ireland, many Liberals and nationalists believed that Carson was bluffing in his threat to use force, and that unionists would come to accept home rule once it had been passed.

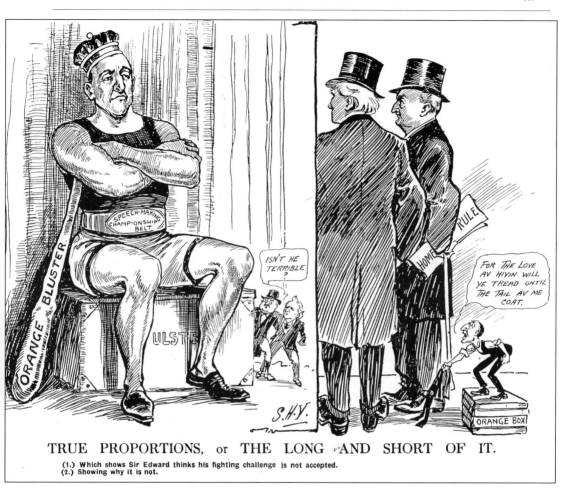

TRUE PROPORTIONS, or THE LONG AND SHORT OF IT.

(1.) Which shows Sir Edward thinks his fighting challenge is not accepted.
(2.) Showing why it is not.

This cartoon by a Dublin artist about whom little is known mocks what it sees as Carson's inflated political self-image. The sketch on the left represents his pompous perception of himself as Ulster's uncrowned king, a giant political heavyweight whose strength rests upon his oratorical powers and use of 'Orange bluster'. Such a show of force, he thinks, will intimidate Redmond and Asquith into submission. The right-hand vignette, however, purports to show Carson's 'true proportions'. Here he appears as a figure of no consequence, a political pygmy perched on his Orange soap box, pathetically trying to attract the attention of Redmond and Asquith, both of whom ignore him. The cartoon neatly encapsulates the failure of many Irish nationalists to appreciate the depth of Ulster unionist opposition to home rule at this time.

SECOND THOUGHTS.

John Redmond. "FULL SHTEAM AHEAD! (*Aside*) I WONDHER WILL I LAVE THIS CONTRAIRY LITTLE DIVIL LOOSE, HE'D COME BACK BY HIMSELF AFTHERWARDS?"

9.13 'Second Thoughts', Partridge, *Punch*, London, 8 October 1913

By the autumn of 1913 Asquith's government was seriously concerned that Ulster rhetoric might soon be translated into Ulster rebellion. Consequently, the Liberal leadership increased its pressure on the Irish Parliamentary Party to concede some form of temporary exclusion for part of Ulster. Redmond was opposed to any such concession, knowing that this would play into the hands of the more militant nationalists in Ireland who opposed his whole home rule policy. However, he realised that his position was weakening as more Liberal ministers began to favour an exclusion scheme, leading to the possibility of a divided cabinet.

This *Punch* cartoon accurately reflects Redmond's dilemma. While four of his five pigs trot happily into the home rule pen, the north-east Ulster animal tries to break free. Redmond's 'second thoughts' – to let the troublesome creature go its own way in the hope that it might later return of its own accord – is an oblique reference to Lloyd George's proposal that Ulster be excluded from home rule for a period of six years.

Spex's cartoon opposite highlights the Irish leader's opposition to any concessions over Ulster. It shows Carson, Redmond and Winston Churchill vying for the new 'home rule

9.14 'Churchill . . .', Spex, *Lepracaun*, Dublin, November 1913

rock' which has just gone on sale in Asquith's imperial candy store. Although the new candy is 'only to be had wholesale', Carson, in Ulster Volunteer Force uniform, wants to buy the Ulster portion of it only, a request supported by Churchill, who had recently advocated special treatment for Ulster in a speech in his Dundee constituency. Redmond objects, however, and insists that home rule be applied to the whole of Ireland or not at all. The cartoon cleverly captures the competing interests at work, and the increasing difficulty of Redmond's and Asquith's respective positions.

9.15 'A Dangerous Game', FCG, *Westminster Gazette*, London, 3 December 1913

By late 1913 the Irish crisis had deeply affected the usual conventions of constitutional government, as well as the normal regard for law and order. The Conservative Party in particular seemed prepared to overstep constitutional legality in its unquestioning support for the Ulster unionists. As far as the Liberals were concerned, the Tories' commitment to the cause of Ulster had more to do with their desire to defeat home rule by any means, and so bring down the government, than to calm unionist fears. Meanwhile, reports from Ulster

A DANGEROUS GAME.

DECEMBER 3.

JOHN BULL : *That's a dangerous game, gentlemen ! If you break through that bank you'll let in a much bigger flood than you are bargaining for !*

that the Ulster Volunteer Force were actively preparing for war prompted the government on 4 December to ban the importation into Ireland of arms and ammunition.

This cartoon from the Liberal *Westminster Gazette* portrays four prominent unionist politicians (from left to right), Carson, Bonar Law, Henry Chaplin and F.E. Smith, so determined to oppose home rule that they are undermining the dyke of law and order which protects society from the forces of anarchy. A worried John Bull admonishes them, fearing their actions might provoke civil war in Ireland, which could lead in turn to violence in Britain.

9.16 'Mixed Menu', Spex, *Lepracaun*, Dublin, December 1913

The industrial unrest which affected much of Europe in the pre-war years also reached Ireland. In Dublin most working-class men were unskilled 'casuals' who were poorly paid and lived in dreadful slum tenements, where malnutrition, disease and high mortality rates were rife. Since 1910, socialist trade union leaders James Larkin and James Connolly had organised a series of strikes demanding better conditions for workers and recognition for their union, the Irish Transport and General Workers' Union. They were opposed by the Dublin Employers' Federation led by William Martin Murphy, a successful businessman and former Irish Parliamentary Party MP.

MIXED MENU.

PAT—" Begorra, this is the quarest Christmas blow-out I ever sat down to.   If the puddin' was cool enough I'd tackle it first, for I'm half afeard most o' them other combustibles 'ud ruin me digestion."

Matters came to a head in September 1913 when Murphy and some 400 employers locked out all union members, leaving 25,000 workers unemployed. There followed a bitter four-month struggle between labour and capital, which united workers, intellectuals and militant nationalists against employers, the Catholic hierarchy and the mainly middle-class Irish Parliamentary Party. The struggle ended in victory for the employers when the strikers were forced back to work in February 1914. While this outcome represented a major blow to the development of socialism in Ireland, the lock-out also acted as a stimulus to the dynamic fusion of nationalism and socialism, which culminated in Connolly's small Citizen Army taking part in the 1916 rising.

This Spex cartoon seeks to represent the volatile nature of Irish politics at the end of 1913. A baffled Pat is confronted by a fiery array of Christmas food, none of which appears to be very appetising. The home rule pudding is too hot, the Ulster haggis too sour, and the other stews and sauces indigestible. 'Murphies' was an Irish expression for potatoes, as well as a coded reference to William Martin Murphy, while 'DMP nut crackers' (as opposed to the usual Christmas crackers) refers to the aggressive methods used by the Dublin Metropolitan Police against the striking workers. Pat's use of 'combustibles' for comestibles (food) may be a Freudian lapse rather than a malapropism.

9.17 'Why They Failed', Greer, *Nomad's Weekly*, Belfast, 24 January 1914

In late 1913 a series of discussions took place between the leaders of the British and Irish parties in an attempt to reach a compromise solution to the divisive home rule question. Negotiations centred on the issue of Ulster's exclusion from an Irish parliament, a concept which Carson had by now come to accept, but which Redmond rejected. Attempts by Asquith and Lloyd George to overcome Irish nationalist opposition failed, leaving the talks process in a state of deadlock by January 1914.

    This Belfast cartoon suggests that both Asquith and Bonar Law are impeded from making progress towards a home rule settlement by their respective Irish political alliances. The two leaders appear as worried parrots, their mouths padlocked and their movement restricted by the chains of Irish nationalism and unionism. Certainly neither Redmond nor Carson could give ground at this point, having built up the enthusiasm and expectation of their supporters. Yet the pressures on all sides were constantly growing, and all leaders were vulnerable to accusations of weakness.

HIS LIMIT.

(The Naked Truth at Last.)

Mr. JOHN REDMOND (divested of his Ulster): "Well, you can have the Ulster, but mind ye, I'll not take off another stitch—no more concessions."

9.18 'His Limit', Greer, *Nomad's Weekly*, Belfast, 21 March 1914

Early in March 1914, Redmond, under sustained pressure from Asquith, reluctantly conceeded the principle of Ulster's temporary exclusion from an Irish parliament. He agreed to a government proposal that individual Ulster counties be allowed to opt out of home rule for a period of six years. The rationale behind this plan was that the Protestant parts of Ulster would, in the course of those six years, realise that they had nothing to fear from home rule, and so willingly accept integration thereafter.

This was the maximum that Redmond was prepared to concede, but it was a dangerous concession. By accepting partition, however temporary, he was effectively conceding that Ireland was two nations, thereby flatly contradicting his assertion of October 1913 that 'Irish nationalists can never be assenting parties to the mutilation of the Irish nation. Ireland is a unit . . . The two-nation theory is to us an abomination and a blasphemy.' Carson, however, totally rejected the six-year time limit and told the Commons on 9 March: 'Ulster wants this question settled now and for ever. We do not want a sentence of death with a stay of execution for six years.'

In this Greer cartoon Redmond is shown to have reached his concessionary limit by surrendering his Ulster (overcoat) to Carson. Though he prates about making 'no more

Home Rule "Noose"!

Mr. Asquith: "I can't understand why you aren't satisfied. It won't be drawn tight for six years."

9.19 'Home Rule "Noose"!', *Pall Mall Gazette*, London, 29 June 1914

concessions' to the unionist leader, the cartoon clearly shows that he is now politically exposed on the path to home rule, feeling all too acutely the 'cruel pang' of compromise of which Churchill spoke. The Conservative *Pall Mall Gazette*, on the other hand, ridicules the whole idea of Ulster's temporary exclusion. Asquith, cast as the Mad Hatter from *Alice in Wonderland*, is incredulous at Carson's reluctance to place his head in the home rule noose on the promise that it will not be tightened for six years. Unionist threats of resistance had by this date been buttressed by a substantial military potential in the form of twenty-five thousand German rifles and much ammunition successfully imported and distributed throughout Ulster by the Ulster Volunteer Force.

9.20 'There's Many a Slip...', Partridge, *Punch*, London, 1 April 1914

The unionists' rejection of a compromise based on exclusion in March 1914 coincided with rumours that the Ulster Volunteer Force was planning to raid arms depots in Ulster. The government's decision that troops should be sent north to protect vulnerable depots alarmed many unionists, who interpreted the announcement as an attempt to coerce Ulster into accepting home rule. Amidst a confusion of military orders and fearing that they were

"THERE'S MANY A SLIP . . ."

being sent to disarm unionists, fifty-eight army officers at the Curragh military camp in County Kildare, led by General Hubert Gough, indicated that they would resign rather than lead their men against Ulster loyalists. The government, fearing a mutiny, summoned Gough to London, where he succeeded in extracting a written assurance from Colonel John Seely, secretary for war, that the army would not be used to impose home rule on Ulster. Although Asquith subsequently repudiated this concession and forced Seely to resign, the damage had already been done and a painful lesson learned: the government could not rely upon the army to enforce home rule in Ireland.

The Curragh incident was a serious blow to the government's authority, and this *Punch* cartoon illustrates its unnerving impact on Asquith's home rule proposals. It shows the prime minister's tentative offer of the cup of self-government to Redmond being dramatically interrupted by the sword of 'army resignations'. The government's irresolute response to loyalist militancy was further underlined a few weeks later by its failure to intervene to prevent the Ulster Volunteer Force gun-running operation.

10

REBELLION AND CIVIL WAR
1914–1923

The First World War, according to R.F. Foster, 'should be seen as one of the most decisive events in modern Irish history. Politically speaking, it temporarily defused the Ulster situation; it put Home Rule on ice; it altered the conditions of military crisis in Ireland at a stroke; and it created the rationale for an IRB rebellion.' The war also proved to be a defining moment for the political fortunes of John Redmond and the Irish Parliamentary Party. In a speech in the Commons on 3 August 1914, the day before Britain declared war on Germany, Redmond offered Asquith's government the support of nationalist Ireland, in the form of the Irish Volunteers, in the impending war effort. This gesture of Irish nationalist goodwill was calculated to impress British public and parliamentary opinion, and galvanise Asquith into placing the Home Rule Bill on the statute book. The tactic paid off when the Home Rule Act received the royal assent on 18 September, despite the walk-out of the entire Conservative opposition in the Commons. Irish self-government was now a legal, though not an actual, reality, as the implementation of the Act was suspended for the duration of the war. The position of Ulster remained ominously unresolved, however, as Westminster reserved the right to make as yet unspecified legislative arrangements for the province.

Buoyed up by this great political triumph, an invigorated Redmond rallied Irish recruits to the British war effort. In an impromptu speech at Woodenbridge, County Wicklow, on 20 September he called on the Volunteers to join the British army and fight 'not only in Ireland itself, but wherever the firing line extends in defence of right, of freedom and of religion in this war'. These rousing words precipitated a dramatic crisis within the Volunteer movement, which led to a split between a majority who supported Redmond's recruitment policy and a minority, among them Eoin MacNeill, Patrick Pearse and Thomas MacDonagh, who opposed it. The former, possibly 180,000 strong, became known as the National Volunteers, while the dissenting 12,000 retained the title of Irish Volunteers.

Whereas constitutional Irish nationalists responded to Britain's war crisis with strategic but none the less heartfelt displays of patriotism, militant separatists demurred. In August 1914 the supreme council of the revitalised IRB decided that a nationwide rebellion should take place before the war ended. Guided by the ancient Fenian dictum that 'England's difficulty is Ireland's opportunity', the small inner circle of the IRB set about planning an insurrection. It was to be led by the Irish Volunteers, supported by Clan na Gael funds from America and German arms. In December 1915 the IRB military council, comprising Pearse, Tom Clarke, Seán Mac Diarmada, Eamonn Ceannt and Joseph Plunkett, secretly decided upon Easter Sunday, 23 April 1916 as the date for the rising. It was these five revolutionaries, together with labour leader James Connolly, commander of the socialist Citizen Army, and Thomas MacDonagh, poet and lecturer, who planned the insurrection.

In the event, key setbacks in the days before the rising was due to take place destroyed their slender chances of success. The *Aud*, a German ship laden with arms, was scuttled by its captain in Queenstown (now Cobh) harbour in Cork, having failed to rendezvous as planned with Sir Roger Casement, a retired Dublin-born colonial civil servant, who was himself arrested in Kerry on Good Friday. The following day the Volunteer commander, Eoin MacNeill, on realising that he had been duped by Pearse and Plunkett into sanctioning special Volunteer manoeuvres, issued an order countermanding all military action. This had the effect of confusing the Volunteers and preventing a nationwide insurrection. It also postponed the start of the rising by one day.

So when, at noon on Easter Monday, Pearse proclaimed the establishment of an Irish Republic from the steps of the General Post Office in Dublin, he knew that military failure was almost inevitable. But Ireland's honour might still be saved by a blood sacrifice, since 'from the graves of patriot men and women spring living nations'. Pearse's words are a reminder that the rising was the product of a specifically Catholic political consciousness – it did, after all, coincide with Easter, the festival which commemorates Christ's resurrection – and as such remains a potent historical testament to the intimate link between religion and nationalism in Ireland.

Lacking widespread popular support, the rebellion was crushed within days and Pearse surrendered unconditionally on Saturday 29 April. He and the other commanders of the rising were imprisoned in Kilmainham jail, where they were hastily tried by court martial and sentenced to death. The first of the executions took place on 3 May when Pearse, MacDonagh and Clarke were shot. Twelve more executions followed over the next nine days. The ferocity of the British response alienated Irish public opinion at home and abroad, especially in America, and elevated the dead rebels to the status of martyrs. Whereas few Irish people, nationalist or otherwise, had supported the rebels during Easter week, the tide of political opinion now turned in their favour. Like many Irish revolutionaries before them, their failure – and their cause – had been ennobled by their deaths.

Unlike 1798 and 1867, however, the ferocity of the government's reponse in 1916 legitimised the violence of the revolutionaries in the minds of a great many Irish people, who were no longer prepared to trust the British government to deliver them into a self-governing Ireland. Nor were they willing to support those Irish politicians who continued to put their faith in 'perfidious Albion'. This had serious implications for Redmond and his party, whose policy of winning home rule by constitutional means was dealt a devastating blow by the rising. In the months that followed, a decisive transformation began to take shape in Irish politics, as public support shifted from the discredited constitutional nationalism of the Irish Parliamentary Party to the militant republicanism of Sinn Féin, reorganised in 1917 under the leadership of Eamon de Valera (1882–1975), the senior surviving commander of the rising.

Although Sinn Féin played no direct part in the rising, the authorities subsequently labelled it the Sinn Féin rebellion, thereby giving the moribund movement and its members an unearned nationalist prestige. With the national mood of resentment provoked by Britain's inept handling of the rising heightened by continuing martial law and the threat of conscription, de Valera sought to translate this new-found prestige into electoral support. Sinn Féin scored a number of by-election successes in 1917, including de Valera's own convincing victory over a home rule candidate in East Clare.

This was the prelude to a spectacular victory in the 1918 general election, when the party won 73 of Ireland's 105 seats and reduced home rule representation to a mere 6. Having declared that its elected members would abstain from attendance at Westminster,

Sinn Féin MPs met in the Mansion House in Dublin on 21 January 1919, declared a sovereign Irish Republic and established a parliament, Dáil Éireann, to legislate for all Ireland. This illegal act was, of course, highly provocative and could not be allowed to go unchallenged by the British authorities. By coincidence, two members of the Royal Irish Constabulary were ambushed and killed at Soloheadbeg in County Tipperary by an Irish Volunteer unit on the very same day as the Dáil was established. This incident marked the start of the Anglo-Irish War, also known as the War of Independence, which was to last until July 1921.

Refusing to negotiate a political settlement, Lloyd George's government sought to pacify Ireland by repressive military means. Cold-blooded killings were carried out by both crown and republican forces. Two additional police units, the Black and Tans and the Auxiliaries, were recruited in Britain from the one million demobilised servicemen to augment the forces of the Royal Irish Constabulary. Their acts of brutality and terror against the Irish civilian population engendered widespread sympathy and support for republican guerrillas and entered deeply into the Irish nationalist consciousness. Throughout this two-and-a-half-year guerrilla war the Volunteers, or, as they came to be known, the Irish Republican Army, were directed by Michael Collins (1890–1922), who also held the post of finance minister in the underground government of the putative Republic. Collins's avowed aim was to make Ireland effectively ungovernable and thereby force the British government to concede independence.

In the autumn of 1919 Lloyd George's coalition government turned again to consider the Irish question. The recommendation of a special cabinet committee that not one but two home rule parliaments be established in Ireland was now adopted as government policy. This was embodied in the Government of Ireland Act passed in December 1920 and effective from 1 May 1921. The Act partitioned Ireland into two jurisdictions, 'Northern Ireland', defined as 'the six parliamentary counties of Antrim, Armagh, Down, Fermanagh, Londonderry and Tyrone, and the parliamentary boroughs of Belfast and Londonderry', and 'Southern Ireland', comprising the remaining twenty-six counties. This Act, the most momentous piece of British legislation to affect Ireland in 120 years, was a compromise solution which failed to satisfy any of the competing strands of Irish political opinion. It was, in effect, a British solution to an Irish problem.

In May 1921 elections were held under the terms of the Act in both parts of Ireland. Northern unionists' initial reluctance to accept the settlement and relinquish the goal of full integration with the United Kingdom soon gave way to a pragmatic resolve to secure comprehensive parliamentary control by returning forty unionist MPs to the fifty-two seat assembly. The Act proved largely inoperative in the south, however, where Sinn Féin leaders rejected its legitimacy and instead used the election to renew their mandate by re-turning 124 members – known as TDs (Teachta Dála) – to the second Dáil, which convened on 16 August 1921.

By then, however, neither side in the conflict could see any immediate prospect of military victory, and a truce was brokered between the British government and the IRA, which came into effect on 11 July. The following day, de Valera led a delegation to London to meet Lloyd George, whose offer of limited independence for a twenty-six-county Ireland within the British Commonwealth proved unacceptable. Further fruitless meetings and correspondence between the two men followed during the next three months. The prime minister finally invited de Valera to send delegates to a London conference which opened on 11 October to determine 'how the association of Ireland with the community of nations known as the British Empire may best be reconciled with Irish national aspirations'.

At the outset, reconciliation seemed an impossibility, given the diametrically opposed demands of the two sides. For the Irish delegation, led by Griffith and Collins, independence and unity were the most important issues. A republic had been proclaimed and died for; it would not be easily relinquished. The twin British priorities were the obverse of the Irish ones: the retention of Ireland within the empire and the maintenance of partition. Nevertheless, after eight weeks of tortuous negotiations, Lloyd George, seizing upon divisions within the Irish team, presented them with an urgent ultimatum: agree to a settlement or face 'war within three days'. Partial Irish sovereignty was available, but not the hallowed republic. His ploy worked, and the six Irish delegates signed the Anglo-Irish Treaty in Downing Street at 2.10 a.m. on 6 December 1921. It was, all knew, a fateful hour, none more so perhaps than Collins, who in signing the treaty predicted that he was signing his death warrant.

The treaty conferred dominion status on the Irish Free State, the new name for the twenty-six counties, which would remain within the British Commonwealth. All members of the Dublin parliament would have to swear an oath of allegiance to the British monarch who would be represented in Ireland by a governor-general. The Free State would have full governmental control over its internal affairs, including the judiciary, police and a limited army, though Britain retained control of certain strategic ports. On the crucial issue of partition, the right of Northern Ireland to opt out from the provisions of the treaty, and so remain part of the United Kingdom, was enshrined in Article 12. If this were to happen, an inter-governmental commission would be appointed to 'determine in accordance with the wishes of the inhabitants, so far as may be compatible with economic and geographic conditions, the boundaries between Northern Ireland and the rest of Ireland'.

The treaty caused deep divisions within the republican cabinet, the Dáil and the country at large. Sovereignty rather than unity – the oath rather than partition – emerged as *the* divisive issue. Pragmatists like Collins defended the agreement as the best available compromise and a stepping stone to full independence, saying that it 'gives us freedom, not the ultimate freedom that all nations desire and develop to, but the freedom to achieve it'. The republican idealists who opposed it, led by de Valera, criticised it for failing to deliver the hoped-for republic, and condemned it as being 'in violent conflict with the wishes of the majority of this nation'.

The protracted and acrimonious Dáil debate which ensued culminated in the narrow ratification of the treaty by 64 votes to 57 on 7 January 1922. De Valera promptly led the anti-treatyites out of the Dáil, while the remaining members proceeded to establish a provisional government under the terms of the treaty. On 16 January 1922 Collins, as chairman of this new body, went to Dublin Castle where a formal transfer of power from the British to the Irish authorities took place. He had, in effect, become the first leader of independent Ireland.

Tension between pro- and anti-treaty forces mounted in the months that followed, as British forces evacuated army barracks throughout the country and the RIC was replaced by an unarmed Irish police force. A blatant challenge to the authority of the provisional government came in April when anti-treaty republicans occupied the Four Courts in Dublin, the centre of the Irish judiciary, and established their military headquarters there. Reluctant to move against his old comrades and precipitate open conflict, Collins played for time. Meanwhile, the Irish general election in June showed that a clear majority of the electorate was in favour of the treaty.

Hopes of peaceful reconciliation between pro- and anti-treatyites were short-lived, however. Two acts of republican defiance – the assassination of Sir Henry Wilson, military adviser to the new Northern Ireland government, by republican sympathisers in London on 22 June, followed by the kidnapping of a leading Free State army commander in Dublin four days later – meant that decisive government action could no longer be postponed. In the early hours of 28 June 1922 the provisional government issued an ultimatum to the republican garrison in the Four Courts to surrender immediately. When the order was ignored, pro-treaty troops began to shell the building with guns and ammunition supplied by the departing British. The Irish Civil War had begun.

The ten months of bloody, brutal fighting that followed not only divided families and communities but also robbed the nation of some of its finest leaders, including Cathal Brugha, Arthur Griffith, Liam Mellows and, aged only thirty-one, Michael Collins, killed in an ambush in his native Cork in August 1922. He was succeeded as chairman of the provisional government by W.T. Cosgrave (1880–1965) in September. Three months later, in the midst of the internecine chaos and to some extent eclipsed by it, the Irish Free State (Saorstát Éireann) formally came into existence, one year after the signing of the treaty. By the time the republicans were ground into submission by the numerically superior and better-equipped government forces in May 1923, as many as four thousand lives had been lost and countless others traumatised by their experiences.

The Civil War represented the worst possible start for the new southern state. Instead of looking forward to the creation of a new society, Irish people were compelled to endure the fierce embrace of the past. The war left a legacy of great bitterness, traces of which are still discernible in Irish life today. The treaty became the central political issue in independent Ireland and the divisions it produced formed the basis for the Irish party system. The two main parties that subsequently came to dominate politics – Fianna Fáil (a Sinn Féin progeny) and Fine Gael (successor to Cumann na nGaedheal) – originated in the divided loyalties of the early 1920s and cast a long shadow over the emergence of other political ideologies. In particular, the struggle for independence arrested the development of embryonic socialist and feminist movements in Ireland, leading to the marginalisation of female and working-class voices in the political life of the new state. This polarisation of Irish politics around attitudes to the national question meant that the country evolved a different political culture to many other European countries, where social and economic divisions often provide the basis for political representation. Over seventy years later, it is these same two parties that continue to dominate the political scene, despite the rising profile of the Labour Party.

10.1 'The Change in Ireland', Rigney, *Bystander*, London, 19 August 1914

During 1914, the failure to reach any compromise over the question of Ulster's exclusion from home rule, together with the continued growth of the rival Volunteer forces north and south, led many to fear that civil war in Ireland was imminent. The Ulster Volunteer Force, which numbered over one hundred thousand men, had already successfully landed thousands of German rifles in April, and the Irish Volunteers followed suit in July, when German arms were landed at Howth. The sudden involvement of Britain in the European war, however, brought an abrupt end to the home rule crisis by altering the dimensions of the Irish problem and introducing new priorities.

The Change In Ireland

Three weeks ago Ireland was divided—so much so that the only point of agreement between Ulster and the Nationalists was in their common vituperation of England and her Government. The Kaiser threatens the power of the British Empire, and—hey presto!—Ulster and the Nationalists make common cause again, but this time to help John Bull

This *Bystander* cartoon by Francis Rigney shows a quizzical and confused John Bull being violently threatened by Redmond's Irish Volunteers on one side and Carson's Ulster Volunteers on the other. His problem seems to be solved, however, when the Kaiser threatens Britain, although his confusion at their sudden conversion remains. Redmond and Carson agreed to suspend their rivalry for the duration of the war and concentrate on supporting Britain's military effort. On the day war was declared by Britain, Redmond, without consulting his colleagues, pledged Ireland's support, and promised that the Irish Volunteers would defend Ireland. He suggested that all British troops be withdrawn from Ireland, stating that its coast 'will be defended from foreign invasion by her armed sons, and for this purpose armed nationalist Catholics in the south will be only too glad to join arms with the armed Protestant Ulstermen in the north'. This stance, which was intended to show that support for home rule was perfectly compatible with loyalty to Britain, was supported by a majority of the Volunteers, though the objections of a militant minority led to a split in the movement.

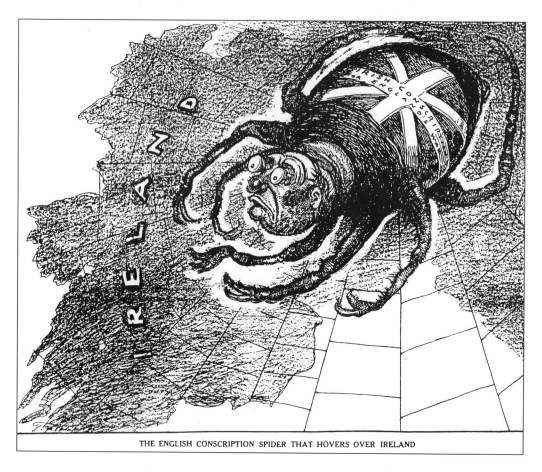

THE ENGLISH CONSCRIPTION SPIDER THAT HOVERS OVER IRELAND

10.2 'The English Conscription Spider...', Fleming, *Irish World*, New York, 21 August 1915

On 18 September 1914 the Home Rule Bill was placed on the statute book, but its operation was suspended for the duration of the war. Two days later Redmond called on Irish nationalists to join the British army. Thousands of Irishmen from all over Ireland responded, despite the opposition of a dissenting nationalist minority. Some two hundred thousand fought in the Great War, but while recruitment was at first popular in Ireland, enthusiasm waned as the conflict dragged on and reports of the slaughter in the trenches reached home.

Reports in the summer of 1915 that compulsory military service was being considered by the government were greeted with dismay by Redmond and his supporters. They

THE RIVAL IRISH RECRUITING SERGEANTS

JOHN BULL—"Bless you my Children"

10.3 'The Rival Irish Recruiting Sergeants', Fleming, *Irish World*, New York,
5 February 1916

knew that conscription would alienate moderate nationalist opinion and play into the
hands of militant republicans like James Connolly, who led an anti-conscription rally in
Dublin in July. The propaganda value of the conscription threat was also exploited by
Irish-American republicans, as the graphic *Irish World* image (opposite) of a predatory
spider attests. Asquith heeded the warnings and exempted Ireland from the provisions of
the Conscription Bill passed in January 1916.

While Redmond opposed conscription, he was nevertheless convinced that a 'union of
hearts' could be created between nationalists and unionists as they fought together in a
common cause. Visiting the front in November 1915, he stated that the Ulster Division
and the Dublin Fusiliers were 'like true comrades and brother Irishmen' and later pronounced: 'Let Irishmen come together in the trenches and spill their blood together and I
say there is no power on earth that when they come home can induce them to turn as
enemies one upon another.'

Nationalist opposition to this position is reflected in this *Irish World* cartoon, which
bitterly indicts the supine attitude of Redmond and William O'Brien to Irish
recruitment for 'England's war'. Although O'Brien led a small nationalist grouping in

rivalry to Redmond's party, the two leaders adopted similar attitudes to the war, hence their joint submission to a complacent John Bull who gratefully accepts this Irish sacrifice. The figure of Erin at the window regards the scene with anger and disgust. The cartoon signals the growing dissatisfaction among Irish-Americans with both wings of the constitutional nationalist movement. As American financial contributions were of major importance, this boded ill for the nationalists' future. The cartoon is particularly striking because it appeared in a neutral country only two months before the 1916 Easter Rising.

WANTED–A ST. PATRICK.

St. Augustine Birrell. "I'M AFRAID I'M NOT SO SMART AS MY BROTHER-SAINT AT DEALING WITH THIS KIND OF THING. I'M APT TO TAKE REPTILES TOO LIGHTLY."

10.4 'Wanted – A St Patrick', Partridge, *Punch*, London, 3 May 1916

Since 1914 Augustine Birrell, the chief secretary for Ireland, and his under-secretary, Sir Matthew Nathan, had allowed armed and uniformed Irish Volunteer units to drill and parade openly and to oppose recruitment to the British army. In this they were following the advice of the Irish parliamentary leaders, Redmond and Dillon, who suggested that it was better to tolerate the extreme nationalists than to suppress them, since this would drive them underground and possibly create martyrs. The Irish Volunteers were generally left alone, therefore, although Birrell was criticised by unionists for not taking a tougher line against them.

Rumours of an intended rising reached Dublin Castle in March and early April 1916, yet the authorities had no definite proof of a rebellious plot until Easter Saturday, when they received news of the arrest of Sir Roger Casement in Kerry. Even then they took no immediate action, on the assumption that this setback had scuppered the rebels' plans. Nathan, moreover, wanted the approval of his superior, Birrell, who was in England, before arresting the Volunteer leaders. (Birrell, like many of his predecessors, was very much an absentee chief secretary who preferred to spend much of his time in London and leave the day-to-day running of Irish affairs to his under-secretary.)

The cartoon opposite, drawn shortly after the rising, is highly critical of Birrell's lax approach to Irish sedition. According to legend, Saint Patrick drove the snakes out of Ireland, but here Birrell, who was sometimes jocularly known as 'Saint Augustine' by contemporaries, is castigated for his failure to banish the reptilian Sinn Féin. As happened regularly in both the British and Irish press, responsibility for the rising is erroneously attributed to Sinn Féin. The movement is also imputed to be in league with Germany, as symbolised by this creature's incongruous dachshund head and pointed helmet. The German association attaching to these dogs caused them to be so reviled in Britain during the war that it was necessary to revive the breed from German stock afterwards. Not long after this cartoon appeared, Birrell was forced to resign as a result of his inept handling of events prior to the rising.

10.5 'The Cause...', Brewster, *Irish Weekly Independent*, Dublin, 13 May 1916

The Easter Rising in 1916 came as a major shock to most people in Ireland and Britain, and many explanations were put forward for its occurrence at this time. The *Irish Weekly Independent* had no sympathy for the rebels, but in cartoon 10.5 by Gordon Brewster it regards the rising as a consequence of the British government's tolerance of violent Ulster opposition to home rule before 1914. A pusillanimous John Bull is confronted by a belligerent Carson, openly flaunting his recent defiance of the government's authority. The suggestion is that the failure of Asquith's government to deal firmly with this Ulster threat convinced militant Irish nationalists to take up arms and defy the government also. 'The effect', therefore, was the rebellion in Dublin which led to the destruction of much of the centre of the city.

THE BROKEN MELODY.

THE MAN WHO "PULLED THE STRINGS."

10.6 'The Broken Melody', Holland, *John Bull*, London, 13 May 1916

John Bull was a radical, independent, but also a warmongering periodical aimed at a working-class readership. In this post-rising cartoon Frank Holland shows the Kaiser unsuccessfully attempting to play 'Irish Rebellion' on the 'Sinn Féin' harp, implying that the insurrection was a failed German-inspired conspiracy. This was not the case, however. Although it quickly became known as the Sinn Féin rebellion, it was actually organised by the IRB, which sent Casement to Germany to seek military aid, but the Germans had so little faith in the planned revolt that they sent only one shipload of arms, much less than was hoped for. So although the proclamation of the Irish Republic referred to 'gallant allies in Europe', the reality was that Germany played little role in the events of Easter week.

10.7 'Maienblüte in Irland', *Kladderadatsch*, Berlin, 21 May 1916

This German cartoon comprises a trenchant comment on the execution of the leaders of the rising in May 1916. It features a British soldier standing sternly by his flag amid a scene of death and carnage, his culpability underlined by the sardonic epigraph – 'the "freedom of small nationalities" is restored in Ireland' – and punning title, which exploits the ambiguity of 'May blossom' and 'May blood'. At this stage of the war the Allies were beginning to devote sympathetic attention to the plight of 'small nationalities' who happened to be living in enemy territory. The cartoonist suggests that this sympathy counted for nothing where, as in Ireland, British interests were involved.

The decision to execute the rebel leaders was politically disastrous from a British government perspective, as it created martyrs for the republican cause and greatly affected

THE IRISHMAN'S BURDEN

10.8 'The Irishman's Burden', Fleming, *Irish World*, New York, 24 June 1916

Irish public opinion. Fifteen men were executed over a nine-day period, despite John Dillon's Commons' warning that the government was 'washing out our whole life work in a sea of blood'. Although Asquith halted the killings after 12 May, Irish political opinion was already beginning to desert constitutional nationalism for a revitalised Sinn Féin.

   The *Irish World* reacted to news of the executions with predictable anti-imperial venom, as this arresting Fleming cartoon indicates. It depicts an Irish republican buckling under the weight of the ferocious British lion, bearing the bloody sword of execution. Redmond's anti-republicanism and Carson's unionism are also indicted, as is the 1914 Home Rule Bill. As government coercion against Irish republicans continued, the editor, Robert Ford, added a new by-line to his paper's masthead, encouraging readers to ask their newsagents for 'the criminal history of the British empire'.

10.9 'Eire . . .', *Irish Nation*, Dublin, 5 August 1916

After the disastrous consequences of the Easter Rising, Asquith realised that the only way to save the cause of moderate nationalism was to try to implement home rule at once. Lloyd George, therefore, was given the task of negotiating a compromise deal between nationalists and unionists during May and June 1916. He dealt with Carson and Redmond separately, and eventually got the latter to accept immediate home rule for the twenty-six

EIRE (to J. E. R.) : *" Take that away—burn it.   If I am to have a place among the Nations I must have a seat at least as good as yonder chair."*

southern counties, on the understanding that the six north-eastern counties' exclusion would be temporary. Carson accepted this deal also, in the belief that Ulster's exclusion would be permanent. When Redmond realised this he immediately renounced the deal, but his position was compromised by his having already agreed to give up areas in Ulster where there were nationalist majorities. This reflected his desperate need to achieve any kind of settlement, but led to the Irish Parliamentary Party being branded as partitionist by its republican opponents, and being heavily criticised by northern nationalists in particular.

This rather crudely drawn cartoon appeared in a short-lived Dublin periodical and illustrates the growing dissatisfaction with home rule politics within nationalist Ireland. It shows an affronted Eire rejecting Redmond's offer of a three-legged home rule chair, the Ulster leg of which has been broken off by Carson. Instead, she demands a seat of better quality, one at least as good as the Speaker's chair in Grattan's parliament of the late eighteenth century. Her demand reflects nationalist impatience with Redmond's ineffectual parliamentarianism and the growing support for the more radical politics of Sinn Féin. Lloyd George, who had attempted to broker a deal between Redmond and Carson, appears in the background as a Chaplinesque clown. He had recently been appointed secretary for war after the death of Kitchener, and departs from the scene with apparently more important matters on his mind than Ireland.

HANDS ACROSS THE FENCE

UNCLE SAM: "Shake, John! We should get together better if it wasn't for this darned fence."

10.10 'Hands Across the Fence', *Star*, London, 4 May 1917

In April 1917 the USA entered the war on the Allied side. This greatly affected the Irish situation and gave much encouragement to those nationalists who desired complete independence. The American president, Woodrow Wilson, had already professed his belief that 'every people has the right to choose the sovereignty under which they shall live', and one of America's stated war aims was 'self-determination for small nations'. The British government, now headed by Lloyd George, realised that the new American alliance would make it even more necessary to appease Irish-American opinion.

This cartoon, which appeared in the radical London evening newspaper the *Star*, reflects the changing reality of war politics. Although Uncle Sam and John Bull can shake hands, the 'fence' impedes closer co-operation. International hostility towards Britain because of its actual, or perceived, policy towards Ireland was widespread, and there was now increased pressure on Lloyd George to abandon coercion and seek a speedy settlement through conciliation.

10.11 'A Bird of Ill-Omen', Maybank, *Passing Show*, London, 28 July 1917

The failure of Redmond's party to secure home rule in the year after the Easter Rising, and his continuing conflict with Carson over Ulster's exclusion, increased the disillusionment

A BIRD OF ILL-OMEN.

"TWEEDLEDUM AND TWEEDLEDEE
AGREED TO HAVE A BATTLE;
FOR TWEEDLEDUM SAID TWEEDLEDEE
HAD SPOILT HIS NICE NEW RATTLE.

"JUST THEN FLEW DOWN A MONSTROUS CROW
AS BLACK AS A TAR BARREL;
WHICH FRIGHTENED BOTH THE HEROES SO
THEY QUITE FORGOT THEIR QUARREL."

Through the Looking Glass

of the Irish public with the Irish Parliamentary Party. This provided the opportunity for Sinn Féin, an amalgam of different groups which was coming increasingly under the direction of republicans, to win over nationalist supporters. During 1917 they made considerable advances, winning by-elections in North Roscommon in February and South Longford in May, constituencies previously held by home rulers. In July a key by-election took place in East Clare. The previous month Lloyd George, in a further attempt to conciliate American opinion, had released the senior surviving leader of the rising, Eamon de Valera. De Valera contested the seat and during the campaign made clear that he wanted a republic. His sweeping victory meant that the majority of the electors had decisively rejected the Irish Parliamentary Party and had opted for the republican ideals proclaimed in 1916.

Many cartoons of the nineteenth and early twentieth centuries draw on Lewis Carroll's *Alice in Wonderland* or, as here, *Alice Through the Looking Glass*. Carson and Redmond are cast as the absurd twins, Tweedledum and Tweedledee, who have 'agreed to have a battle' over the 'nice new rattle' of home rule. They are comically protected by a motley collection of armour, including a saucepan and coal scuttle as helmets, and several speeches secured by bands of red tape. The 'monstrous crow' which frightens them has the body of Sinn Féin and the head of de Valera, fresh from his recent East Clare by-election victory. Despite this clear and present danger, however, Redmond and Carson, unlike Tweedle-dum and Tweedledee, were unable to forget their 'quarrel'.

The Clare by-election occurred in poignant circumstances, as it was caused by the death in action of Major William Redmond, younger brother of John. It was Daniel O'Connell's by-election victory in the same county in 1828 which had set in motion the chain of events leading to Catholic emancipation in 1829.

A TEST OF SAGACITY.

Mr. LLOYD GEORGE. "LADIES AND GENTLEMEN, WITH THE LETTERS I HAVE PLACED BEFORE HIM OUR LEARNED FRIEND WILL NOW SPELL OUT SOMETHING THAT SIGNIFIES THE GREATEST HAPPINESS FOR IRELAND."
THE PIG. "I CAN'T MAKE THE BEASTLY THING SPELL 'REPUBLIC.'"

10.12 'A Test of Sagacity', Partridge, *Punch*, London, 18 February 1920

Lloyd George reacted to the growing violence of the Anglo-Irish War, which had begun in January 1919, with his usual combination of coercion and conciliation. While prosecut-ing a sustained military campaign against the guerrilla offensive of the IRA, he also set up a special cabinet committee under the chairmanship of unionist Walter Long to advise the

"THE RESOURCES OF CIVILISATION."

Mr. Lloyd George. "STICK TO IT, BONAR. POOR OLD SISYPHUS NEVER HAD AN IMPLEMENT LIKE THIS."

10.13 'The Resources of Civilisation', Raven-Hill, *Punch*, London, 20 October 1920

government on the best means of securing an Irish settlement. The committee eventually settled on the idea that Ireland should be divided into two parts, with each being granted home rule. Thus, all Irish people would to be able to enjoy self-government, while Britain would benefit from being able to distance itself from Irish affairs, and thus remove a contentious issue which had frequently caused it embarrassment on the international stage. Accordingly, the Government of Ireland Bill was introduced in February 1920, which proposed the establishment of two separate parliaments in Dublin and Belfast.

The *Punch* cartoon opposite casts Lloyd George as a music hall entertainer introducing his performing pig to his audience, an image which testifies to British cartoonists' continuing reliance on bestial tropes to represent the Irish character. In this instance, the porcine stereotype may be seen in either of two ways. From one perspective, it ridicules Irish nationalists' stubborn cleavage to the republican ideal, which is seen as, literally, pigheaded; from another, the pig may be seen as an astute animal with a very clear idea of what he wants and who is not prepared to be deflected by Lloyd George. While northern unionists reluctantly came to accept the proposal of a home rule parliament of their own, de Valera and the Sinn Féin leadership in the south were implacably opposed to the idea. An Irish republic remained their goal, and the cartoon accurately reflects the disparity between Lloyd George's offer and the nationalists' demand.

The *Punch* cartoon above adapts another familiar Anglo-Irish cartoon motif, the myth of Sisyphus, to comment on the political situation in the autumn of 1920. Although Lloyd George was a Liberal, he was leader of a Conservative-dominated coalition government at this time. But since both British parties were now distancing themselves from their former Irish allies, he firmly believed that a united coalition front, backed up by military strength, could force both parts of Ireland to accept the Government of Ireland Bill, which was then in its third reading in the Commons. Raven-Hill concurs with this assessment, suggesting that the coalition lever will enable Lloyd George and the Conservative leader, Bonar Law, to secure the Bill's acceptance and bring about the settlement of the Irish question. The cartoon title refers to a speech made by Gladstone in October 1881, in which he denounced Land League violence by proclaiming that 'the resources of civilisation against its enemies are not yet exhausted'.

The Government of Ireland Bill finally became law on 23 December 1920, despite opposition from both unionists and nationalists in Ireland and Britain. The political measure never took effect in the form intended, however, though it did leave a long-term legacy in the form of the Northern Ireland parliament. *Punch*'s optimism ultimately proved to be unfounded, therefore, and later cartoonists would again have recourse to the Sisyphus image to reflect the seemingly intractable nature of the Anglo-Irish relationship.

"Were Not We, Too?"

[The forces of law and order were entitled to the support of every honest citizen, Liberal as well as Conservative, for we were all under the same protection. (Cheers.)"—Mr. LLOYD GEORGE at the Conservative Club.]

10.14 'Were not we, too?', Low, *Star*, London, 6 December 1920

Throughout the Anglo-Irish War, the British government refused to concede publicly that its opponents, the IRA, constituted a proper army. Instead, Lloyd George continually referred to it as 'a murder gang' to be dealt with by the police, supported by the army, and not vice versa. (A similar approach underpinned Britain's 'criminalisation' and 'Ulster-isation' policies in Northern Ireland in the 1970s.) So although troops were used to counter IRA violence, a campaign was launched to find English recruits for the Royal Irish Constabulary, as young Irishmen were not joining.

These new recruits, the first of which arrived in Ireland in March 1920, were mainly demobbed soldiers. They were quickly labelled the 'Black and Tans', as they wore army khaki trousers and dark green police tunics because of a shortage of police uniforms. A further smaller force, called the Auxiliaries, was mainly made up of ex-army officers and numbered approximately one thousand men by the end of the year. Both groups were greatly lacking in proper police discipline and soon earned a gruesome reputation as a result of their retaliatory attacks on civilians in the wake of IRA violence. The British government was prepared to condone these ferocious reprisals, if not actually encourage them, in the hope that they would deter people from supporting the IRA. In fact, the reprisal policy proved counter-productive and boosted republican support.

The British cartoon (opposite) by New Zealand-born David Low (1891–1963), a political radical who later worked for the Conservative *Evening Standard*, is one of a number in which he explicitly and trenchantly criticises the government's repressive policy in Ireland during the Troubles. As the epigraph indicates, it was drawn in response to a recent speech by Lloyd George in which he called for universal public support for 'the forces of law and order'. Low seizes on this phrase to expose the hypocrisy of the prime minister's remarks when applied to the many innocent civilian victims of British brutality in Ireland, the ghost of which poses the terse, searching question: 'Were not we, too?' Britain's disregard for the rule of law in Ireland is deftly underscored by the image of the two portly club members who seem to bask in the glow of the prime minister's specious sentiments. Five days later, rampaging Auxiliaries and Black and Tans burned property to the value of £3 million in Cork city in retaliation for an earlier IRA ambush.

10.15 'The Problem Play', Partridge, *Punch*, London, 14 September 1921

After the truce between the IRA and the British forces became effective on 11 July 1921, de Valera, as president of Dáil Éireann, went to London to meet Lloyd George for preliminary discussions. A state of deadlock quickly emerged, however, as de Valera insisted upon an independent all-Ireland republic, whereas Lloyd George was only willing to concede limited dominion status for the twenty-six counties. Much correspondence between the two men followed during the next two months, as they sought to find a compromise solution and so move beyond the precarious truce to a final negotiated settlement.

In September Lloyd George received a letter from de Valera while on a fishing holiday at Gairloch in the Scottish Highlands. In it the Sinn Féin leader asserted Ireland's right to sovereign independence. The prime minister refused to recognise this declaration, but instead invited an Irish delegation to attend a conference in London on 11 October, 'with a view to ascertaining how the association of Ireland with the community of nations known as the British Empire may best be reconciled with Irish national aspirations'. This

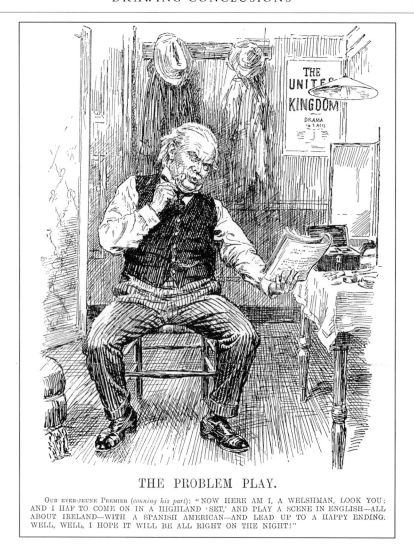

THE PROBLEM PLAY.

Our ever-jeune Premier (*conning his part*): "NOW HERE AM I, A WELSHMAN, LOOK YOU:
AND I HAF TO COME ON IN A HIGHLAND 'SET,' AND PLAY A SCENE IN ENGLISH—ALL
ABOUT IRELAND—WITH A SPANISH AMERICAN—AND LEAD UP TO A HAPPY ENDING.
WELL, WELL, I HOPE IT WILL BE ALL RIGHT ON THE NIGHT!"

proposal, known as the 'Gairloch formula', formed the basis for the negotiations which
eventually resulted in the signing of the Anglo-Irish Treaty on 6 December 1921.

This *Punch* cartoon cleverly parodies Lloyd George's dilemma on the eve of the talks
process by highlighting the diverse backgrounds of the two main players. He is cast as a
jeune premier, that is, an actor who plays the part of the hero, rehearsing his role in a three-
act 'problem' play, suggestively entitled 'The United Kingdom'. The Welsh-born
premier, who was renowned for his acting ability on the political stage, is shown learning
his English lines, which were conceived in Scotland, for a play about Ireland. To confuse
matters further, the actor playing opposite him, de Valera, was born in America to an Irish
mother and a Spanish father. He is therefore uncertain about the prospect of a happy ending, but hopes, in time-honoured theatrical fashion, that 'it will be all right on the night'.

Low's cartoon in the *Star* (opposite), on the other hand, reduces the crucially divisive
issue of the constitutional status of a new Ireland to the stuff of pantomime by casting

10.16 'Irish Freedom...', Low, *Star*, London, 21 September 1921

de Valera and Lloyd George as elderly relatives squabbling over the naming of the 'Irish Freedom' baby. The British premier's choice was eventually accepted by the Irish delegation, from which de Valera absented himself, when they signed the treaty three months later. This conferred dominion status on the newly named Irish Free State, an outcome rejected by de Valera and his fellow radical republicans in Sinn Féin because it fell far short of full sovereignty. Many years later, however, he succeeded, through subtle and tenacious statecraft, in changing the name and status of the adolescent state, so that Ireland could at last declare herself a sovereign nation.

10.17 'The Joy-Jig-Jazz', Low, *Star*, London, 8 December 1921

After two months of intensive negotiation and much soul-searching, the Anglo-Irish Treaty was signed in 10 Downing Street in the early hours of 6 December 1921. The general reaction in southern Ireland was one of relief, although republican extremists were quick to register their anger and dismay at the Irish delegation's failure to deliver full independence. Northern unionists reacted angrily also, seeing in the Boundary Commission clause a threat to the future existence of the Northern Ireland state.

In Britain the treaty was welcomed by many people as the final solution to a problem that had plagued the nation for centuries, a sentiment captured by Low in this celebratory cartoon. Collins and Lloyd George dance a jig on the grave of the 800-year-old 'Irish

Trouble', while a ghostly figure plays the British national anthem. The suggestion that disillusioned republican die-hards (bottom left) slouched into exile is rather misleading, however. While the anti-treatyites withdrew from parliament, they remained a formidable oppositional force in the country as a whole, as the ten-month Civil War revealed. This war also proved that Low's report of the death of the 'Irish Trouble' was greatly exaggerated, and his burning of his other, less sanguine Irish cartoons decidedly premature.

10.18 'The Glittering Gates', Booth, *Dublin Opinion*, Dublin, March 1922

On 7 January 1922, after a lengthy and impassioned debate, the Anglo-Irish Treaty was approved by the Dáil by a narrow majority of seven votes. An emotional de Valera responded by leading the anti-treatyites out of the chamber and resigning his position as president of the Republic. Meanwhile, Collins and Griffith, the two key supporters of the treaty, prepared to take control of the provisional government. This body was set up to facilitate the transfer of power from Britain and the subsequent transition to full government, which, under the terms of the treaty, was due to take effect from 6 December 1922, exactly one year after the agreement was signed.

THE GLITTERING GATES

ST. DAVID LLOYD GEORGE : " In you go."
ARTHUR : " Righto, it'll be heavenly."
MICHAEL : " I'm a bit doubtful, but I'll try it for a while."
EAMONN : " I'll go below ; it may be easier to get out ! "

This cartoon comes from the first issue of a new comic monthly, *Dublin Opinion*, which became the main source of political and social satire in independent Ireland. It continued regular publication until the early 1970s, and at its peak sold over seventy thousand copies per issue, a unique achievement for a magazine of its kind. As its name suggests, it was mainly concerned with southern society and politics, though it occasionally commented on northern affairs with a gentle sense of irony.

This sketch, by the magazine's founding editor, Arthur Booth, depicts Lloyd George as Saint Peter at the 'glittering gates' of a 'heavenly' Irish Free State, offering the key to Griffith, Collins and de Valera. A revolver hangs by his side, however, hinting that a more earthly form of persuasion might yet be necessary to concentrate Irish minds. Griffith, who was most supportive of the treaty, appears keen to enter, but Collins is more dubious, given his strong links with the anti-treatyites, especially in the IRA. Having already decided to stay out, de Valera prepares to descend into the hell of 'immediate and terrible war'. This phrase is borrowed from Lloyd George, who used it as a threat to Collins and Griffith on 5 December 1921 in order to coerce them into signing the treaty. By March 1922 de Valera was himself using such inflammatory language to conjure up the spectre of civil war, and Booth suggests this terrible prospect seemed preferable to him than Free State entrapment. This prospect became a reality on 28 June 1922, when the Irish Civil War erupted in Dublin.

UNDER NEW MANAGEMENT

10.19 'Under New Management', *Fleming, Irish World*, New York, 13 January 1923

On 6 December 1922, at the height of the Civil War, the Irish Free State became a constitutional and political reality. William T. Cosgrave was confirmed in the post of president of the executive council, with Kevin O'Higgins as vice-president. Richard Mulcahy was given the onerous defence portfolio, while veteran anti-Parnellite T.M. Healy became the first governor-general of the new state. The following day, a pro-treaty deputy, Sean Hales, was killed in an IRA ambush in Dublin. The new cabinet responded by authorising the execution without trial of four republican prisoners, Rory O'Connor, Liam Mellows, Joe McKelvey and Dick Barrett. These were the latest in a series of government executions, which had earlier claimed the life of Erskine Childers, one of the most influential anti-treatyite republicans.

The ruthlessness of these episodes horrified many in Ireland, Britain and America, and prompted the *Irish World*'s Fleming to draw this scathing anti-government cartoon. It casts the new Irish regime as a firm of butchers, 'Cosgrove, Mulcahy & Co', which has taken over the business of their British predecessors. Their opening announcement that they kill only 'prime young Irishmen' and respond promptly to British orders comprises a searing indictment of the new government's reliance on British military and financial support in their war against the IRA. The advertisement for 'freak steaks' parodies the new state's title, which the *Irish World* frequently lampooned as the 'Irish Freak State'. But perhaps the most lacerating detail of all is the savage slogan attributed to the new managers, 'We Kill All Our Own', which conveys a satiric scorn of Swiftian proportions.

IRELAND'S EVIL GENIUS.

Mr. De Valera. "MUCH AS I LOVE YOU, I AM COMPELLED BY CIRCUMSTANCES TO LEAVE YOU. BUT ONLY FOR A TIME."
Erin (*wearily*). "WELL, MAKE IT AS LONG AS YOU CAN."

10.20 'Ireland's Evil Genius', Raven-Hill, *Punch*, London, 6 June 1923

The Civil War ended in May 1923, soon after the death of the IRA chief of staff, Liam Lynch. Although de Valera was the political leader of the republican movement, he had exercised little influence over the course of the war. On 24 May, however, he issued a dramatic message to the 'soldiers of the Republic', calling upon them to cease military operations. To the republican forces, this cessation represented a cease-fire, not a surrender. As de Valera put it: 'Military victory must be allowed to rest for the moment with those who have destroyed the Republic.' Thus, the IRA was told to conceal its arms for future use. At a parliamentary level, de Valera's anti-treaty Sinn Féin party refused to recognise the new Free State government or take its seats in the Dáil, thereby absenting itself from the democratic process.

Punch welcomed de Valera's departure from Irish constitutional politics with this querulous cartoon. In it he appears as a grim-faced, malevolent figure, bidding a temporary farewell to his beloved Erin. She is wholly unperturbed by his departure, and actually hopes that his exile might prove permanent. History revealed this to be wishful thinking on a grand scale, however, as de Valera soon returned to play a centrally influential role in the shaping of modern Ireland over the next fifty years.

11

FROM FREE STATE TO REPUBLIC
1923–1959

In August 1923 the Irish Free State electorate entrusted the formidable task of building a state from the rubble of revolution to W.T. Cosgrave's renamed pro-treaty party, Cumann na nGaedheal. As in many post-revolutionary societies, the intractability of inherited realities dictated that tradition rather than experiment characterised the policies and practice of the new government. The Cosgrave administration was naturally conservative in character and showed a notable degree of continuity with the *ancien régime*, so much so that Ronan Fanning has observed that the new state was marked, 'not by a commitment to cast off British influence, but by an extraordinary fidelity to British models'.

While the army and police force were fundamentally restructured, the political institutions, civil service and legal and educational systems did not change radically after independence. The government's systematic attempt to revive the Irish language, which led to Gaelic becoming the language of instruction in primary schools and a prerequisite for employment in certain state posts, represented a rare, and ultimately futile, attempt to translate revolutionary idealism into post-revolutionary reality. The boast of one of the leading ministers of the new state was justified: the first generation of Irish self-governors showed themselves to be the most conservative of revolutionaries.

The conservative instincts of Cosgrave and his colleagues were deepened by their overriding need to legitimise and consolidate their authority throughout the twenty-six-county state. While the abstentionism of de Valera's Sinn Féin strengthened the government's parliamentary authority, the defeated republican forces posed a serious extra-parliamentary threat to the legitimacy of the new regime, as the assassination of the vice-president and minister for justice, Kevin O'Higgins, in July 1927 graphically demonstrated. Fearful of a return to the anarchy of civil war, the government courted the support of those sectors of society with vested interests in the maintenance of political and economic stability: businessmen, prosperous farmers and an increasingly influential Catholic hierarchy.

The result was a polity characterised by fiscal prudence and social conservatism. Economic policy was based on a commitment to develop the dominant agricultural sector at the expense of the weak industrial sector. Episcopal concerns about public morality led to laws being passed to protect the nation's purity from such perceived moral contaminants as films, novels and divorce. Such measures helped create an authoritarian and censorious social climate which inhibited cultural expression and confirmed Ulster Protestants' perception that the largely homogeneous Catholic south was becoming a strongly confessional state, thereby hardening the partitionist divide.

The reality of partition was formally consolidated in 1925 following the deliberations of the Boundary Commission, which was established under the treaty to readjust the border between Northern Ireland and the Free State. Negotiations ended ignominiously for the southern government when Cosgrave signed a tripartite agreement with British

Prime Minister Stanley Baldwin (1867–1947) and James Craig to accept the territorial status quo, thereby effectively ending Dublin dreams of reunification. While the fiasco of the Boundary Commission deepened the conviction of militant republicans that partition could be removed only by physical force, it strengthened the resolve of de Valera and his followers to abandon abstentionism and enter the constitutional arena.

Thus, in May 1926 de Valera launched a new republican party, Fianna Fáil, dedicated to the establishment of an independent, self-sufficient, Irish-speaking united Ireland by constitutional means. The party won forty-four seats in the 1927 general election, after which he took the crucial decision to lead his deputies into the Dáil, formally taking the odious oath of allegiance to the British monarch, while informally denying he was doing so. The party's transition from parliamentary opposition to government occurred five years later in 1932, when de Valera succeeded Cosgrave as president of the Irish Free State and began sixteen years of uninterrupted Fianna Fáil rule.

De Valera's primary political objective was to expunge all references to the British crown from the Irish constitution in order to bring about his cherished goal of full Irish sovereignty. Within months of coming to power he initiated war with Britain on two fronts, constitutional and economic. His constitutional crusade began with the abolition of the oath of allegiance and the downgrading of the office of governor-general. In 1936 he took advantage of the abdication of King Edward VIII to remove the crown from the existing constitution, and the following year succeeded in having a new constitution adopted by plebiscite which made Éire, the new name for the Free State, a de facto republic. On the economic front, from July 1932 de Valera withheld land annuity payments due to Britain under the Land Acts of the late nineteenth and early twentieth centuries. When Britain retaliated by imposing tariffs on Irish produce entering the United Kingdom, the Anglo-Irish 'economic war' began. It lasted until the spring of 1938 and caused disruption to the economies of both countries.

These years also witnessed a fundamental economic shift away from free trade towards a policy of industrial protectionism, the corollary of de Valera's vision of frugal self-sufficiency and pastoral isolation, which he so eloquently evoked in his celebrated Saint Patrick's Day radio broadcast of 1943:

> The Ireland which we have dreamed of would be the home of a people who valued material wealth only as a basis of right living, of a people who were satisfied with frugal comfort and devoted their leisure to things of the spirit; a land whose countryside would be bright with cosy homesteads, whose fields and villages would be joyous with the sounds of industry, with the romping of sturdy children, the contests of athletic youths, the laughter of comely maidens; whose firesides would be forums for the wisdom of serene old age. It would, in a word, be the home of a people living the life that God desires that men should live.

This sonorous vision encapsulated de Valera's conception of Ireland as a Gaelic, Catholic utopia in an unprincipled, materialist world. It was a dream that bore little relationship to Irish reality, however, as the high levels of poverty, unemployment and emigration which characterised his premiership attest.

The Anglo-Irish Agreement of 1938 which brought the trade war to an end also provided for the return to the state of the three ports (Berehaven, Cobh and Lough Swilly) retained by the British under the treaty, thus making Irish sovereignty a twenty-six-county reality. The first exercise in national sovereignty occurred in September 1939 when de Valera proclaimed Ireland's neutrality on the outbreak of the Second World War or, as it was known in Ireland, 'the Emergency'. While partition was the ostensible reason for Irish neutrality, non-participation in the war was also desirable from the point of view of internal state security – there were fears that an IRA–Nazi pact might destabilise the state – and the economy. But whereas the proclamation of neutrality was a straightforward affair, its preservation required considerable diplomatic skill.

De Valera demonstrated adroit statecraft in maintaining Ireland's formal non-alignment, not least in his rejection of Prime Minister Churchill's seductive offers of Irish unity in return for Allied alignment. As the conflict went on, however, the government's officially neutral stance was belied by its covert support for the Allied war effort, which involved the sharing of Irish air space and intelligence information with Britain, and a passive acquiescence in the steady stream of Irish recruits to the British forces. Yet Ireland's policy of friendly neutrality did not prevent Churchill from launching an imperious attack on de Valera's isolationism in his victory broadcast of May 1945, to which the latter issued a restrained and dignified response.

The immediate post-war years were characterised by socio-economic gloom brought about by continuing shortages of food and fuel, rising prices, increasing unemployment (despite high emigration) and a series of poor harvests. A Fianna Fáil administration, jaded after sixteen years in power, bore the brunt of popular dissatisfaction in the 1948 general election and was replaced by a five-party coalition government under the premiership of Fine Gael's John Costello (1891–1976). The impact of this new government on Anglo-Irish relations was immediate and dramatic. On 7 September 1948, during an official visit to Canada, Costello announced his government's intention to declare Ireland a republic and secede from the Commonwealth. This involved revoking the 1936 External Relations Act, which authorised the king to act in the appointment of Irish diplomatic representatives on the advice of the Irish government. Repeal legislation was passed by the Dáil in December and the formal inauguration of the Republic of Ireland followed on Easter Monday 1949, the thirty-third anniversary of the 1916 Rising.

Not surprisingly, these precipitous constitutional manoeuvres provoked alarm among northern unionists, who viewed them as yet another putative threat to partition. Renewed fears of a recrudescent southern irredentism prompted Prime Minister Basil Brooke (1888–1973) to extract guarantees from Clement Attlee's Labour government that Northern Ireland's constitutional position within the United Kingdom would be safeguarded. The resultant Ireland Act of June 1949 affirmed 'that in no event will Northern Ireland or any part thereof cease to be part of His Majesty's dominions and of the United Kingdom without the consent of the parliament of Northern Ireland'. This retaliatory Act disabused southern anti-partitionists of their lingering unificatory notions and proved yet again, in the words of Fanning, that 'the achievement of sovereignty took precedence over the aspiration to unity in the minds of those who controlled the destiny of independent Ireland'.

Costello's ideologically disparate coalition finally crumbled in the spring of 1951 in the aftermath of a controversy over the introduction of a state medical service for mothers and children by the socialist minister for health, Dr Noel Browne. His 'mother-and-child' scheme, which proposed to offer free healthcare to mothers and children under sixteen, was successfully opposed by Catholic churchmen, thereby revealing the extent to which ministerial freedom continued to be circumscribed by episcopal influence. Fianna Fáil was returned to power in the resultant election but only as a weak, minority government, which gave way to a second Costello-led coalition in 1954.

Three years later the redoubtable de Valera, now seventy-five and almost blind, was elected taoiseach for the final time, as Fianna Fáil began another unbroken sixteen years in office. When, in June 1959, this colossus of modern Irish politics finally resigned the leadership of his party to become the country's third president, the state he had so profoundly shaped was ready to embrace social, economic and cultural changes so far-reaching as to render his cherished myth of a pastoral, Gaelic Ireland finally and utterly obsolete.

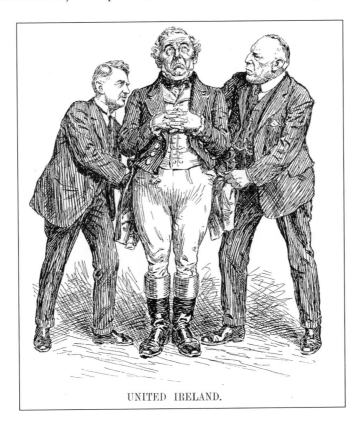

UNITED IRELAND.

11.1 'United Ireland', Partridge, *Punch*, London, 9 December 1925

When the Civil War ended in May 1923 the minds of many Irish nationalists turned to the issue of the Boundary Commission, to be established under Article 12 of the treaty if, as had happened in December 1922, Northern Ireland opted out of the Irish Free State. Craig's refusal to appoint a Northern Ireland representative, coupled with political instability in Britain, delayed the start of the commission until 6 November 1924, when it sat under the chairmanship of Justice Richard Feetham, an English-born South African judge. Feetham's narrow interpretation of a crucial but ambiguous passage of Article 12 effectively ruled out the possibility of any substantial revision of the border, as dismayed nationalists learned in a leaked *Morning Post* report in November 1925. Eoin MacNeill, the Free State representative, resigned from the commission in protest and an alarmed

CELEBRATING THEIR "VICTORY"

11.2 'Celebrating Their "Victory"', *Irish World*, New York, 19 December 1925

Cosgrave quickly signed an agreement with Craig and Baldwin to suppress the commission's report and accept the existing border on 3 December 1925.

Cartoons 11.1 and 11.2 provide widely contrasting views of the outcome of the Boundary Commission. Partridge views the settlement from a wholly British perspective by focusing on the financial rather than the political aspect of it. The cartoon refers to Article 2 of the December agreement, which relieved the Free State government of its liability for part of the British national debt, as stipulated by the treaty. *Punch* clearly believed that the British Exchequer was the real loser in the settlement, hence this image of Cosgrave (left) and Craig picking the pockets of a blithely unaware John Bull.

The suggestion that this constituted a 'United Ireland' is rather fanciful, however, since it ignores the widely differing reactions to the agreement within the profoundly polarised world of Irish politics. While northern unionists were both relieved and delighted at the consolidation of partition, northern nationalists felt betrayed and abandoned by Dublin. The settlement also reinforced the conviction of hard-line republicans that unity could only be achieved by physical force, while prompting the more moderate de Valera to pursue the path of constitutional politics.

The American *Irish World* takes an altogether different view of the Boundary Commission, seeing it as an utter fiasco from an Irish republican perspective. This republican newspaper adopted a strenuously anti-Cosgrave line throughout the 1920s and reserved special animus for his inept handling of the 1925 negotiations. In this cartoon John Bull and Craig are represented as conspirators in a sinister pact to 'dismember' Ireland. While they jubilantly toast their 'famous victory', the forlorn figure of the Free State cowers outside, the victim of their devious machinations. Craig's defiant utterance – 'Not an inch' – would be echoed repeatedly by his unionist successors whenever they felt the constitutional link between Northern Ireland and Britain to be under threat from unreconciled nationalists.

THE MAN WHO SWALLOWED THE OATH.

Irish Republican Elector (*to Mr. de Valera*). "I'D NEVER HAVE SENT YE TO THE PARLIAMENT IF I'D THOUGHT YE'D BREAK YOUR WORD AND GO THERE; AND, NOW THAT YE *ARE* THERE, WHERE ARE YE?"

11.3 'The Man Who Swallowed the Oath', Raven-Hill, *Punch*, London, 24 August 1927

The centrally divisive issue of the oath of allegiance to the British crown in the politics of post-treaty Irish republicanism is the subject of this cartoon. De Valera emerged from prison in July 1924 anxious to enter parliamentary politics and wrest control of anti-treaty Sinn Féin from hard-line republican abstentionists. The Boundary Commission débâcle

confirmed his commitment to constitutionalism and prompted him to propose a motion
at the Sinn Féin convention in March 1926 that, provided the oath was abolished, 'it
becomes a question not of principle but of policy whether or not republican representatives' enter the Dáil. When he failed to secure the support of the majority of the delegates,
he resigned as Sinn Féin president and launched his own political party, Fianna Fáil, on
16 May 1926.

Within a year, Fianna Fáil had dramatically supplanted Sinn Féin as the popular voice of
Irish republicanism. In the June 1927 general election the party won forty-four seats compared with Sinn Féin's paltry total of five. Still unwilling to pledge allegiance to the king in
order to enter parliament, de Valera and his followers initiated a campaign for a constitutional referendum on the oath. The assassination of Kevin O'Higgins by IRA opportunists
on 10 July forestalled their efforts, however, and enabled the government to regain the
initiative by introducing a Bill which required all future parliamentary candidates to
promise to take the oath if elected. Faced with this stark prospect, de Valera decided to
enter the Dáil. Thus, on 11 August, in a tortuous display of intellectual casuistry, the
Fianna Fáil leader signed the oath without reading or repeating the actual words, while
simultaneously informing the Dáil clerk: 'I want you to understand that I am not taking
any oath nor giving any promise of faithfulness to the King of England or to any power
outside the people of Ireland.'

Punch shows an uncomfortable de Valera being attacked by an angry Fianna Fáil supporter for his volte-face over the oath. Not only is he criticised for breaking his election
promise, his political judgement is also called into question, as the Cumann na nGaedheal
government survived a vote of no confidence by one vote on 16 August, despite the
combined opposition of Labour and Fianna Fáil. A second general election was held in
September, and while Cosgrave's party was returned to office, Fianna Fáil's strong showing confirmed their potential as a party of future government.

11.4 'Administering the Oath . . .', Low, *Evening Standard*, London, 10 March 1932

In the general election of February 1932 Fianna Fáil won seventy-two seats, fifteen more than Cumann na nGaedheal. The following month de Valera formed the first Fianna Fáil government with Labour Party support. The revision of the terms of the treaty was central to his plans for government, and while he took the oath in order to assume office, he soon informed Westminster of his intention to abolish it.

The Low cartoon opposite satirises de Valera's undisguised contempt for the oath by showing him administering a ludicrously contradictory pledge to a motley collection of would-be deputies with the aid of a Gaelic dictionary. The cartoon features several anti-Irish tropes familiar from cartoons of the Victorian era, including an Irish bull, pig and stereotypical brogue. The 'Spectre of "The Trouble"' has a more recent vintage, however, and refers to the (unrealised) expectation in some quarters that de Valera's accession to power would herald a recrudescence of IRA violence.

PRACTISING THE SPLITS

IN PREPARATION FOR A PERFORMANCE BEFORE THE DAIL.

Mr. de Valera. "THIS IS NOT GOING TO BE QUITE SO PAINLESS AS I HAD HOPED."

[In support of the opposition offered by the Variety Artists' Federation to the Children and Young Persons Bill a performance was to have been given in the House of Commons last week by young acrobats to prove the painlessness of their feats; but it was not permitted.]

11.5 'Practising the Splits...', Raven-Hill, *Punch*, London, 13 April 1932

Relations with Britain dominated de Valera's first months in office. He retained the external affairs portfolio for himself and orchestrated a systematic campaign to dismantle the imperial superstructure of the Free State and enable Ireland to become a de facto republic. One of the first targets of his republican crusade was the office of the governor-general, the king's representative in Ireland. The incumbent, James MacNeill, was snubbed by government ministers on official occasions before being replaced in May by Donal Ó Buachalla, a political nonentity who acquiesced in the further down-grading of the office.

De Valera's attack on the oath of allegiance was more direct and uncompromising, as evinced by his introduction of the Removal of the Oath Bill on 20 April 1932. This Bill struck at the heart of the imperial connection and was central to de Valera's aim of transforming the twenty-six counties from a British dominion to an Irish republic. In cartoon 11.5 Raven-Hill suggests that the Irish leader would overreach himself through this proposed constitutional manoeuvre. The cartoon shows a perplexed premier trapped in a painfully contorted position in his quest for sovereignty. The image ironically calls to mind Collins's famous description of the treaty as a stepping stone to full sovereignty, a concept vehemently rejected by de Valera during the 1921 treaty debates, but one which he increasingly came to adopt in practice when in government.

THE PARTLY-ALL-IN ECONOMIC WRESTLERS.
"As the boys could not agree on a referee, the contest is still going on without one. I've forgotten what round it is, but at any moment now the boys may, or may not, leave their corners!"

11.6 'The Partly-All-In . . .', CEK, *Dublin Opinion*, Dublin, October 1936

In June 1932 the Fianna Fáil government withheld land annuities payable to the British

Treasury by Irish tenants who purchased their farms under the Land Acts of the late nineteenth century. De Valera argued that the state was absolved from this financial liability, which amounted to over £3 million a year, under the terms of the 1925 Boundary Commission agreement. His proposal that the matter be submitted to an international court for arbitration was refused by the British, who insisted on a Commonwealth tribunal. When negotiations proved fruitless, the British government imposed a 20 per cent duty on Irish livestock exports to the United Kingdom in July. The Irish government retaliated by imposing tariffs on British coal imports and the 'economic war' began. Hostilities lasted for almost six years, during which time the Irish economy generally, and the farming community in particular, suffered great hardship.

The cartoon opposite by *Dublin Opinion* editor Charles E. Kelly (1904–81) takes a rather sardonic view of the Anglo-Irish tariff war. It casts the two premiers, Baldwin and de Valera, as wrestlers engaged in a prolonged stand-off, having failed to agree on a mutually acceptable referee. The non-contest is presided over by Britannia and Éire, neither of whom appears to be particularly interested in the outcome. The drawing reflects the sense of stalemate which prevailed after four years of retaliatory economic action by both governments.

The first move to resolve the impasse came a year later in November 1937, when de Valera raised the prospect of a negotiated settlement with Neville Chamberlain (1869–1940), the new British prime minister. Talks began in London in January 1938 and ended successfully with the signing of the Anglo-Irish Agreement on 25 April, whereby the Irish government agreed to a one-off payment of £10 million to settle the land annuities dispute and duty-free trade between the two countries resumed. Britain also agreed to return the three Irish ports which it retained under the terms of the treaty, namely, Berehaven, Cobh and Lough Swilly.

11.7 'The President's Blotting Pad', *Dublin Opinion*, Dublin, January 1937

One of the factors which encouraged de Valera to seek *rapprochement* with Chamberlain in the autumn of 1937 was that by this date he had succeeded in effectively revising the 1921 treaty out of existence by means of a new constitution. Having spent his first years in office systematically modifying the imperial character of the 1922 constitution, he eventually announced his intention to replace it with a new one in May 1936. He was greatly helped in his efforts by the British abdication crisis which broke in late November of that year.

On 11 December, the day after King Edward VIII abdicated, the cabinet decided to eliminate all references to the king and governor-general from the existing constitution as far as internal Irish affairs were concerned. The accompanying External Relations Act empowered the king to act on behalf of the Free State in certain external matters, on the advice of the Irish government. Such opportunism brought closer de Valera's proclaimed goal of full Irish sovereignty and cleared the way for the publication of a new constitution on 1 May 1937, which was ratified by the Dáil in June and passed by referendum on 1 July.

This *Dublin Opinion* cartoon, which appeared four months before the draft constitution was published, comprises a witty amalgam of de Valera's putative jottings. The sketch suggests that the president had no clear constitutional vision but was casting around for models to imitate. Hence his memoranda to consult the American Declaration of Independence, Lincoln's Gettysburg address and the Parnell monument in Dublin's O'Connell Street for ideas. The jottings labelled 'Ceremonial Head of State' refer to the creation of the new office of president, an elected figurehead with limited political powers, with the

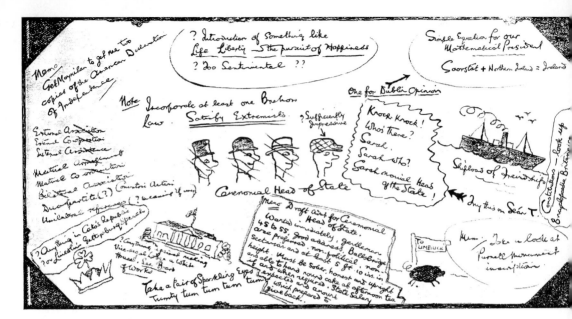

The President's Blotting Pad.

Reproduction of the actual blotting-pad used by President de Valera during the final drafting of the New Constitution.

title of 'taoiseach' being given to the head of government. The note about the inclusion of a Brehon law, the legal system of pre-colonial Gaelic Ireland, refers to de Valera's concern to satisfy hard-line republicans, while the 'simple' equation 'Saorstát [Free State] + Northern Ireland = Ireland' is a droll allusion to his own cherished ideal of a thirty-two-county sovereign Irish republic.

In fact, de Valera stopped short of proclaiming a republic in 1937 on the grounds that the nation was not yet unified. Nevertheless, Articles 2 and 3 asserted the Dublin government's constitutional right to exercise jurisdiction over the six northern counties, a claim which has been the target of much unionist resentment until their proposed removal by referendum in May 1998.

11.8 'Will yiz shut up . . .', CEK, *Dublin Opinion*, Dublin, June 1937

The new constitution eventually came into operation on 29 December 1937 and remains the fundamental law of the state. One article which attracted little criticism at the time but subsequently led to widespread disquiet is that which refers to the position of women. Article 41 enshrines the idea that a woman's natural and proper place is in the home as a full-time wife and mother. It reflects the patriarchal consensus that underpinned official attitudes to women in post-independence Ireland, a consensus which enabled successive governments to enact a series of discriminatory laws curtailing women's political, economic and reproductive rights. The fact that no woman contributed to the drafting of the constitution further underlines this female marginalisation.

The *Dublin Opinion* cartoon opposite is an amusing yet accurate representation of Irish women's domestic confinement, both actual and constitutional, in de Valera's Ireland. Its implied criticism of women's subordination is quite advanced for its time, especially when one considers the chauvinism that characterised much contemporary social and political

" Will yiz shut up, all o' yiz, while your father's explainin' me position under the New Constitution !"

debate. It was not until the 1970s and the emergence of a vibrant Irish feminist movement that many of the discriminatory laws against women began to be changed and the patriarchal bias redressed. Ireland's first female minister was appointed in 1979 and eleven years later the Republic elected its first woman president, Mary Robinson, whose victory was widely seen as a symbolic milestone in Irish women's painful journey towards full and equal citizenship.

11.9 'The Doctor . . .', CEK, *Dublin Opinion*, Dublin, November 1938

By 1938 de Valera's Fianna Fáil government had wrought substantial changes in both the internal and external affairs of the Irish Free State or, as it was now known, Éire. However, one major political problem remained unresolved: partition. Despite de Valera's continual rhetorical attacks on the iniquity of the border and illegitimacy of the Northern Ireland state, both remained intractable realities which no amount of constitutional revisionism could remove. Indeed, Article 3 of the new constitution effectively acknowledged this fact in its declaration that laws enacted by the Dáil should apply to the twenty-six counties only, 'pending the reintegration of the national territory'.

This Charles E. Kelly cartoon wittily juxtaposes de Valera's rhetorical commitment to Irish unity with his tacit acceptance of partition in reality. The 'doctor', holding an incongruous stethoscope, appears to have no practical remedy to reunite Éire with her severed left arm, which is shown autonomously beating an Orange Lambeg drum across the partitionist divide. All he can offer her is his vague hope that this 'very peculiar case' might

THE DOCTOR: "It's a very peculiar case, Miss Rosaleen, but I am not without hope that I will be able to do something to bring you and your other arm together."

somehow be resolved in the future, a sentiment which reflects the consistent failure of the Fianna Fáil government to comprehend the complexity of the partition issue and devise an effective northern policy during its first sixteen years in office.

11.10 'Eamon Defying the Lightning', Shepard, *Punch*, London, 17 July 1940

In the months leading up to the outbreak of the Second World War, de Valera expressed his government's intention to adopt a policy of neutrality, citing the continued existence of partition as a justification. On 2 September the Dáil unanimously affirmed the state's neutral stance for the duration of the war, which was termed 'the Emergency' in Ireland. This declaration represented an unequivocal assertion of Irish sovereignty and a clear determination to pursue an independent foreign policy in international relations. Though the state showed itself to be a 'friendly neutral' towards the Allies as the war progressed, de Valera maintained an official stance of non-alignment throughout, although he came under considerable pressure from Britain and later America to enter the war on their side at various times.

EAMON DEFYING THE LIGHTNING

Cartoons 11.10 and 11.11 appeared at a time of grave danger for Britain. France had fallen to the Germans in June 1940, leaving Churchill effectively alone in the fight against Hitler. The Battle of Britain raged from July to October, with the Luftwaffe competing with the RAF for vital air supremacy over the English Channel, as a prelude to a German invasion of Britain. All the while, de Valera remained aloof, having set his face against direct involvement. The first cartoon by Ernest Shepard (1879–1976), illustrator of *Winnie the Pooh*, presents de Valera's neutral stance in a somewhat ambiguous light. He is shown in defiant, almost heroic, mode, defending Ireland from the Nazi lightning with only his (paper) policy of neutrality and a shillelagh for protection. The rural setting is entirely consonant with the taoiseach's social vision of a rural, Gaelic idyll where 'cosy homesteads' of the kind drawn here were represented as beacons of moral rectitude.

The left-wing Low takes an altogether more scathing view of Irish neutrality, however. He shows German submarine officers drinking a toast to 'Neutral Eire' in anticipation of the imminent occupation of the country. In fact, Ireland's peripheral geographical location meant that its occupation never became strategically vital to the security of the Nazis or the Allies, though Hitler did toy with the idea of invading Britain from Ireland in July and December of 1940. However, the British anti-submarine campaign was seriously impaired

NEUTRAL EIRE
NO REFUELLING BRITISH FLOTILLAS
& AIRCRAFT TO PROTECT THE TRADE
BY WHICH BRITAIN & EIRE LIVE

"GOD BLESS EIRE'S NEUTRALITY — UNTIL THE FÜHRER GETS THERE"

11.11 'God Bless Eire's Neutrality...', Low, *Evening Standard*, London, 8 November 1940

by the denial of the right to use Irish ports. Both drawings are underpinned by varying degrees of incomprehension and incredulity at the Irish leader's non-aligned response to the fascist threat.

11.12 'Lambs Mourn Butcher!...', *Daily Mirror*, London, 4 May 1945

De Valera's adroit management of Ireland's neutrality during the war years ended in an episode of high controversy in May 1945, when he responded to news of Hitler's suicide by paying a formal visit to the German envoy to Ireland, Dr Eduard Hempel, to express his condolences. The taoiseach justified his actions on the grounds of diplomatic protocol and pointed out that it was consistent with his government's non-partisan stance; he had made a similar visit to the American embassy in April following the death of Roosevelt.

Such justifications received short shrift from the international community, however, which regarded the visit as a grave moral and diplomatic error. Sir Winston Churchill was particularly incensed by de Valera's action, and used his victory broadcast of 13 May to contrast Éire's treachery with Northern Ireland's loyalty. Three days later, de Valera magnanimously excused Churchill's intemperate attack as post-war euphoria in a restrained reply which won him much acclaim.

Lambs mourn butcher! (SENSATION!)

This caustic *Daily Mirror* cartoon pre-empted Churchill's angry broadcast by several days. It features de Valera and the Portuguese dictator, António Salazar, another neutral leader who also formally mourned Hitler's death, paying tearful tributes to the German 'butcher'. A bitter gloss (bottom right) reinforces the cartoon's trenchant message: 'The neutrals who but for the sacrifices of the Allies would also have been murdered.'

11.13 'Mr Costello the Cutter', Shepard, *Punch*, London, 27 October 1948

Sixteen years of Fianna Fáil government came to an end following the February 1948 general election. De Valera was replaced as taoiseach by Fine Gael's John Costello, who headed a five-party coalition government. Within months of taking office, Costello dramatically announced his government's intention to repeal the 1936 External Relations Act and declare Ireland a republic. This announcement, made at a press conference in Ottawa on 7 September, surprised many in Dublin and London, including some members of his own cabinet.

Formal cabinet approval for Costello's actions came a month later, and repeal legislation was introduced in the Dáil in November. On 21 December the Republic of Ireland Act was passed with all-party support, and Éire seceded from the Commonwealth to become the Republic of Ireland on 18 April 1949. Thus, Costello completed the process of dismantling the treaty which de Valera had initiated in 1932, thereby fulfilling the latter's

MR. COSTELLO THE CUTTER

"I'm going to take it back to Tara's halls."

proclaimed strategy of April 1933: 'Let us remove these forms one by one, so that this state
we control may become a republic in fact; and that, when the time comes, the proclaiming
of the republic may involve no more than a ceremony, the formal confirmation of a status
already attained.'

Shepard's *Punch* cartoon aptly captures the audacity of Costello's diplomatic initiative. It
shows the taoiseach bestride a flagpole in the act of removing the Irish harp from the royal
standard, the symbol of British monarchy. His express intention is to return it to Tara in
County Meath, the seat of the ancient Irish high kings and symbol of the original unity of
Ireland. In the modern era Tara was the site of a massacre of United Irish rebels in 1798 and
of one of O'Connell's 'monster meetings' in 1843. The phrase 'Tara's halls' comes from
'The Harp that Once', one of the most famous songs of Ireland's national poet of the nineteenth century, Thomas Moore, author of a number of enormously popular sentimental
nationalist ballads.

11.14 'A plague...', JOD, *Dublin Opinion*, Dublin, August 1956

The 1950s were a time of prolonged economic stagnation in Ireland. Unemployment
reached a record seventy-eight thousand in 1957, pushing the already soaring emigration

" A plague on both your houses !"
(with apologies to " *Romeo and Juliet* ")

rate even higher. Over four hundred thousand people left Ireland in the decade from 1951 to 1961, the greatest exodus since the 1880s. Many of de Valera's mythic cosy homesteads became all too real ruined cottages during these years, as economic necessity forced thousands of mostly rural Irish men and women to seek employment opportunities elsewhere. Meanwhile, politicians dithered, unable or unwilling to stop this national haemorrhage; some even regarding emigration as an inevitable and not altogether unwelcome social fact.

Whereas nineteenth-century Irish migration was mainly to America, the vast majority of mid-twentieth-century Irish emigrants settled in Britain, where they played a major role in the post-war rebuilding programme. The 1948 British Nationality Act recognised the 'special position' of citizens of the Irish Republic, and Britain continued to treat Irish immigrants as Commonwealth citizens even after the 1949 Ireland Act. Cartoons 11.14 and 11.15 provide contrasting perspectives on this post-war Irish immigration. This first, by JOD (James O'Donnell), indicts the leaders of the two main political parties, Fianna Fáil and Fine Gael, for their indifference to the plight of the country's economic victims. De Valera and Costello, who was then in his second term as coalition taoiseach, are cast as the heads of the feuding families in Shakespeare's *Romeo and Juliet*, the Montagues and the Capulets, while a disaffected 'Paddy Mercutio' heads for the emigrant boat to Britain.

The cartoon by Michael Cummings (1919–97) views the same phenomenon from a rather jaundiced British perspective. By the early 1960s immigration control was

11.15 'Begorrah...', Cummings, *Sunday Express*, London, 19 November 1961

becoming a major issue in British politics. Though most of the debate centred on restricting the entry of migrants from the Caribbean and the Indian sub-continent, immigrants from the Irish Republic were also regarded as a social liability in some quarters. In the autumn of 1961 Harold Macmillan's Conservative government introduced the Commonwealth Immigrants Bill, which passed through the Commons in July 1962. In its original form the Bill included a provision to restrict Irish immigration, but this was subsequently dropped on the basis that it would be impossible to patrol the border between the Republic and Northern Ireland.

Cummings emotively juxtaposes post-war Irish immigration to Britain with Britain's history of colonialism in Ireland. The cartoon portrays the southern Irish as aggressive latter-day invaders who are wilfully exploiting Britain's relaxed entry laws. The clear implication is that the Irish want it both ways; they are unwilling to tolerate the 'fearful English' in Ireland, yet object to proposed restrictions on their own entry to Britain. Not only does this imputation have racist undertones, it also rests upon a spurious equation of immigration and colonial occupation.

12

UNIONISM AND NATIONALISM IN NORTHERN IRELAND
1920–1968

The Northern Ireland state came into existence as a result of the Government of Ireland Act which finally passed through the Westminster parliament on 23 December 1920 and took effect in May 1921. This Act provided for the setting up of two governments and two parliaments in Ireland, one for the six counties which were to form Northern Ireland, the other for the remaining twenty-six counties in southern Ireland. Each of these parliaments would be concerned exclusively with government of its own part of Ireland, while matters which concerned the United Kingdom as a whole would continue to be decided at Westminster, and MPs from both parts of Ireland would continue to sit there. The UK parliament was to retain the power to override the Irish parliaments, a measure which was to prove very important many years later.

In the south the Act was virtually a dead letter as Sinn Féin refused to recognise it. Northern unionists had not wanted such an arrangement and only came to accept it as 'a supreme sacrifice'. They would have preferred to remain directly under the United Kingdom parliament but, as Charles Craig, brother of James, the first prime minister of Northern Ireland, told the Commons in 1920: 'We believe that so long as we were without a Parliament of our own constant attacks would be made upon us, and constant attempts would be made . . . to draw us into a Dublin Parliament. We see our safety, therefore, in having a Parliament of our own.'

Many British and southern Irish politicians viewed the partition settlement as a temporary measure, envisaging an eventual reconciliation between north and south. The 1920 Act reflected this by setting up a Council of Ireland, consisting of northern and southern representatives, to facilitate the process. This notion of an all-Ireland dimension to north–south relations was to remain a feature of subsequent British governments' attempts to resolve the Irish question up to the present day. However, the concept of a unitary state was to remain anathema to northern Protestants, who continued to fear that their religious interests and economic well-being would be jeopardised in any all-Ireland parliament dominated by a Catholic majority.

Northern unionists quickly came to appreciate the merits of having their own state as a protection against enemies both within and without. These enemies were the Catholic minority in the north, many of whom refused to accept the legitimacy of the Northern Ireland state, and the different southern political parties and groups, including the IRA, who wished to achieve a united Ireland. British politicians themselves could not be fully trusted, as northern unionists feared that at some time in the future a Westminster government might be tempted for its own reasons to negotiate a deal with the south, by which unionist interests would be overridden, and they would be forced into the southern state.

Having reluctantly accepted a parliament of their own, the unionists were able to force a major concession from the British government regarding the area of the new state. This was not to be the nine counties of the historic province of Ulster, but rather the six north-eastern counties, which meant that the overall Protestant majority in the new state was 65 per cent, whereas in a nine-county Ulster it would have been only 55 per cent. Although unionists in the three excluded counties of Cavan, Monaghan and Donegal complained bitterly about being sacrificed, Northern Ireland leaders wanted a solid Pro-testant majority in order to establish the long-term security and safety of their new state.

This territorial arrangement was even more objectionable to the 450,000 Catholics (one-third of the population) who were incorporated into the new state against their wishes. There were nationalist majorities in the counties of Fermanagh and Tyrone, in the city of Derry and in Newry, and considerable nationalist numbers in north and west Belfast and south Armagh. Whilst desiring an independent united Ireland, many of these would have preferred continued direct rule from Britain to the new arrangements, and greatly resented their changed status as a powerless minority in a Protestant state domin-ated by their unionist opponents.

This solution which had been agreed at Westminster, therefore, left many people in Ulster angry and resentful. What seemed the simplest and quickest answer to politicians in Britain was not seen the same way in Ireland. If the two communities in Northern Ireland were to enjoy their separate allegiances in peace, it was going to demand great tact, skill and tolerance from the new Northern Ireland government, and close supervision by the body with final responsibility for the new state, the United Kingdom parliament at Westminster.

However, the reality of British political life was that since the end of the First World War and the signing of the Versailles Treaty, Lloyd George's coalition government had been trying to distance itself from Ireland and the Irish problem. The government was deeply divided, including both home rulers and unionists among its leading members. The 1920–21 settlement which resulted in partition and the creation of two states was a compromise forced upon reluctant Ulster unionists and equally reluctant Irish nationalists. It certainly suited most members of the British government, in that it no longer directly ruled either part of Ireland, and the settlement effectively removed the irritant of Irish issues from British political life for the first time since 1800. It was not, however, a solution to the Irish question, the problematic terms of which now focused on Northern Ireland.

This desire to keep the Irish question at arm's length meant that British governments consistently declined to intervene in the internal politics of Northern Ireland until Harold Wilson's Labour government was reluctantly forced to send in troops as a result of the civil disturbances in August 1969. While this political stance was understandable from a British point of view, given the previous troubled history of entanglement, in the long run it amounted to a grievous abdication of responsibility, the repercussions of which became starkly obvious in the late 1960s.

The new state got off to a bad start, being born amidst sectarian violence, bloodshed and IRA attacks. Between July 1920 and July 1922 over 550 people died in inter-communal violence, with Catholics suffering most. Thousands of Catholics were driven out of their jobs and some twenty-three thousand forced out of their homes. All of this contributed to a deep sense of alienation felt by the Catholic minority, most of whom refused to recognise the new state. Nationalist MPs initially refused to sit in the new Northern Ireland parlia-ment, so that at a time when the institutions of the new state were being formed, one-third of its citizens were refusing to participate in its structures. Although most nationalists came to a reluctant acceptance of the new state eventually, their unwillingness to participate actively, plus the distinct bias by the unionist establishment against a community which it viewed as the enemy within, as a 'fifth column', meant that from the beginning many of the institutions were heavily weighted in favour of unionists.

The power of the Protestant majority was strengthened by the abolition of proportional representation in local (1922) and national (1929) elections and by the gerrymandering of constituency and local government boundaries, particularly in Derry city, to maintain unionist majorities. The Special Powers Act of 1922 gave to government extralegal powers of arrest and imprisonment without trial, while an armed police force, backed up by an openly sectarian B Special reserve police, meant that constant control could be exercised over the suspect Catholic community.

Catholics responded by withdrawing into their own communities and creating their own socio-economic networks. Many took shelter within their religious associations and social and sporting fraternities. They harboured a bitter resentment against what they saw as the social and economic discrimination that was practised against them, particularly in the areas of public and private job allocation, and in local authority housing. Protestant supremacy in Northern Ireland was reinforced by this Catholic repudiation of the state. The character of life in both communities was parochial and partisan, and the deeply defensive nature of Northern Ireland unionists meant that its leaders were men who were dogged, conservative and narrow-minded, rather than outward-looking, imaginative and creative. The sectarian strife and turmoil which attended the inception of the state was to remain, and the close connection between security forces and the Northern Ireland Protestant community revealed a fatal lack of consensus over the very existence of the state.

The heavy unemployment and social distress of the 1930s produced few examples of working-class solidarity across the religious divide, with the notable exception of the 1932 unemployment riots in Belfast which were non-sectarian in nature and for a brief moment united the Catholic working class of the Falls Road with the Protestant working class of the Shankill Road. More usually, the depression of the 1930s revealed the pernicious relationship between economic recession and sectarian violence. Widespread riots occurred in the early 1930s, reaching their peak in July and August 1935 when 13 people were killed, more than 600 wounded and over 2,000 driven from their homes. The comparative peacefulness of the next twenty-five years served only to disguise the inherent divisions of a fractured society.

Tensions between the north and the south continued throughout the Stormont years. In 1934 the prime minister, James Craig, now Lord Craigavon, famously boasted to the Northern Ireland House of Commons in the new parliament buildings at Stormont that 'we are a Protestant parliament and a Protestant state'. When challenged, he argued that this was merely a riposte to similar boasts in the south that it was a Catholic state for a Catholic people. Three years later, de Valera's new Irish constitution of 1937, with its distinctly republican and Catholic character, confirmed Northern Ireland Protestant prejudices and reinforced their need to defend their existing institutions.

The war years of 1939–45 brought new jobs and greater prosperity. This eased the sectarian tension, as did the shared experience of German bombing raids on Belfast. The number out of work fell from an average of 25 per cent in the 1930s to 5 per cent in 1942–45. Yet in good times as in bad, the level of unemployment in Northern Ireland remained substantially higher than in Britain. The shipbuilding, engineering and aircraft industries which had been in decline now made an important contribution to the United Kingdom's war effort. However, despite Lord Craigavon's declaration that 'we are all King's men', the British government did not attempt to apply conscription to Northern Ireland, out of fear of the reaction this would provoke from nationalists.

The south's neutrality and its refusal to let Britain use its ports greatly increased Northern Ireland's strategic importance to Britain. Unionist fears of an ultimate British sell-out of Northern Ireland to nationalist Ireland were given credence in June 1940 with the revelation that Churchill's government had made an offer to de Valera to support the principle of Irish unity in return for southern Ireland's support in the war. Craigavon declared that he was 'disgusted' by 'such treachery to loyal Ulster'. When the war ended, however, Churchill and most of the British political leadership felt they owed a debt to unionists for their loyalty, in contrast to their frustration at the southern government's neutrality. The war had led to very different experiences for the people of the north and the south and had reinforced the divisions between the two parts of Ireland, and between London and Dublin.

Unionists were initially alarmed at the advent in 1945 of a British Labour government under Clement Attlee (1883–1967), given Labour's traditional sympathy with the Irish nationalist cause. However, the Northern Ireland and Labour governments soon found little difficulty in working together. When the taoiseach, John Costello, announced his decision in 1948 to make the south a republic and withdraw from the Commonwealth, Northern Irish unionist interests and British defence interests coincided. The cabinet secretary, Norman Brooke, wrote: 'So far as can be foreseen it will never be to Great Britain's advantage that Northern Ireland should form part of a territory outside His Majesty's jurisdiction.' Attlee's Ireland Act of 1949 revealed the Labour government's hostile reaction to Costello's declaration of a republic, and Britain's new appreciation of Northern Ireland, by affirming that it would not cease to be part of the United Kingdom 'without the consent of the parliament of Northern Ireland'. This was the firmest guarantee that the unionists had ever won from Britain and effectively copper-fastened the existence of the Northern Irish state.

After 1945 the introduction to Northern Ireland of British welfare state measures benefited the poorer classes in society. The post-war years also saw a marked improvement in the prospects and conditions of the Catholic minority who were disproportionately represented among the unemployed and unskilled. Indeed northern Catholics became significantly better off than their co-religionists in the south. However, this improvement in many ways served to highlight other grievances such as voting iniquities, discrimination in employment and housing, and a general exclusion from political and economic power. Modernising welfare legislation came up against the sectarian parochialism of the past, to produce a combustible mixture which by the 1960s had grave implications for the stability of the state. The triumphalist and uncompromising behaviour of the unionist majority in the 1940s and 1950s did little to help reconcile nationalists to accept the 1920–21 settlement.

In the 1950s and 1960s, however, there was a growing tendency among Catholics to see their future within a Northern Ireland context rather than in an all-Ireland state. A new Catholic leadership was prepared to acquiesce in the constitutional status quo, with the proviso that Catholics received fairer treatment and were offered better opportunities. This was reflected in the failure of Operation Harvest, the violent IRA campaign of 1956–62 against British rule in Northern Ireland, which resulted in eighteen deaths. The aims of the IRA seemed irrelevant to Catholics in the north and, in ending the campaign in 1962, the IRA blamed northern nationalists for not supporting it. It was soon to concentrate on achieving socialist objectives by political means, rather than Irish unity by military means.

The 1960s began as a decade of hope. In the south the aged figure of de Valera had been replaced by a much more pragmatic leader in Sean Lemass. In the north the increasingly ineffective premiership of Basil Brooke came to an end. His continuing failure to promote economic development led to the moderate unionist Captain Terence O'Neill (1914–90) being appointed prime minister in 1963. O'Neill hoped to modernise Northern Ireland by improving its economic performance and by 'building bridges between the two traditions' in the north. He also believed that reconciliation between the Republic and the north was necessary for progress, and was prepared to move away from the siege mentality of many of those unionists who had been associated with the formation of the state. However, there were numerous obstacles to change in both communities in the north, and the ancient divisions in the region survived intact.

O'Neill's most dramatic gesture was his invitation to Sean Lemass to visit Northern Ireland in January 1965, the first such meeting for forty years. He also encouraged economic collaboration and cross-border co-operation. However, O'Neill's modest reform proposals alarmed many traditional unionists, some of whom gathered around the imposing figure of Ian Paisley (1926–), leader of the Free Presbyterian Church. They began to campaign under the slogan 'O'Neill must go'. In the meantime, many younger Catholics wished to abandon the policy of remaining aloof from the state which had been followed since 1921, seeking instead to play a greater role in political life in order to achieve equal citizenship within Northern Ireland. A much larger, ambitious, educated Catholic middle class had emerged whose aims were not to overthrow the state but rather to reform its structures and institutions by applying British standards of justice. It rapidly became dissatisfied with the gap between O'Neill's actual performance and his gestures, many of which seemed merely cosmetic. In 1967 the Northern Ireland Civil Rights Association was formed, inspired by the American civil rights campaign of Martin Luther King, and began a peaceful campaign of street protests and demonstrations to end discriminatory practices.

Most of these events went unnoticed in Britain and attracted only sporadic attention from Wilson's Labour government, until the media began to pay increasing attention to rising sectarian tension. In October 1968 the Northern Ireland government banned a proposed civil rights march in Derry. The march went ahead and there was a violent clash with the police, who were widely criticised for the unrestrained batoning of unarmed demonstrators. As television images of the incident were shown across the world, the sectarian flame was re-ignited and community relations dramatically deteriorated. It was apparent that a new version of the Irish question was emerging, successive British governments having for too long neglected their responsibilities. Labour ministers belatedly came to realise the seriousness of the situation, and saw that if it deteriorated further they would be dragged in. O'Neill made a television broadcast on 9 December 1968 beginning with the ominous statement 'Ulster stands at the crossroads'. He continued: 'What kind of Ulster do you want? A happy respected province . . . or a place continually torn apart by riots and demonstrations, and regarded by the rest of Britain as a political outcast?' In 1968 few realised how long and painful would be the road upon which Northern Ireland was about to embark.

THE KINDEST CUT OF ALL.

WELSH WIZARD. "I NOW PROCEED TO CUT THIS MAP INTO TWO PARTS AND PLACE THEM IN THE HAT. AFTER A SUITABLE INTERVAL THEY WILL BE FOUND TO HAVE COME TOGETHER OF THEIR OWN ACCORD—(ASIDE)—AT LEAST LET'S HOPE SO; I'VE NEVER DONE THIS TRICK BEFORE."

12.1 'The Kindest Cut of All', Partridge, *Punch*, London, 10 March 1920

In 1920 Lloyd George was faced in the south of Ireland with full scale guerrilla war waged by the Irish Volunteers, now calling themselves the Irish Republican Army. This Anglo-Irish War soon spread north, where it led to widespread sectarian conflict and the worst violence for over one hundred years. The 1920 Government of Ireland Act was the prime minister's compromise solution. The Act partitioned Ireland along the six-county border, but as a gesture to the nationalist desire for unity, a Council of Ireland was proposed, comprising twenty representatives from each of the Irish parliaments. The council was initially to have modest powers over some minor issues, but it was hoped that these would increase over time, leading to 'the eventual establishment of a parliament for the whole of Ireland' with the mutual consent of Dublin and Belfast.

The Partridge cartoon opposite accurately conveys the prevailing sense of public uncertainty about Lloyd George's ingenious proposal, as well as his own private doubts. It portrays the partition of Ireland as a new and untried 'trick', the outcome of which is far from certain. Though all nine Ulster counties are about to be severed on the magician's map, only six were eventually partitioned. As a result of Ulster unionist insistence, the three predominantly Catholic counties of Donegal, Cavan and Monaghan were separated from the (mainly Protestant) other six, which became the state of Northern Ireland in 1920. In the event, the Welsh wizard's magic act failed to work. Sinn Féin refused to recognise the southern parliament and Ulster unionists remained implacably opposed to the proposed council, which they saw as a device to entice them into a united Ireland. An attempt to set up a similar council was made in 1974, only to be again blocked by unionist opposition, spearheaded by the Ulster Workers' Council general strike. No Council of Ireland has ever met to date, though a similar proposal is contained within the Anglo-Irish Framework Document of 1995, and was a key element of the 1998 peace negotiations.

IRELAND'S KING.

Dublin. "THEY TELL ME 'TWAS A GRAND TIME YE HAD WID A VISIT FROM YOUR KING!"

Belfast. "IS IT JEALOUS YE ARE? BY THE SAME TOKEN HE'S YOUR KING TOO; AN' HE'LL PAY YE A VISIT FAST ENOUGH IF YE'LL BE AFTER PUTTIN' YOUR HOUSE IN ORDER AN' ASKIN' HIM."

12.2 'Ireland's King', Partridge, *Punch*, London, 29 June 1921

On 22 June 1921 King George v paid a much-publicised visit to Belfast to open the new Northern Ireland parliament in Belfast City Hall. His speech had been carefully crafted, with considerable input from Lloyd George, and was greeted as a wonderful success by Ulster unionists. Although nationalist and Sinn Féin MPs refused to attend the parliament, the king made a dramatic appeal for conciliation after over two years of bitter fighting during the Troubles. He stated: 'May this historic gathering be the prelude of a day in which the Irish people, north and south, under one parliament or two, as those parliaments may themselves decide, shall work together in common love for Ireland upon the sure foundation of mutual justice and respect.'

The speech was very warmly received by public opinion in Britain, and a number of newspapers urged the government to attempt a settlement with Sinn Féin. Lloyd George had no appetite to attempt the military suppression of the south of Ireland and, with the Ulster question apparently resolved by the establishment of the Northern Ireland state, he was keen to exploit this opportunity to initiate a negotiated settlement. With de Valera also anxious for peace, Lloyd George proposed a truce which came into effect on 11 July 1921.

In cartoon 12.2 Partridge presents a softer, feminine image of both parts of Ireland. A contented, well-dressed, industrious northerner chats amicably to her more impoverished southern neighbour across a stone wall, symbolising the border. The suggestion is that if Dublin, and, by implication, Sinn Féin, were to seek a compromise, then they would receive a favourable response from Britain. Partridge stresses that George v is the king of the whole of Ireland, and this issue of allegiance to the king was to become a major obstacle during the treaty negotiations. The cartoon is indicative of the favourable response of the British press to the king's Belfast speech.

THE MOON MAYBE?

12.3 'The Moon Maybe?', Brewster, *Irish Weekly Independent*, Dublin, 19 November 1921

From the beginning, the Northern Ireland state was dependent upon Britain. In particular it relied upon Westminster to finance welfare measures and the cost of maintaining law and order. The Northern Ireland government was repeatedly forced to go cap in hand to the British government to request special grants, and to fight the reluctance of Treasury officials to agree to them. A particularly onerous cost was that of the Ulster Special Constabulary, later known as the B Specials, set up in 1920, which became in practice an exclusively Protestant force, and one that was greatly resented by Northern Irish Catholics.

The Gordon Brewster cartoon opposite represents Britain's growing impatience with the financial demands of northern unionists. It depicts Lloyd George as an impatient nanny upbraiding a petulant and demanding child, Craig. Although surrounded by playthings and presents, the infantile northern premier still demands more from its grown-up minder. This reflects the fact that Craig refused to be satisfied with the existing concessions and insisted that, since Ulster unionists had not wanted a parliament of their own and had only reluctantly accepted one in order to help Britain solve its Irish question, it was Britain's responsibility to sustain and support the northern state in every way. Inevitably, British frustration with the political and financial policies of unionist leaders led to an uneasy relationship between the two. However, Britain's great reluctance to become directly involved in the affairs of Northern Ireland resulted in her frequently giving in to the demands of her junior partner.

LAST ULSTERMAN (to last Sinn Feiner): " I won't have it ! " (They both expire.)

12.4 'Last Ulsterman . . .', Low, *Star*, London, 2 December 1921

The violent conflict between Catholics and Protestants in Northern Ireland, which started early in 1920, continued on well after the 1921 treaty. Over five hundred people were killed in inter-communal violence between July 1920 and July 1922. Belfast experienced the worst atrocities, where an estimated 11,000 Catholics were forced out of their jobs and 23,000 driven from their homes. The deep-seated nature of this conflict and the sectarian passions it inspired were incomprehensible to most people in Britain, especially at a time when hostilities in the south had ceased. The Low cartoon (12.4), published just four days before the treaty was signed, is representative of the British view that the northern conflict consists of two equally intransigent and irrational opponents who are prepared to fight each other until the bloody end rather than accept a compromise settlement. Although death and destruction lie all around them, the integrity of their quarrel remains intact.

THE MAD BULL.

FARMER CRAIG. "IF YOU CAN'T KEEP THAT BRUTE ON YOUR SIDE OF THE FENCE I SHALL DEAL WITH HIM AS I THINK FIT."

FARMER COLLINS. "WELL, BETWEEN YOU AND ME, I WISH TO GOD YE WOULD."

12.5 'The Mad Bull', Partridge, *Punch*, London, 15 February 1922

The 1921 treaty brought relative peace for a short while to the south of Ireland, but its effect on Northern Ireland was to increase the bloodshed and civil strife which had been ongoing since 1920. De Valera and his supporters refused to accept the treaty, and loyalists, particularly those living near the border, feared that the terms of the agreement which made provision for the establishment of a Boundary Commission would result in significant parts of Northern Ireland being transferred to the new Free State. The IRA, although divided on the treaty, was still determined to try to overthrow the Northern Ireland state and began a military campaign in January 1922, during which they killed policemen, took hostages, and attacked RIC barracks. The situation deteriorated in the next few months, both in Belfast and the countryside, as IRA volunteers, loyalists and police engaged in shootings, assassinations and bloody reprisals. Statistically, Catholics suffered most in terms of casualties and in being driven out of their homes and businesses.

The *Punch* cartoon opposite shows the IRA bull having broken through the boundary fence and rampaging out of control on the northern side. An irate 'Farmer Craig' warns a perplexed 'Farmer Collins' of the consequences of his failure to control his marauding beast. The cartoon cleverly illustrates Collins's ambiguous attitude to the IRA in early 1922. Although he had played a major part in organising the movement, he was by now president of the pro-treaty provisional government of the south. He nevertheless continued to support some IRA activity against the northern state, while opposing republican violence in the south, where he realised that there was a real danger of civil war between treaty and anti-treaty forces, and that most IRA activists were anti-treatyites. In this delicate situation he could not publicly denounce the IRA, nor could he privately control them. Thus Partridge suggests that Collins would be glad to get rid of the problem and pass it on to Craig.

At the time, many Protestants believed that the IRA was trying to revise the border between north and south through violence. Craig and Collins met three times in early 1922 in an attempt to end the violence, and to reach agreement on the boundary issue and other questions, but with little lasting success. Ironically, when the Civil War in the south broke out in June 1922 and IRA members began to fight each other, there was a great reduction in violence in the north. Collins himself was killed in August 1922 by anti-treaty forces at the age of thirty-one. Craig died peacefully in 1940, aged sixty-nine.

12.6 'Ulster Arithmetic', Shemus, *Weekly Freeman*, Dublin, 16 September 1922

From the inception of the Northern Ireland state, unionists were most concerned about maintaining the status quo, defending the state from external and internal foes, and safeguarding unionist solidarity. The refusal of many northern Catholics to accept the new state meant that they denied themselves a role in shaping and influencing the new institutional structures. Moreover, the siege mentality of the Protestant population meant that despite their numerical superiority, they feared being outvoted by Catholics at some time in the future. Accordingly, a number of measures were introduced to prevent this from happening, one of the earliest of which was the government decision of 11 September 1922 to abolish proportional representation in local government elections, a move which greatly antagonised the Catholic population and reinforced their sense of alienation.

The *Weekly Freeman* cartoon takes an ironic view of what ' "Ulster" arithmetic' means. It shows a stern Craig explaining the political facts of life to a young Ulsterman. He suggests that Ulster does not need anything as sophisticated or democratic as proportional representation, which could only help minority parties to gain access to political power. Hard-headed Orangemen could and should rely on a simple sectarian head count to

" ULSTER " ARITHMETIC.

SIR JAMES CRAIG—Proportional Representation, laddie, means confusion in "Ulster."   Cut out such
new-fangled stuff. Every Orangeman knows how many beans make five !

guarantee their political hegemony. Unionists were indeed anxious to regain local councils which they had lost in the 1920 elections, and this was one way of doing so.

In 1929 Craig abolished proportional representation for parliamentary elections in an effort to reduce the number of seats won by the Labour Party and Independent Unionists, and to return political life to the old single issue of nationalists versus unionists. No British government was willing to intervene to oppose this policy, despite the anger of nationalists who saw it as a breach of faith, PR having been inserted in the Government of Ireland Act for their protection. The result was that these measures, together with others relating to the redrawing of electoral boundaries and the raising of the property qualification for the local government franchise, gave northern unionists an almost complete domination of public and political life.

12.7 'Ulster Will Fight, Etc', Shemus, *Weekly Freeman*, Dublin, 7 July 1923

Sir Edward Carson was by nature a passionate supporter of the Union, and had hoped to use the Ulster question to break home rule for the whole of Ireland. Only reluctantly did he come to accept the inevitability of the six counties' exclusion, and later became sad-dened and depressed at the way in which southern Irish unionists had been abandoned. In a famous speech in the House of Lords in December 1921, shortly after the signing of the Anglo-Irish Treaty, he bitterly attacked some of his former friends, declaring: 'What a fool

ULSTER WILL FIGHT, ETC.

CARSON TO SOUTHERN UNIONIST EXILES—" I'm sorry I ever told you to trust England !"
SOUTHERN UNIONIST CHORUS—" We're sorry you ever told us to trust Ulster !"

I was! I was only a puppet, and so was Ulster, and so was Ireland, in the political game that was to get the Conservative Party into power.'

In this cartoon a scowling Carson, whose health suffered severely from depression, apologises to a group of southern unionists for having told them to trust 'England'. The almost exclusively Protestant southern unionists, who were a small minority in the Irish Free State, respond by expressing their resentment at having been abandoned so easily by their northern counterparts, so that Ulster could be saved from nationalist home rule. Northern nationalists could well have made similar criticisms of their counterparts in the south, as they had been effectively abandoned by pro-treaty Sinn Féin in 1922. Unlike southern unionists, however, northern nationalists made up a substantial minority of the population and never became fully reconciled to the new state.

12.8 'The Long View', Partridge, *Punch*, London, 14 May 1924

A key element of the treaty was the setting up of a Boundary Commission to determine the division between Northern Ireland and the Irish Free State. The existing border had been arbitrarily drawn along ancient county boundaries, but there were substantial areas along this border where people's political sympathies lay with the other side. For the first four years of Northern Ireland's existence, unionists were frightened that sizeable areas might be taken from them and given to the new southern state; indeed during the treaty negotiations, Lloyd George had strongly hinted at this in order to entice the Sinn Féin representatives to sign. At the insistence of the Irish government, the Boundary Commission was finally set up in late 1924. Craig's government refused to co-operate with it, and

THE LONG VIEW.

JOHN BULL (*to the PRESIDENT OF THE IRISH FREE STATE*). "I DON'T SAY THIS IS THE BEST FENCE I'VE EVER SAT ON; BUT, IF YOU HOPE ONE DAY TO DISPENSE WITH IT ALTOGETHER, I SHOULDN'T RAISE TOO MUCH TROUBLE ABOUT IT NOW."

made military preparations to resist any enforced boundary changes. While the commission was deliberating, Craig called a general election in April 1925, using an election cry which became a catch phrase of loyalism, 'Not an inch'.

This *Punch* cartoon reveals the reality of the situation. The British government had no desire to reopen the old wounds of Ireland and its internal boundaries and, with many other problems to deal with, simply wanted to maintain the status quo. Thus, John Bull is depicted advising the Irish president, William Cosgrave, not to make 'too much trouble' during the Boundary Commission negotiations, as it may upset the currently peaceful relationships within the two islands, and make the likelihood of eventual unification even more remote. Although Cosgrave appears sceptical, in reality the Irish government, having just experienced a bloody civil war over the treaty, had no real enthusiasm for reopening the whole border issue and exacerbating existing divisions within the Free State.

In the event, the three governments agreed to suppress the Boundary Commission report, which recommended only minor territorial changes and confirmed the existing border. This represented a major victory for Craig, and a painful realisation by northern Catholics that they would have to accept the reality of their position in the new state. The nationalist 'Shemus' takes a more jaundiced view of the negotiations, therefore. His cartoon opposite implies an unequal contest between the gargantuan and belligerent Craig and the nervous, insignificant Cosgrave. Clearly, Craig intends to concede nothing, and is determined to bluster his way through.

AS BELFAST WOULD LIKE IT.

"I am prepared to sit down and discuss this question with Mr. Cosgrave."—Sir James Craig.

12.9 'As Belfast Would Like It', Shemus, *Weekly Freeman*, London, 6 September 1924

12.10 'And They Call this Freedom!', Fleming, *Irish World*, New York, 23 February 1929

In October 1924 a general election was due to take place in Britain and Northern Ireland. During the campaign, de Valera, who was standing in one of the northern constituencies, declared publicly that he was going to cross the border to speak in favour of anti-treaty republican candidates. The northern government issued an order banning him from the state, but he defied this and was arrested in Derry. He was tried in Belfast and sentenced to a month in solitary confinement. This episode gained him valuable publicity in Ireland and boosted the cause of Sinn Féin in the south. In February 1929 he got himself arrested again in Northern Ireland, when he attempted to speak at a meeting in Belfast in defiance of an exclusion order against him which was still in force. De Valera, who was adept at gaining publicity for himself and his Fianna Fáil party, was again sentenced to a month in jail and again received enormous media coverage, especially in America, where he had been assiduously building up political and financial support for his party and his proposed daily newspaper, the *Irish Press*, among the powerful Irish-American lobby.

The republican *Irish World* supported de Valera's opposition to the treaty and partition, and frequently indulged in savage attacks on Cosgrave's pro-treaty ministers, depicting them as mere lackeys of Britain. This cartoon represents de Valera in an embattled but heroic pose, imprisoned in the so-called 'free' southern state and criticising the denial of democratic rights to Irish nationalists in the north. It is made very obvious that power in Northern Ireland lies not with the Belfast government, but rather with Britain in the shape of John Bull. According to the *Irish World*, it was Britain that was responsible for the maintenance of the partition of Ireland, and this remained a constant theme in its cartoons of the 1920s and 1930s.

CALM OVER STORMONT,
or
A WARRIOR RESTS.

12.11 'Calm Over Stormont . . .', CEK, *Dublin Opinion*, Dublin, March 1938

During the 1930s Northern Ireland suffered a period of economic and social stagnation. The staple industries of shipbuilding and linen were in decline, Britain was largely indifferent and southern Ireland hostile. There was no effective leadership from an ageing Craig and little attempt to introduce innovative or imaginative economic planning. Instead, unemployment rose rapidly, average income per head fell to less than 60 per cent of the United Kingdom average, transport systems were antiquated, and housing conditions for many of the working class were dreadful.

This Charles E. Kelly cartoon reflects the prevailing sense of government indifference to economic crisis. It depicts Craig as a stately warrior sleeping peacefully in the new parliament buildings at Stormont Castle, still purring the 'No Surrender' refrain, while outside the economic problems loom large. By 1938 the prime minister was in poor health and had little control of his government, with few cabinet meetings being held. Thus the state was virtually rudderless at a time when effective actions and policies were needed.

THE SPIRIT OF THE ALIEN BARBARIAN

12.12 'The Spirit of the Alien Barbarian', *Irish World*, New York, 20 August 1938

Sectarian riots returned to Northern Ireland in the 1930s after a period of relative calm.
The worst incidents took place during the Orange marches in the summer of 1934 and
particularly in 1935, when 13 people were killed and over 300 families, mostly Catholic,
were driven from their homes. The republican *Irish World* regularly reported on such
incidents and firmly placed the blame on Orange mobs, the police and B Specials. In this
striking 1938 cartoon the ghost of Cromwell is seen instructing a police officer, whose
uniform is reminiscent of that of a Black and Tan soldier, to stir up 'the fierce fires of
bigotry' by attacking Catholic houses and churches. Background images of Orange
atrocities reinforce the sense of Catholic oppression. The *Irish World* laid the ultimate blame
for this carnage upon successive British governments which, it claimed, had kept Irish
people divided for centuries in order to maintain British imperialism. The imagery of
Cromwell was a highly emotive one for northern Catholics, implying that the historic
wrongs of the mid-seventeenth century were being repeated in the 1930s.

"*I wonder why I seem to be against Partition in a half-Continent like India, and in favour of it in a little island like Ireland. . . .*"

12.13 'I Wonder Why . . .', CEK, *Dublin Opinion*, Dublin, June 1946

In 1945 a new Labour government under Clement Attlee came to power in Britain and soon began the process of granting independence to India. Despite widespread inter-communal violence between Hindus and Muslims, Attlee's government initially opposed the idea of partitioning the sub-continent, before ultimately conceding the division into two states of India and Pakistan in 1947. In this cartoon Kelly highlights the contrasting

British view of partition in India and Ireland. John Bull is depicted in a gentle light, as a somewhat perplexed and pensive Labour figure, with his Fabian text beside him, yet still surrounded by the trophies and trinkets of empire. He wonders why he is opposing partition in India, despite its religious and political divisions, yet supporting partition in a small country like Ireland, with similar, but less pronounced, religious differences. The implication behind the cartoon is that a mistake has been made in Ireland in the past, and that a new Labour government might rectify it.

12.14 'Ill-paid Eire Worker...', *Voice of Ulster*, Belfast, January 1948

In the immediate years after the end of the Second World War Northern Ireland benefited from the considerable sums of money which Britain was willing to pay to support new welfare measures. The economy also improved, largely because of an increased demand for Northern Ireland's linen, ships and machines caused by a worldwide shortage of goods. The overall result of these changes was a significant improvement in the material welfare of the people, as the northern economy became more prosperous than the south.

The *Voice of Ulster* was a Belfast unionist magazine which appeared in the 1940s and continually compared the economic advances that were being made in the north with the continuing poverty and underdevelopment which prevailed in the south. In this cartoon an impoverished southern agricultural worker, surrounded by socio-economic problems, looks enviously at the industrial progress of Northern Ireland. The 'black north' was a derogatory phrase often used by southern Catholics to describe the overwhelmingly Protestant nature of the northern state, though here it is given an ironic twist by the unionist cartoonist.

SIR BASIL: "DEV COULDN'T CRACK IT, SO YOU'D BETTER GIVE UP THE BIG IDEA."

12.15 'Sir Basil . . .', *Voice of Ulster*, Belfast, March 1948

In February 1948 a general election was held in the south of Ireland. De Valera's Fianna Fáil government, which had been in power since 1932, was defeated by a new coalition of parties led by John Costello. One of these parties, Clann na Poblachta, was strongly republican in character and was led by Seán MacBride, son of one of the leaders of the 1916 Rising. This Belfast cartoon surveys these political developments from a unionist perspective. It shows Eddie McAteer, a leading Northern Ireland Nationalist MP, encouraging the new southern burglar to crack the 'Ulster safe'. Sir Basil Brooke, northern prime minister since 1943, looks on unperturbed, sure in the knowledge that the would-be safe-cracker will have no more success than his predecessors. The message that Ulster is 'safe' in Brooke's hands is underscored by the image of him holding the key to the city of Derry, which famously refused to surrender to the forces of James II during the siege of the city in 1689. The cry of 'No Surrender' was as valid to unionists in 1948 as it was in the late seventeenth century.

THE BABY SITTER

12.16 'The Baby Sitter', CEK, *Dublin Opinion*, Dublin, June 1949

In late 1948 Costello dramatically announced his intention to declare Ireland a republic and to leave the Commonwealth. When this duly happened in 1949, it stimulated a rapid response from both the Northern Irish and British governments. Basil Brooke called an election for February 1949 to strengthen the unionist position, and turned it into a virtual referendum on the issue of partition. Attlee's Labour government retaliated to Costello's action by passing the Ireland Act in June 1949, which affirmed that 'in no event will Northern Ireland or any part thereof cease to be part . . . of the United Kingdom without the consent of the Parliament of Northern Ireland'. The effect of this was to reinforce partition and strengthen the Unionist Party's hold on the Protestant population. The Stormont parliament was now the key means of defending Northern Ireland's constitutional position.

   This Dublin cartoon shows a relaxed and feminised Brooke contentedly looking after the partition baby, which now has its soother in the form of the British guarantee. The parents, John Bull and Britannia, are about to leave the house of Ulster, confident that all will be peaceful. For the next twenty years successive British governments continued this policy of parental neglect until forced to attend to their domestic duties by the renewal of the Troubles in 1968–69.

12.17 'Excuse me, Mother . . .', JOD, *Dublin Opinion*, Dublin, November 1955

During the early 1950s many northern nationalists became increasingly frustrated at their inability to secure state reforms by constitutional means. They gradually began to

" Excuse me, Mother, but I think your show is slipping."

withdraw support from their parliamentary representatives in favour of republican groups associated with the IRA and the use of physical force. In the May 1955 Westminster general election, Republican Party candidates, half of whom were in jail for arms raids on military barracks in Northern Ireland, stood in all twelve constituencies. The election results were a major success for republicans, who won the two seats of Fermanagh–South Tyrone and Mid-Ulster, and attracted the largest anti-partition vote since 1921.

Since both republican MPs were serving ten-year prison sentences for a raid on Omagh barracks in 1954, the British attorney-general proposed a parliamentary motion in July that the seat held by the new Mid-Ulster MP, Tom Mitchell, be declared vacant and a by-election held. When Mitchell was re-elected with an increased majority at the August by-election, a Belfast election court ruled that he and fellow republican MP Phil Clarke were ineligible for election and that their seats should be awarded to the defeated Unionist candidates. The Westminster parliament voted in favour of this decision and so the Unionist candidate for Mid-Ulster, Charles Beattie, entered the Commons in the autumn of 1955. The affair reflected badly on the democratic process in both Britain and Northern Ireland, as the constituents were now represented by an MP who had twice been rejected by them. The controversy was widely reported in the European and American press, and this *Dublin Opinion* cartoon reflects the criticism levelled at Westminster, the 'mother of parliaments', for sanctioning such undemocratic practice.

There was an even more bizarre sequel to the affair when it became known in December that Beattie was a member of three national insurance tribunals and as such held offices of profit under the crown which made him ineligible to serve as an MP. Early in 1956, therefore, he was disqualified by a select Commons committee and another by-election was held in May. Although Mitchell failed to win this time because of the intervention of a Nationalist candidate, he still won the vast majority of the Catholic vote. This increasing Catholic support for republicanism was reflected in the IRA's decision to launch Operation Harvest, its new campaign against the Northern Ireland state, on 11 December 1956.

13

TRANSFORMATION AND MODERNISATION
IN THE REPUBLIC 1959–1998

The year 1959, which saw the appointment of Sean Lemass (1899–1971) as taoiseach, is widely regarded as the *annus mirabilis* of modern Ireland, the date which marks the beginning of the belated economic modernisation of the nation. In place of de Valera's vision of a rural, introspective, self-sufficient Gaelic idyll, the pragmatic Lemass, who retained power until 1966, envisaged an industrialised, entrepreneurial, outward-looking meritocratic society. The blueprint for this new Ireland was supplied by the influential secretary of the department of finance, T.K. Whitaker, whose 1958 report entitled *Economic Development* formed the basis for Lemass's ground-breaking First Programme for Economic Development of the same year. This was a five-year plan (1958–63) for economic expansion which emphasised the need to replace the protectionist principles of previous decades with free-trade policies, increase state investment in productive enterprises, and attract international investment in export-oriented Irish industries.

Efficiency and competitiveness became the new watchwords as tariff barriers were dismantled, access to international markets sought, and capital grants and tax concessions offered to foreign firms. An eagerness to engage in European economic co-operation was signalled by Ireland's application in 1961 for membership of the European Economic Community, to which it eventually gained admittance in 1973. Meanwhile, two economic agreements with Britain (the 1960 Anglo-Irish trade pact and the 1965 Anglo-Irish Free Trade Area Agreement) paved the way for full free trade between the two countries by 1975. There was, as a 1960s *Time* magazine feature on Ireland proclaimed, 'New Spirit in the Oul Sod'.

This radical redirection of economic policy produced dramatic results over the next decade as over three hundred foreign-owned companies were established nationwide, national income rose, unemployment fell, emigration slowed dramatically, the Republic's population increased, and the material prosperity of the majority of its citizens leapt to unprecedented heights. Sweeping social and cultural change paralleled this sudden economic expansion. Increased affluence fuelled a growth in materialism which was fed in turn by the nation's exposure to the glitzy international world of consumer capitalism through the rise of tourism and foreign travel, the relaxation of the film and book censorship laws, and the advent in 1962 of that most potent agent of cultural change, television.

Telefís Éireann played a major part in accelerating the trend towards liberalism in 1960s Ireland. Innovative home-made programmes, such as the talk show the *Late Late Show*, provided a forum for the public discussion of hitherto taboo subjects (especially those relating to sexual morality) and in the process subjected the values, attitudes and often the representatives of traditional Ireland to close critical scrutiny. Indeed, so concerned was one reactionary Irish politician by the corrosive influence of such programmes on the moral fabric of the nation that he boldly proclaimed that 'there was no sex in Ireland before television'! The dismay of Irish traditionalists was further deepened by the social radicalism of the Second Vatican Council (1962–65). The innovations of Pope John XXIII sent shock waves through the conservative Irish Church and set it on a turbulent course of readjustment to the unpropitious realities of an increasingly secular and sceptical social order.

In the diplomatic sphere, the later years of Lemass's premiership were marked by a historic breakthrough in relations between the Republic and Northern Ireland. In January and February 1965 Lemass officially met his northern counterpart, Captain Terence O'Neill, first in Belfast and then in Dublin, to discuss matters of mutual economic concern. This symbolic encounter ended a forty-year cold war between the two governments and raised hopes of increased co-operation in the future. But while this new spirit of *rapprochement* was broadly welcomed in the south, O'Neill's conciliatory diplomacy, coupled with his mildly reformist social policies, alienated many conservative Ulster Unionists and ultimately led to the splitting of unionism into 'official' and 'unofficial' strands.

The year 1966 brought Ireland's political and cultural divisions into fresh focus as nationalists and unionists celebrated the fiftieth anniversaries of two glorious events in their respective historical traditions, namely, the Easter Rising and the heroic sacrifice of the Ulster Division at the Battle of the Somme. Though none could have known it at the time, two other events of that year, each in their way legacies of 1916 – the blowing up of Nelson's Pillar in Dublin by the IRA and the shooting of three Catholic men in Belfast by the revived Protestant paramilitary group the UVF – were ominous portents of the violent re-eruption of ancient antagonisms which were to engulf Northern Ireland before the decade was out.

The onerous political responsibility for responding to the northern Troubles and managing their impact on the southern state fell to Jack Lynch (1917–), the mild-mannered Corkman who succeeded Lemass as taoiseach in 1966. The arrival of British troops on the streets of Derry and Belfast in August 1969, albeit to an initial welcome from the minority Catholic community, coupled with the sight of refugees streaming into makeshift shelters in the Republic, shattered southern complacency and re-ignited smouldering nationalist resentments within the republican ranks of Lynch's Fianna Fáil government. Following an initial implied threat to intervene to defend Catholics against Protestant attack, Lynch pledged his government to a more realistic policy of peaceful resolution of the northern problem, while retaining a long-term aspiration to Irish unity.

His moderate stance did not receive universal cabinet support, however, as the dramatic events of May 1970 were to prove. In that month two senior ministers, Neil Blaney and Charles Haughey (1925–), were sacked from the Irish government and charged with conspiring to import arms and ammunition into the Republic for use in the north. Although the 'arms crisis', as it was known, ended with the acquittal of both men, the ability of Lynch's government to contain political violence was tested repeatedly throughout the tumultuous early seventies, most notably after the introduction of internment in August 1971 and in the emotional aftermath of Bloody Sunday in January 1972. Southern revulsion at the killing of thirteen unarmed civilians by British paratroopers in Derry city resulted in the burning of the British embassy in Dublin following an angry mass demonstration on 2 February.

As civil conflict intensified north of the border, the Republic joined the EEC in January 1973 along with Britain and Denmark, thus placing the northern issue within a broader diplomatic setting. The immediate material effects of membership were muted by the fact that the Republic's accession coincided with the first major economic recession of the seventies induced by the 1973 Middle East oil crisis. When the crisis abated, however, it became clear that membership of the EEC was having a transformative socio-economic impact on the country. The expansion of trade links with its European partners reduced the nation's economic dependence on Britain and the psychological baggage that went with it. A new economic self-confidence manifested itself in the Republic's decision to join the European Monetary System in 1979, while Britain stayed out. European grants and subsidies greatly benefited the Irish agricultural sector, while the application of European laws improved workers' rights and promoted greater social tolerance. Overall, Ireland's positive experience of EC membership has engendered strong pro-European loyalties in the majority of its citizens, in marked contrast to the Euro-sceptical attitudes of many Britons.

In 1973 Fianna Fáil was replaced in office after sixteen years by a Fine Gael–Labour coalition government led by Liam Cosgrave (1920–), son of the first Irish prime minister. Cosgrave continued Lynch's northern policy of quiet diplomacy. The high watermark of his government's influence on Northern Irish affairs came at the Sunningdale Conference of 1973. The Dublin delegation secured a formal acceptance by both British and Northern Irish representatives of a southern Irish dimension in the future government of the region, in return for which Cosgrave agreed that any change in the status of Northern Ireland must have the consent of the majority there. However, the proposed instrument of southern influence, a Council of Ireland to deal with matters of mutual concern in the island as a whole, never materialised and disappeared from the political agenda following the collapse of the power-sharing executive in May 1974.

In June 1977 Fianna Fáil returned to power with its biggest ever parliamentary majority. Two years later, Lynch resigned as taoiseach and was succeeded by Charles Haughey, whose appointment occurred within months of Margaret Thatcher (1925–) becoming Britain's first female prime minister. The accession to power of these two charismatic and controversial leaders heralded the dawn of a new phase in Anglo-Irish relations which was characterised by an inter-governmental approach to Northern Ireland based on a growing recognition by both the British and Irish governments of the failure of internal initiatives to resolve the Troubles. The search for new institutional structures began with a meeting of the new premiers in May 1980, and was advanced at the first summit meeting between them in Dublin in December, at which they agreed to establish joint Anglo-Irish studies groups to explore matters of common concern. Although the constitutional position of the north was not discussed at this meeting, they did agree to examine 'the totality of relationships within these islands' at their next meeting in 1981.

By then, however, relations between London and Dublin had deteriorated because of Britain's inept handling of the Maze hunger strikes. Diplomatic coolness hardened into outright estrangement in the spring of 1982, when the Irish government refused to support Britain's military conflict with Argentina over the Falkland Islands on the grounds that to do so would endanger Ireland's traditional policy of neutrality. Anglo-Irish relations remained strained until the autumn of 1983, by which time Haughey's Fianna Fáil government had been replaced by another Fine Gael–Labour coalition under the premiership of Garret FitzGerald (1926–).

Unlike Haughey, whose republican rhetoric alienated many northern unionists, FitzGerald aspired to a pluralist unitary state to be achieved by consent, in which the cultural identities and religious convictions of all the people of Ireland would be afforded equality of status and mutual respect. Prompted by Northern Ireland's Social Democratic and Labour Party leader John Hume (1937–), he set about convening an all-Ireland conference in early 1983 to consider how such a state might be achieved. The result was the New Ireland Forum, which met for the first time at Dublin Castle in May 1983. Over the next twelve months representatives of constitutional nationalist parties from both parts of Ireland deliberated on the shape of a new Ireland.

The resultant Forum report recommended a unitary state as their preferred option, while retaining joint Irish–British authority over Northern Ireland and some form of federal or confederal state as possible alternatives. Despite the fact that all three options were brusquely dismissed by Mrs Thatcher following an Anglo-Irish summit at Chequers in November 1984, the report set the political agenda for a process of patient diplomacy between Irish and British government ministers and their civil servants which culminated in the signing of the Anglo-Irish Agreement by the two premiers at Hillsborough Castle, County Down, on 15 November 1985.

The agreement, the most historic Anglo-Irish accord since the 1921 treaty, granted the Irish government a consultative role in certain stated aspects of Northern Ireland affairs through an inter-governmental conference, serviced by a secretariat staffed by civil servants from both countries, based at Maryfield near Belfast. If this measure boosted the hopes of northern nationalists that their interests and aspirations might be advanced, the two governments' affirmation of the majority's right to decide on the constitutional future of Northern Ireland was intended to allay unionist fears of forcible absorption into a united Ireland. Such reassurance fell on deaf ears, however, as an outraged unionist community proclaimed its vehement opposition to the agreement through street demonstrations, civil disobedience and acts of intimidation and violence. Sustained unionist opposition continued over the next three years, yet failed to weaken the two governments' resolve to implement the terms of the agreement, and so avoided a repeat of the collapse of the 1974 power-sharing experiment.

Despite the diplomatic success of the Hillsborough accord, the late 1980s proved to be a time of recurring tensions in Anglo-Irish relations. Charles Haughey's return to power in 1987 coincided with a period of renewed controversy over the extradition of terrorist suspects from the Republic to face charges in Britain and Northern Ireland. A number of highly publicised cases of Irish courts' refusal to extradite suspects, for diverse reasons, led to mutual recriminations between Dublin and London. Relations were further strained by Irish disquiet over the British judiciary's inequitable treatment of Irish people as exemplified by the release on appeal of the 'Guildford Four', 'Birmingham Six' and 'Maguire Seven', all of whom had been wrongfully imprisoned for terrorist offences in the 1970s. Matters began to improve in the 1990s, however, helped by the personal friendship which developed between the two new premiers, John Major (1943–) and Albert Reynolds (1932–), and the emergence of a mutual desire to bring about a peaceful settlement in Northern Ireland.

In the internal politics of the Republic, FitzGerald's crusade to make the south more attractive to northern unionists suffered a setback when his government's attempt to legalise civil divorce was defeated in a 1986 referendum. This was the second significant political victory of the decade for the forces of Catholic reaction in the Republic, following their successful campaign to have a constitutional prohibition on abortion adopted in 1983. The liberal cause received a significant symbolic boost in 1990, however, when the feminist lawyer Mary Robinson (1944–), who had earlier resigned from the Irish Labour Party in protest against the Anglo-Irish Agreement being imposed upon unwilling unionists, became Ireland's first female president. Her victory was widely seen both as a triumph for the advocates of a secular, pluralist agenda and as a striking assertion of the public identity of Irish women, for so long silenced and marginalised in society. Women's political prominence was further enhanced when a record number of female candidates (twenty) was elected to the Dáil in the 1992 general election. As Robinson herself memorably declared in her victory speech, the hand that rocked the cradle was now rocking the system.

The 1980s was a difficult decade for the Irish economy. The recession triggered by a further oil crisis in 1979 was compounded by reckless government borrowing, leading to increased levels of unemployment and emigration, particularly among the young, many of whom went to Britain. There was a corresponding rise in urban poverty and criminal activity, much of it drug-related, as Dublin earned an unwanted reputation as 'the heroin capital of Europe'. Ten years later, however, Ireland was projecting an altogether different international image.

As the 1990s unfolded, tangible signs that Irish society was becoming more liberal emerged. In 1992 the laws on abortion were modified in the aftermath of the infamous 'X' case, in which a fourteen-year-old rape victim was initially prevented by a court injunction from travelling to Britain to have an abortion. Homosexuality was decriminalised in 1993, and two years later a second referendum to remove the constitutional prohibition on divorce received the assent of the electorate, albeit by the narrowest of margins. But perhaps the most striking feature of Irish life in the 1990s is the degree to which public confidence in the moral and political authority of the institutions of church and state has been profoundly undermined by a series of crises and controversies.

A number of financial scandals in the Irish business world in the early part of the decade was followed by a lengthy tribunal of inquiry into the beef processing industry, which uncovered evidence of fraud and corruption involving businessmen and government ministers. The weakening of the authority of the Catholic Church has been marked by equally dramatic public scandals. In May 1992 the Bishop of Galway, Eamonn Casey, was forced to resign following the revelation that he had fathered a son by an American divorcée in the 1970s and used Church funds to pay for his upkeep. Two years later, a crisis over the extradition to Northern Ireland of a paedophile priest who had for years been protected from civil prosecution by the Church authorities led to the collapse of the Fianna Fáil–Labour coalition government. Revelations of an even more tumultuous nature emerged in the summer of 1997, when a government tribunal of inquiry into payments to politicians found that the former taoiseach, Charles Haughey, had accepted secret financial gifts from a millionaire Irish businessman which he had failed to disclose.

The cumulative effect of these controversies has been to raise fundamental questions about the nature and practice of democracy in contemporary Ireland, questions which inevitably engender cynicism in the minds of Ireland's young, articulate and self-confident population. Paradoxically, such alienation from the democratic process in the Republic coincided with a renewed momentum towards democracy in Northern Ireland, generated by the peace process. This is one of the many curious paradoxes that characterise a society in which the forces of rapid change have produced an uneasy contiguity of the traditional and the modern or, as some would have it, the postmodern.

In another of those stray coincidences that retrospectively acquire symbolic significance, the day of the IRA ceasefire in Northern Ireland, 31 August 1994, was also the day on which the investment bank Morgan Stanley favourably compared the Republic's thriving economy with the East Asian 'tiger' economies, thereby launching the concept of the

'Celtic tiger'. By the end of 1996 the Republic was producing more wealth per head of population than the United Kingdom and could boast the highest growth rate in the EU. A mood of ebullient self-confidence took hold of the nation, born of this extraordinary economic growth and a cultural vibrancy that has made Ireland one of the most popular tourist destinations in Europe. Not only this, Irish culture at the end of the century has become increasingly internationalised through the work of writers like Seamus Heaney and Roddy Doyle, the films of Neil Jordan and Jim Sheridan, the music of U2, the spectacular Irish dance show *Riverdance*, and what is perhaps the most incongruous example of reverse colonisation, the Irish theme pub.

Yet the Celtic tiger's alluring stripes conceal a dark underbelly. Ireland's sudden economic prosperity has meant little for many sections of the population. Thousands continue to live below the poverty line and problems of social inequality remain stubbornly persistent. Soaring levels of violent and organised crime have led to the introduction of a panoply of anti-crime measures, the harshest of which are designed to combat the rise in drug trafficking. Moreover, the country's improved economic situation has made it attractive to asylum seekers and refugees, whose arrival has prompted the implementation of some of the toughest immigration controls in Western Europe. At a more fundamental level, nagging doubts remain about the sustainability of Irish economic growth, given its heavy reliance on foreign capital rather than an indigenous industrial base. In all of this, the paradoxes resonate: a nation whose history is defined by the experience of emigration, which has scattered its citizens all over the globe, is now showing itself reluctant to receive the scatterings of others, at a time when its national prosperity is being underwritten by transnational wealth.

Yet the mood of the nation remains overwhelmingly buoyant as the new millennium approaches, even if Ireland's cosmopolitan present sometimes looks more like its confessional past. This was nowhere more evident than in the controversy caused by President Mary McAleese (1951–) when, within weeks of her inauguration, she accepted communion at a Church of Ireland ceremony in Dublin in December 1997. Whereas her action was forthrightly condemned by some senior Catholic churchmen, who regarded it as a blatant breach of canon law, many ordinary Irish people took a less dogmatic view. To them, the president's gesture represented a welcome act of ecumenism and a tangible expression of her genuine desire to 'build bridges' with other religious traditions on the island. To see it as such is to hope that the deep divisions of the past might yet be healed by future dialogue and understanding, and that the process of peace and justice in Ireland might be spiritual as well as political, personal as well as formal.

" All the same, dearie, it's nice to be talking trade instead of history."

13.1 'All the same, dearie . . .', CEK, *Dublin Opinion*, Dublin, March 1960

The election of Sean Lemass, minister for industry and commerce, as taoiseach in June 1959 accelerated Ireland's embryonic economic recovery. Lemass, an ardent advocate of free trade, foreign investment, export-led economic growth and greater European integration, quickly came to personify the nation's new-found vigour, optimism and buoyancy. By the end of 1960, he was presiding over a rapidly expanding economy characterised by rising industrial growth rates and falling levels of unemployment and emigration.

Closer economic association with Britain was a central feature of Lemass's fundamental reappraisal of Ireland's economic policy. His eagerness to replace the protectionism of the de Valera era, of which he had been one of the chief architects in the 1930s, with a more outward-looking economic attitude to meet the challenges of the 1960s led to the signing of an Anglo-Irish trade pact in London on 13 April 1960. This *Dublin Opinion* cartoon reflects the new spirit of friendship and co-operation in which these trade negotiations took place. A matronly Britannia and a youthful Erin, age-old adversaries in the political sphere, are shown enjoying a moment of economic détente, each having set aside her respective national emblems. Though the agreement itself did not satisfy the Irish demand for unrestricted free trade between the two countries, it was an important first step towards the eventual achievement of that goal.

"You go first, Macmillan, and see how deep it is."

13.2 'You go first, Macmillan . . .', JOD, *Dublin Opinion*, Dublin, June 1961

Lemass's commitment to trade liberalisation did not end at Britain's shores; membership of the recently formed EEC was his ultimate objective. Indeed, the two issues were inextricably linked from an Irish perspective, given the country's heavy economic dependence on Britain as an export market. So when Lemass learned of the intention of Prime Minister Harold Macmillan (1894–1986) to seek immediate British entry in April 1961, he felt his government had little option but to follow suit. Thus, the Republic formally applied for membership of the EEC on 1 August 1961, the day after Britain submitted its application.

   This *Dublin Opinion* cartoon accurately reflects the invidious position in which Lemass found himself in the early summer of 1961. While his comment to Macmillan suggests that he would prefer to await the political and economic consequences of Britain's Common Market membership before deciding Ireland's fate, the rope on his ankle reveals the precarious nature of his actual predicament. Macmillan himself seems somewhat dubious about Britain's membership prospects and appears to have little relish for his swim. His fears proved to be well-founded in reality, as Britain's application was vetoed by French President Charles de Gaulle in January 1963, a rejection which adversely affected Ireland's application also.

" *Remind him about the Irish at Fontenoy, Jack, and he'll let you in.*
Then I'll follow . . . "

13.3 'Remind him about . . .', JOD, *Dublin Opinion*, Dublin, February 1967

Four years elapsed before the two countries again sought EEC membership. Both reapplied on 11 May 1967, only to have their joint endeavour again thwarted by the anglophobic de Gaulle. This cartoon wittily imagines the circumstances of this latest setback to Anglo-Irish economic hopes. It shows Macmillan's successor as prime minister, Labour's Harold Wilson (1916–95), advising the new Irish premier, Jack Lynch, on how to overcome French opposition for their mutual benefit. He suggests that Lynch exploit French goodwill towards Ireland by reminding de Gaulle of the Battle of Fontenoy in 1745, where the heroic exploits of the Irish Brigade in the army of King Louis xv led to a famous French victory. Lynch's notes suggest that he is thinking along similar lines, though the historical event he has in mind is revolutionary France's support for the United Irishmen at Bantry Bay in 1796. Ironically, both events refer to periods when Britain was at war with France.

In 1969 the new French president, Georges Pompidou, allowed negotiations on Britain's entry to begin, thereby enabling Ireland's dormant application to be revived also. Ireland and Britain eventually became full EEC members on 1 January 1973.

13.4 'Sit down, Murphy . . .', JAK, *Evening Standard*, London, 8 May 1970

On 6 May 1970 one of the most serious political crises in the history of the southern state occurred when Taoiseach Jack Lynch sacked two members of his cabinet, Charles Haughey, minister for finance, and Neil Blaney, minister for agriculture, on the suspicion

" Sit down, Murphy, your Luger's showing ! "

that they were plotting to import arms illegally for use by Northern Ireland nationalists. The 'arms crisis', as it became known, had its origins in the outbreak of civil conflict in the north in August 1969, which prompted the small republican faction within the Fianna Fáil government to make contact with leading IRA figures with a view to offering financial and military aid.

The sackings, which sent shock waves through Anglo-Irish relations, were followed by the arrest of the two ex-ministers on 28 May on charges of attempted gun-running. The charges against Blaney were dropped in July, but Haughey was returned for trial in September, along with three others, including an Irish army officer. Though all the defendants were acquitted the following month, the allegations indelibly tarnished Haughey's political reputation and delayed his rise to power, which culminated in his election as taoiseach in 1979.

This cartoon by JAK (Raymond Jackson) is a scathing attack on the propriety of Irish parliamentary politics at this time. It implies that the Fianna Fáil government is collectively involved in illegal arms smuggling, with the tacit approval of Lynch, the only clearly identifiable politician in the drawing, sitting silently on the front bench. As the crisis unfolded, some cabinet members claimed that Lynch privately knew and approved of the planned gun-running despite his official denials, though these allegations have never been proved.

13.5 'We shall all stand . . .', Nick, *Irish Times*, Dublin, 20 August 1971

The introduction of internment without trial by the Northern Ireland unionist government on 9 August 1971 pushed the state to the brink of civil war. It triggered a major
upsurge in sectarian violence which left several dead and over six thousand people homeless, most of them Catholic. Many of these sought refuge in the south, where makeshift
refugee camps were hurriedly set up to accommodate them. Lynch, who had no advance
notice of the decision by his northern counterpart, Brian Faulkner (1921–77), deplored the
move and called for the replacement of Stormont by a power-sharing executive.

   Meanwhile, John Hume and Ivan Cooper, two leading members of the constitutional
nationalist SDLP, initiated a campaign of civil disobedience which resulted in their arrest in
Derry on 18 August. The following day Lynch came out in support of their action, as
reflected in this *Irish Times* cartoon. The remark which the cartoonist Nick Robinson (husband of the future Irish president, Mary) ascribes to the taoiseach is an ironic parody of a
phrase Lynch used in a famous television broadcast two years earlier, when he announced
that the Irish government 'can no longer stand by and see innocent people injured and
perhaps worse' as bitter sectarian rioting engulfed the north. In the event, Lynch's threat
proved to be mere rhetoric, though some members of his cabinet contrived to intervene on
behalf of northern nationalists.

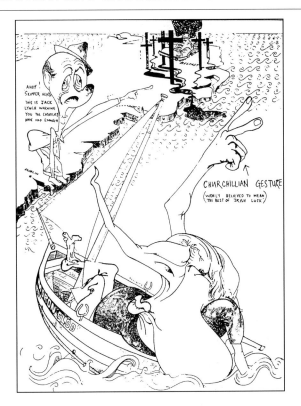

13.6 'Ahoy! Skipper Heath...', Scarfe, *Sunday Times*, London, 22 August 1971

Gerald Scarfe's cartoon reflects the strained nature of Anglo-Irish relations in the wake of Faulkner's regressive action. An angry Lynch points to a blood-soaked Northern Ireland and warns the British prime minister, Edward Heath (1916–), that continuing violence against Catholics will produce dire consequences. Heath, whose government had ultimate responsibility for Northern Ireland's affairs, is shown to be flagrantly indifferent to the crisis, preferring to relax aboard his yacht, the 'Moron Clod' (a corruption of 'Morning Cloud'). Such a scarifying indictment of Britain's mismanagement of the Troubles by a British cartoonist was rare in 1971, when many Fleet Street artists were beginning to revive century-old stereotypes to denounce IRA violence.

13.7 'Whom the gods destroy...', Fitz, *United Irishman*, Belfast, September 1973

In March 1973 responsibility for managing the Republic's response to the escalating northern crisis passed from Jack Lynch to Liam Cosgrave, leader of the new Fine Gael–Labour coalition government. Within a week of the coalition's formation, the British government published its proposals for a power-sharing Northern Ireland assembly involving unionists and nationalists. Included in the proposals was a provision for a Council of Ireland which would give Dublin a consultative role in northern affairs. While Cosgrave welcomed this proposed measure, Northern Ireland was of secondary importance to the maintenance of security and stability within the Republic. Increasing IRA activity in the south prompted

—WHOM THE GODS DESTROY THEY FIRST MAKE MAD.

him to propose a series of stringent security measures against subversives shortly after taking office, and it is these which are the subject of this cartoon.

It comes from the *United Irishman*, a monthly republican newspaper founded in Belfast in 1948, which became the organ of the Official IRA following the split in the republican movement in January 1970. It features a deranged Cosgrave about to light the fuse of a large bomb which carries references to recent security controversies in the south. Several relate to cross-border security issues, including extradition and British army incursions into the Republic. There is also an allusion to the recent trial for armed robbery of Kenneth Littlejohn, who claimed to be an MI6 agent working to infiltrate the Official IRA.

But the cartoon's main point, suggested by the threatening letter from Prime Minister Heath and the 'Anglo-friendly match', is that by capitulating to British pressure Cosgrave is effectively colluding in the destruction of the republican ideal of a united Ireland. Cosgrave's party, Fine Gael, was, of course, the successor to the pro-treaty Cumann na nGaedheal, which his father had led, and which in the 1920s had accepted the Free State compromise in place of the much sought after republic. The cartoonist is also warning Cosgrave that British policy in Ireland will always be based on subjective assessments of its own interests, a fact that Irish politicians ignore at their peril. On 17 September 1973 Cosgrave met Heath in Dublin to discuss the setting up of a Council of Ireland, which was finally agreed upon at the Sunningdale Conference in early December.

13.8 'What worries me...', Turner, *Irish Times*, Dublin, 2 September 1976

Cosgrave's coalition government was beset by a series of threats to internal state security from both loyalist and republican paramilitaries during the mid-seventies. Among the most alarming incidents were the killing of thirty-three people by loyalist car bombs in Dublin and Monaghan in May 1974, the greatest loss of life in any one day of the Troubles; the IRA kidnapping of Dutch industrialist, Tiede Herrema, in 1975; the unrest generated by the death of republican hunger-striker Frank Stagg in 1976; and the IRA assassination of the British ambassador, Christopher Ewart-Biggs, in July of that year.

The last atrocity prompted the government to declare a state of national emergency and introduce an Emergency Powers Bill to permit the detention of terrorist suspects for seven days without charge. This draconian legislation mirrored the Prevention of Terrorism Act introduced in Britain and Northern Ireland following the Birmingham pub bombings in November 1974. A third measure, a Criminal Law Bill, sought to strengthen the powers of the security forces and increase prison sentences for those convicted of terrorist offences.

This sketch by Martyn Turner, an English-born cartoonist who has been one of the most incisive satirical commentators on Irish and Anglo-Irish affairs since the seventies, expresses reservations about the sweeping nature of these proposed new laws and their implications for civil liberties in Ireland. The Irish president, Cearbhall Ó Dálaigh, was equally concerned, and referred the Emergency Powers Bill to the Supreme Court to test its constitutionality. His intervention was publicly criticised by the minister for defence,

Patrick Donegan, whose description of Ó Dálaigh as a 'thundering disgrace' precipitated a dramatic constitutional crisis which resulted in the president's resignation on 22 October 1976. Incidentally, Cosgrave, a keen horseman, had once referred to his opponents within his own party as 'mongrel foxes'.

"I say, Maggie, you'll never guess who they've picked up under the SUS law!"

13.9 'I say, Maggie...', JAK, *Evening Standard*, London, 22 May 1980

The election of Charles Haughey as taoiseach in December 1979 marked a shift in the Dublin government's approach to Northern Ireland and Anglo-Irish relations. In his address to the annual Fianna Fáil party conference in early 1980 Haughey declared that his government's first political priority was to end partition. He went on to say that Northern Ireland was 'a failed political entity' and called on the British government to declare 'their interest in encouraging the unity of Ireland, by agreement and in peace'. The new British prime minister, Margaret Thatcher, did not share his political diagnosis. On the eve of her first meeting with Haughey on 21 May she told the Commons that the constitutional future of Northern Ireland was solely a matter for the people of the province and the British government. The meeting itself was cordial, however, and a joint communiqué issued afterwards emphasised the two governments' commitment to closer political co-operation.

JAK's cartoon probes beneath this public display of Anglo-Irish harmony to expose the underlying political tensions between the two premiers. It shows the British foreign

13.10 'Mind you . . .', Turner, *Irish Times*, Dublin, 10 December 1980

secretary, Lord Carrington, informing Thatcher that Haughey has been detained under Britain's SUS law, which allowed arrests to be made on suspicion. The cartoon implicitly questions Haughey's fitness to be leader on the basis of his republican sympathies and his role in the arms crisis of 1970, which was currently being re-examined in the Irish media on the basis of new evidence. As such, it echoed the bitter attack on Haughey's 'flawed pedigree' by opposition politicians following his election as taoiseach five months earlier.

The second meeting between the two leaders in December 1980 took place in a heightened political atmosphere. On 27 October seven republican H–Block Maze prisoners began a hunger-strike as a further protest against prison regulations as part of their ongoing campaign for political status. Thatcher immediately refused to make concessions and the strike was still in progress when she and Haughey held their first summit meeting at Dublin Castle on 8 December. The leaders agreed to establish joint Anglo-Irish study groups to examine a range of issues, 'including possible new institutional structures' which might better accommodate 'the totality of relationships within these islands'.

Problems arose immediately afterwards, however, when the Irish side exaggerated the significance of the agreement by suggesting that progress had been made towards Irish re-unification. This prompted denials from London and provoked alarm among northern unionists, many of whom suspected that a secret deal was being hatched by London and Dublin. Turner's cartoon reflects the divisive impact of Haughey's optimistic interpretation of the December communiqué, while at the same time highlighting the difficulty of achieving consensus in the increasingly polarised realm of Anglo-Irish politics in the early 1980s. In such a heavily politicised zone, multiple meanings could, and still can, attach to even the most innocuous remark.

"... on the other hand I think I should tell you that this action does not have the full support of Italy or Ireland!"

13.11 '... on the other hand...', JAK, *Evening Standard*, London, 19 May 1982

Relations between Dublin and London reached a new low following the outbreak of war between Britain and Argentina over the Falkland Islands or Malvinas in April 1982. The Irish government initially supported a United Nations resolution calling for an immediate Argentinian withdrawal from the islands and co-operated, albeit reluctantly, with an EEC trade embargo. The mood changed, however, following the sinking of the Argentinian battleship, the *General Belgrano*, on 2 May. The Irish defence minister accused Britain of aggressive action and called for a cessation of hostilities pending a diplomatic solution. This move angered the British, as did Ireland's subsequent withdrawal from the EEC embargo. In this cartoon JAK derides Ireland's refusal to support Britain's war effort by implying that the country is virtually alone in its opposition, and is, in any case, an insignificant voice in the international community. The Italian government is also criticised for its reluctance to endorse Britain's position.

13.12 'F.O.R.U.M. R.E.P.O.R.T. . .', Turner, *Irish Times*, Dublin, 17 November 1984

The November 1982 general election in the Republic resulted in the formation of a Fine Gael–Labour coalition government headed by Garret FitzGerald. Within months of gaining office, the new taoiseach, strongly influenced by SDLP leader John Hume, announced the establishment of an all-Ireland forum in which Irish constitutional nationalists might agree a blueprint for a political settlement on the island. The New Ireland Forum first met in May 1983 and its report was published twelve months later.

While the report acknowledged the legitimacy of the unionist tradition, its main conclusion was that 'the desire of nationalists is for a united Ireland in the form of a sovereign, independent Irish state' to be achieved by consent. Two other proposals were outlined, namely, a federal Irish state and joint sovereignty. Although the report was rejected by the British government, it regenerated the faltering Anglo-Irish political process and led directly to a summit meeting between FitzGerald and Thatcher at Chequers on 19 November 1984.

Turner's *Irish Times* cartoon succinctly summarises the differing expectations of the two leaders in advance of the Chequers summit. Whereas FitzGerald hoped to win British support for the report's proposals, Thatcher was intent on getting Dublin to agree to greater cross-border security co-operation. The outcome was disastrous for the Irish side. At a post-summit press conference Thatcher haughtily dismissed all three of the report's options, thus humiliating FitzGerald and provoking nationalist fury. Once the ensuing furore subsided, however, Irish and British officials recognised the need to redouble their efforts to find a political solution to the Northern Ireland problem. The result was the Anglo-Irish Agreement of November 1985.

'As far as I can make out, Messrs Paisley and Powell are stating that they refuse to have their destiny influenced by a foreign power!'

13.13 'As far as I can make out . . .', Gibbard, *Guardian*, London, 15 November 1985

The agreement gave Dublin a limited consultative role in the administration of Northern Ireland, while at the same time offering a unionist guarantee that 'any change in the status of Northern Ireland would only come about with the consent of the majority of the people of Northern Ireland'. It met with vociferous and violent unionist fury, as this *Guardian* cartoon indicates. It shows two of the most implacable unionist MPs, Enoch Powell and Ian Paisley, attacking the co-signatories, Thatcher and FitzGerald. Gibbard detects a fundamental irony in this display of unionist resistance to having 'their destiny influenced by a foreign power', given the presence of American cruise missile bases in Britain, and the implications this had for the government's defence policy. By locating the agreement in this geo-political context, the cartoon serves as a reminder that the Anglo-Irish dispute is itself part of a wider 'totality of relationships', which raises questions about the limits of sovereignty and the nation state.

13.14 'The Time Travellers', Blotski, *Fortnight*, Belfast, 23 June 1986

One of the defining characteristics of Garret FitzGerald's political career was his deep commitment to the achievement of greater social pluralism in the Republic. This prompted him to launch a 'constitutional crusade' in September 1981 to create 'a genuine republic on the principles of Tone and Davis'. He criticised the sectarian nature of the Republic's constitution and laws and spoke of the need to make the south more acceptable to northern unionists. His liberal agenda drew the wrath of many conservative Catholics, however, and worried some members of the hierarchy.

The first test of strength between the forces of liberalism and conservatism resulted in a victory for the latter when a constitutional referendum to prohibit abortion was passed by a majority of two to one in September 1983. Undaunted by this defeat and the divisiveness it engendered, FitzGerald continued to promote liberal social reforms throughout the rest of his premiership. In February 1985 his coalition government succeeded in passing a Bill to legalise the sale of contraceptives to adults, despite opposition from Catholic traditionalists.

The following year the government introduced a Bill to remove the constitutional ban on divorce, but this was comprehensively rejected in a referendum in June 1986. A disappointed FitzGerald admitted that the outcome was 'a set-back to the long-term prospect of the two parts of Ireland coming closer together politically' and a rebuff to northern unionists.

This cartoon by Blotski, pseudonym of Ian Knox, from the independent Northern Ireland magazine *Fortnight* portrays the taoiseach's dilemma at this time. It shows him wrestling for control of a 'divorce' time machine with Kevin MacNamara, the then Catholic archbishop of Dublin and a staunch conservative. FitzGerald is vainly trying to redirect the capsule towards a 'pluralist secular future', where he hopes to join his fellow time travellers, unionist leaders Ian Paisley and James Molyneaux. They, however, admit to be going backwards at an even greater pace!

By June 1986 unionist protests against the Anglo-Irish Agreement had resulted in the effective breakdown of local democracy in the north, culminating in the dissolution of the Northern Ireland assembly on the day this cartoon appeared. Meanwhile, the south was in the grip of a religious fervour generated by sightings of so-called 'moving statues', which many liberal commentators regarded as a manifestation of a residual medievalism in Irish religious belief. Divorce was eventually legalised in the Irish Republic in February 1997.

13.15 'Willoughby . . .', JAK, *Evening Standard*, London, 2 December 1988

The issue of extradition, which had long been a source of friction between Westminster and Dublin, came into renewed focus in the aftermath of the signing of the Anglo-Irish

"Willoughby, are you absolutely certain the Irish spell "extradition" with one T?"

Agreement. The British government envisaged closer cross-border co-operation between the security forces and a greater willingness on the part of the Republic to hand over suspects wanted for terrorist offences in Britain. Irish concerns about the fairness of the British justice system resulted in the refusal of some extradition requests, however, while others were rejected due to errors in warrants issued by the British Crown Prosecution Service.

A number of high-profile cases, including that of Evelyn Glenholmes, Scotland Yard's most-wanted IRA suspect, led to acrimonious exchanges between the two governments during 1986 and 1987. Then, in November 1988, a major row flared up over the refusal of the Belgian government to extradite Father Patrick Ryan to Britain to face charges of conspiracy to murder and cause explosions, because of a faulty extradition warrant. Ryan was deported to the Irish Republic instead, amid much hostile criticism from Prime Minister Thatcher. Her fury deepened in December when the Irish attorney-general rejected Britain's extradition request for Ryan on the grounds that he could not be guaranteed a fair trial.

This *Evening Standard* cartoon satirises the Irish judiciary's scrupulous attitude to British extradition warrants in the late 1980s, some of which were turned down on the basis of technical inconsistencies, including typographical errors. A new extradition row broke out in March 1990 when the Irish Supreme Court refused to extradite two Maze escapees on the grounds that their lives would be in danger if they were re-imprisoned in the north. Former Fermanagh–South Tyrone MP, Owen Carron, was released from custody the following month after a warrant for his extradition was rejected also. Both decisions provoked intense unionist anger and led to a sharp deterioration in London–Dublin relations.

13.16 'The Introduction of Internment . . .', Turner, *Irish Times*, Dublin, 19 February 1992

In February 1992 the Republic was plunged into its second abortion crisis inside ten years when the High Court ruled that a pregnant fourteen-year-old girl, the victim of rape, did not have the right to travel to Britain for an abortion. This judgment, which provoked a massive public outcry, was quickly reversed by the Supreme Court on the grounds that there was a 'real and substantial risk' to the life of the hapless girl, known as 'Miss X', who had threatened to commit suicide. This decision in turn aroused the ire of pro-life activists, who were dismayed that the judgment undermined the intended effect of the 1983 constitutional ban on abortion. In the ensuing debate questions were raised about Irish women's civil liberties and the right of the state to intervene in the sphere of private morality, issues which are strikingly illustrated in Turner's cartoon. Its stark imagery and emotive internment analogy comprise an acerbic indictment of the attorney-general's initial decision to seek a court injunction to prevent the schoolgirl from travelling for an abortion, while at the same time evoking something of the victim's terrible plight.

Cartoon 13.17, also by Turner, is an equally forceful representation of the wider ramifications of the 'X' case for Ireland's relations with Britain and the rest of Europe. The abortion controversy coincided with a public debate about the Maastricht treaty on closer European union and its ratification by Ireland through a constitutional referendum set for June 1992. The two issues became entangled when it transpired that the European courts, so often the final arbiter in matters of national concern, were powerless to adjudicate on the issue of a woman's right to travel, because of the Irish government's earlier

13.17 'Suggested New Wording...', Turner, *Fortnight*, Belfast, May 1992

insertion of a treaty protocol explicitly preventing them from doing so. Unable to persuade the heads of the other eleven EC member states to amend the protocol and desperate for a pro-Maastricht vote, the government pledged itself to resolve the abortion question by referendum in the autumn of 1992.

Turner searingly indicts the government's inept handling of the whole affair by suggesting a sardonic new protocol wording which highlights the state's ostrich-like attitude to the social reality of abortion, whereby approximately four thousand Irish women travel to Britain each year for terminations. His image of an anxious-looking Britain bearing Ireland's unwanted pregnancies recasts the historical colonial relationship between the two countries in contemporary socio-sexual terms and offers an arresting new gloss on the meaning of 'mother' country. In the subsequent November referendum the Irish electorate voted in favour of allowing women access to abortion information and the right to travel abroad for a termination, while rejecting a proposal to allow abortions to be carried out in Ireland in certain extreme cases.

13.18 'I'm sorry Father...', Bell, *Guardian*, London, 18 November 1994

In November 1994 Ireland was convulsed by a dramatic political crisis arising from a dispute between the leaders of the coalition government, Taoiseach Albert Reynolds (Fianna Fáil) and his deputy, Tánaiste Dick Spring (Labour), over the appointment of the attorney-general, Harry Whelehan, to the presidency of the High Court. Spring objected to this key appointment because he was dissatisfied with Whelehan's explanation of the delay in processing warrants for the extradition of a paedophile priest, Father Brendan Smyth, to Northern Ireland to face charges of child sexual abuse. The taoiseach initially defended the integrity of his attorney-general and went ahead with the appointment. But when the tánaiste subsequently revealed that information concerning an earlier case, which could have expedited Smyth's extradition, was withheld from him, Reynolds was forced to resign as taoiseach and make way for a new coalition government.

These extraordinary developments deepened the public mood of cynicism about the political process and further undermined people's confidence in the institutions of church and state. Steve Bell's cartoon response is typically risible; he exploits the comic potential of the religious aspect of the controversy by exposing the penile pun in the tánaiste's first name. On the other hand, in cartoon 13.19 Martyn Turner succinctly captures the widespread sense of anger and dismay at the flawed nature of political, religious and legal authority in Ireland. Cardinal, judge and politician stand indicted before an incredulous public in their well-fitting feet of clay, all having failed the test of accountability, transparency and honesty. The gaunt and angry figure on the right who signifies the victims of these discredited institutions is, significantly, female, representing the many Irish women and girls who have suffered through the years as a result of the diktats of a male-dominated church and state.

13.19 'Irish Pantomime', Turner, *Guardian*, London, 19 November 1994

13.20 'The Condition of Ireland . . .', Rowson, *Sunday Tribune*, Dublin, 8 December 1996

In a survey carried out in the aftermath of the collapse of the coalition government in November 1994 a massive 82 per cent of respondents expressed the view that a 'sleaze factor' had entered Irish politics. British public opinion at this time was equally concerned about parliamentary corruption, largely as a result of newspaper allegations about government ministers asking Commons' questions in return for cash payments. Mounting political pressure forced the prime minister to establish a government inquiry under Lord Nolan to investigate these allegations, which led in turn to the appointment of a new parliamentary commissioner for standards, Sir Gordon Downey, in 1995. The 'cash for questions' scandal rumbled on, however, re-erupting in the autumn of 1996 when two of those at the centre of the row, former minister Neil Hamilton and parliamentary lobbyist Ian Greer, dropped their libel action against the *Guardian* newspaper hours before the court case was due to begin.

The closing months of 1996 witnessed a dramatic revival of the sleaze factor in Irish politics also. Media reports alleged that payments had been made to serving and retired cabinet ministers by millionaire businessman Ben Dunne, who had been ousted as chairman of Ireland's biggest retail group by his sister, Margaret Heffernan, following his well-publicised arrest for cocaine possession in Florida in 1992. The resignation of Communications Minister Michael Lowry on 2 December prompted the government to appoint retired Judge Gerard Buchanan to investigate the extent of these payments, amid sensational rumours that the former taoiseach, Charles Haughey, had himself received over £1 million from Dunne while in office.

Martin Rowson's doleful cartoon (opposite, top) effectively illustrates the stifling cumulative impact of these sleaze allegations upon the Irish political establishment, while also directing a sharp side-swipe at British parliamentary malpractice. The nation appears

submerged beneath a putrid mass of political corruption which has obscured the workings of democracy and disorientated the democrats themselves. The morass, like the contemptuous public mood it created, seems bottomless.

13.21 'Oh! – that £1.3 million . . .', Willson, *Sunday Times*, London, 13 July 1997

On receipt of Judge Buchanan's interim report in February 1997, the Dáil set up a tribunal of inquiry under the chairmanship of Mr Justice Brian McCracken, a High Court judge, to investigate the 'payments to politicians' scandal. The inquiry centred on the secret payment of £1.3 million to Charles Haughey by Ben Dunne, a claim which Dunne admitted under oath, but which Haughey initially denied. In July, however, the former taoiseach's veracity was dramatically challenged and he was forced to make a terse public confession of guilt. The subsequent tribunal report severely criticised Haughey and Michael Lowry, former minister and serving Fine Gael TD, leaving their reputations in ruins and casting a shadow over the integrity of all elected representatives in the Republic.

Richard Willson's sketch graphically represents the sensational climax of this compelling national drama, described by one *Irish Times* journalist as 'a moment of such epic significance that no history of post-war Ireland would be complete without it'. It shows the apparently absent-minded former taoiseach being led to the site of the secret cache by his accuser, Ben Dunne (right), and the tribunal chairman, Justice McCracken. Haughey's eventual acknowledgement that he received £1.3 million from Dunne was accompanied by his assertion that he had no recollection of ever having received the money, thus revealing an attitude towards the truth as jesuitical as that of Eamon de Valera towards the oath of allegiance.

13.22 'Oh hello...', Knox, *Irish News*, Belfast, 1 November 1997

13.23 'Next Week's News', Turner, *Irish Times*, 22 November 1997

The 1997 Irish presidential campaign was remarkable for several reasons, not least because four of the five candidates were women. History was made when Mary McAleese, an academic and lawyer from Belfast, became the first Northern Irish Catholic nationalist to be elected to high political office in the Republic. Her victory was a defining event for northern nationalists at a potentially historic moment in the peace process and also represented a desire on the part of the southern electorate for a new post-nationalist identity based on inclusivity and diversity. McAleese herself articulated this desire, both in her campaign theme of 'building bridges' and in her inaugural speech, when she spoke of her vision of an Ireland 'where difference is celebrated with joyful curiosity and generous respect' and of a people 'at ease with the flowering diversity that is now all around us'.

Throughout the campaign, McAleese was compared with her predecessor, Mary Robinson, with whom she shares a similar legal and academic background. This tended to obscure some important differences between the two women, one of which the Ian Knox cartoon opposite suggests is their contrasting attitudes to Articles 2 and 3 of the Irish constitution which claim jurisdiction over Northern Ireland. These articles were a 'core value' of the republican Fianna Fáil party which, together with the Progressive Democrats, nominated McAleese for the presidency. They were also endorsed by many northern nationalists, though unionists regarded them with the utmost antipathy. As the cartoon indicates, Robinson had been among those in favour of sending these 'unwanted items' to northern unionists as a conciliatory gesture. However, Knox suggests that the new president and Fianna Fáil taoiseach, Bertie Ahern (1951–), may take a somewhat different view, judging by their rather perturbed reaction to the outgoing president's generosity. Subsequent events soon proved otherwise, however, as Ahern successfully spearheaded the government campaign to have Articles 2 and 3 removed from the constitution in the southern referendum on the Good Friday agreement in May 1998.

Despite ill-judged attempts to smear her during the campaign, McAleese recorded the biggest winning margin ever in an Irish presidential contest. The nation had little time to bask in the glow of her historic victory, however, as Martyn Turner's cartoon suggests. Within days of the election, the Republic was immersed in a legal crisis precipitated by the improper appointment of court clerks, followed by yet another abortion controversy. Such all too familiar developments prompted Turner to imagine this comic sequence of future events which, given the nation's propensity to surprise even the most inured observers, may not be as far-fetched as they seem!

14

POLITICAL VIOLENCE IN NORTHERN IRELAND
1969–1993

In the winter of 1968–69 the Northern Ireland prime minister, Terence O'Neill, came under increasing pressure from three sources. First, the predominantly Catholic civil rights movement was demanding widespread reform of the state to end the gerrymandering of electoral boundaries, to allocate public housing on a fair basis, to disband the B Specials and to introduce 'one man, one vote' in local council elections. Second, there was a growing number of unionist critics of O'Neill, the most extreme of whom was the Reverend Ian Paisley, who feared that O'Neill's concessions to the nationalist minority were weakening the unionist position. Third, Wilson's Labour government in Britain was beginning to grow more concerned about the increasing unrest in Northern Ireland.

On 4 January 1969 a march from Belfast to Derry organised by students at Queen's University Belfast and other civil rights supporters was attacked by some two hundred loyalists, including members of the B Specials. That night, amid widespread unrest in Derry, the police went on the rampage in the Catholic Bogside area of the city. Sectarian passions were rising to a level unknown for many years and undermining any goodwill that O'Neill's modest reforms had earned him from the nationalist population. Ultraloyalists like Paisley and some within O'Neill's own party saw the civil rights movement as a republican plot aimed at bringing down the northern state, not merely reforming it. In desperation, O'Neill called a general election in February, hoping to strengthen his hand, but the splits within unionism widened, and his own position was further undermined by the relative success of more hardline loyalist candidates. Of the 52 seats in the Stormont parliament, unionists won 39, but 10 of these went to anti-O'Neillites, with 2 undecided. O'Neill resigned in April, a beaten man, to be replaced as prime minister by his cousin, the lacklustre figure of James Chichester-Clark (1923–). To add insult to injury, O'Neill's seat at the subsequent by-election was won by his arch-enemy, Paisley.

Sectarian clashes grew more frequent during the summer of 1969. British civil servants sent over to Belfast from London to oversee reforms were totally unfamiliar with the political culture, historical complexities and sectarian passions which confronted them. The heightened tension during the traditional Orange marches in July led to rioting in Belfast, but the climactic moment of no return occurred in Derry in August, following disturbances during a Protestant Apprentice Boys' march in the city. The B Specials played a critical role in these events. They attempted to enter the Catholic Bogside area but were prevented by the residents who, believing that their homes were about to be attacked, erected barricades and hurled petrol bombs at the police. Three days of serious rioting followed, and this spread to Belfast where Protestant mobs attacked Catholic areas of the city, sometimes assisted by armed B Specials.

It was soon clear that the Northern Ireland police was incapable of subduing the violence and maintaining law and order. During the night of 14 August, 6 people died as a result of the riots and over 400 houses were severely damaged. On the same date, the Labour government reluctantly took the decision to send in British troops to restore order. They were greeted warmly by the Catholic population, who saw them as saviours, infinitely preferable to the armed police, while Protestants looked on hesitantly, realising that the unionist regime was no longer sole master of its own house.

The presence of British troops on the streets of Belfast and Derry was to change fundamentally the nature of the Northern Ireland problem. Having ignored the state it created for almost fifty years, an ill-prepared British government was now dragged into its affairs, with little thought being given to the long-term implications. There was uncertainty amongst all groups as to whether the army was there to protect the Catholic population, to subdue revolution, or to shore up a discredited regime. The officer commanding British troops, Lieutenant-General Sir Ian Freeland, perceptively warned that the initial 'honeymoon period between troops and the local people is likely to be short-lived'. Wilson's government, which now had effective overall responsibility for maintaining order, continued to work through the unionist government at Stormont in the unrealistic hope of keeping the northern problem at a distance. The expectation was that the army would be able to keep the peace while some reforms were made to the running of the state, and that normality would resume under a reorganised unionist government. However, the short-term reforms which Wilson's government forced the Northern Ireland administration to concede only served to antagonise further many Protestants, and failed to reconcile Catholics, a growing number of whom were coming to regard Northern Ireland as a 'failed political entity' and to see security and justice in a new united Ireland.

The IRA had been much criticised in some Catholic areas for its failure to defend besieged Catholic communities during the rioting of August 1969. In January 1970 it split into two groups. The Official IRA, the so-called 'Red' faction, retained its socialist objectives, but a breakaway group, the Provisional or 'Green' IRA, soon became the dominant body. The movement quickly established itself in Catholic housing estates and spent much of 1970 training its volunteers and acquiring weapons. The Provisionals' aim was to drive the old enemy, the British army, out of Northern Ireland and to bring about the unification which had been denied them in 1921.

Gradually, the IRA began to attack British troops and the first soldier was killed in February 1971. By this time the Labour government in Britain had been replaced by Edward Heath's Conservative administration, which tended to see the IRA as the basic problem together with the Catholic community which gave it active or tacit support. This new emphasis on a security response to what was a political problem further alienated Catholics from the British government and its unionist allies at Stormont, and led to the army being perceived in Catholic housing estates as an army of occupation, which was exactly what the Provisionals were arguing.

In August 1971 the London government made the disastrous decision to accept the Northern Ireland government's advice and introduce internment without trial for IRA suspects. Internment was very much a one-sided operation against the nationalist population. No loyalists were included among the 342 men arrested. Many innocent people were detained, internees were brutalised and tortured, violence escalated and Catholic disenchantment deepened. Indeed Catholic and Protestant fears were such that there was a massive movement of people to 'safe areas', producing the largest enforced population movement in Europe since 1945. The final straw came on 30 January 1972 when British paratroops killed thirteen unarmed civilians during a civil rights march in Derry, on what became known as Bloody Sunday. The British government, having tried to work through the Stormont regime, finally realised that it would have to accept full responsibility for policy in Northern Ireland. Accordingly, in March 1972 Heath's government suspended the Northern Ireland parliament and established direct rule from London through a Northern Ireland secretary of state.

Initially intended as a temporary measure, direct rule was to become a permanent feature of the state. The fall of Stormont was regarded by unionists as a victory for the Provisional IRA. Many Protestants felt betrayed by Britain and felt very deeply insecure about their future. A number of paramilitary organisations were formed in Protestant working-class areas to counter-balance the activities of the Provisionals and carry out attacks on Catholic areas. As the IRA increased its campaign of shootings and bombings, 1972 became the most violent year of the Troubles with 467 deaths in Northern Ireland, 321 of which were civilian casualties.

Catholic political self-confidence was growing, particularly as the British government was coming to accept the fact that the nationalists' aspiration towards unity required formal acknowledgement, and that the Dublin government might in some way be involved in an overall solution. The core problem for the British government, however, was how to reconcile the opposing interests of nationalists and unionists. In both groups there were different factions. Within nationalism, those republicans represented by Sinn Féin saw the British presence as the key problem and refused to participate in constitutional politics, while more moderate nationalists, represented by the SDLP, were willing to co-operate with the government to reform the northern state. Within unionism, extreme loyalist groups objected to concessions to nationalists, and to the involvement of the Dublin government in northern affairs, which they considered would weaken the link with Britain.

For a great many years, Northern Ireland unionists had co-operated so closely with British Conservatives that they were, for practical purposes, one party. In the early 1970s, however, the unionists broke this alliance and became a separate force in United Kingdom politics. In 1971 the previously monolithic Ulster Unionist Party had split when Ian Paisley broke away to form the Democratic Unionist Party. The DUP, although smaller in numbers than the 'official' unionists, was dominated by the imposing figure of Paisley and adopted extreme positions on most matters. Its roots were more working class than those of the Ulster Unionists, and its members tended on the whole to be Presbyterian, while the 'officials' represented a broader range of Protestantism, including a higher proportion of members of the Church of Ireland.

By 1972 it was apparent to the British government that military measures alone could not solve the problem and so during the next twenty-five years a series of political initiatives was attempted. All of these took place against a background of killings and bombings in Northern Ireland and Britain, while successive governments sought to contain the political violence through emergency legislation. The first major initiative took place in November 1973 when the British government, while guaranteeing Northern Ireland's position in the United Kingdom, proposed to set up an elected Executive in which power was to be shared by moderate unionists and nationalists. A Council of Ireland was also proposed, which would allow Dublin an ill-defined role in Northern Ireland affairs.

There was, however, much unionist opposition to these proposals, and in particular to the Council of Ireland, which was seen as a threat to the Union. Amid increasing unrest, groups of loyalist workers, calling themselves the Ulster Workers' Council, declared a general strike in May 1974. They were aided by loyalist paramilitary groups such as the Ulster Defence Association. Despite widespread intimidation, Wilson's new Labour government was unwilling to use the army to break the strike and support the power-sharing Executive. The result was the ignominious collapse of the five-month-old Executive on 28 May 1974, and a confirmation of loyalists' belief that they could effectively destroy by force any political plan put forward by Britain which they opposed.

For the rest of the 1970s there was little sense of plan or purpose to British policy in Northern Ireland, but rather a further emphasis on security measures. In 1973 the IRA took its bombing campaign to England. Following major bombings in London, Guildford and Birmingham, the Labour government rushed through the Prevention of Terrorism Act in 1974, part of which enabled the authorities to ban suspected terrorists from entry into Britain and to banish them to Northern Ireland, although still an integral part of the United Kingdom. Within Northern Ireland itself, the mid-1970s saw an increasingly vicious series of bombings and 'tit-for-tat' sectarian murders. In an attempt to restore the appearance of normality, the British government adopted a new strategy of 'Ulsterisation' in 1976, whereby the prominent role of the army was replaced by an emphasis on the primacy of the RUC.

In 1976 'special category' (political) status for paramilitary prisoners was also removed in an attempt to criminalise those convicted of political offences. This move precipitated a grave crisis in the prisons which came to dominate northern politics in the late 1970s. Republican prisoners, demanding political status, refused to wear prison clothes and went on a 'blanket protest', later followed by a 'dirty protest'. Finally, in March 1981, they began a series of hunger strikes in their H-Block cells in the Maze prison near Belfast in order to regain political status. The hunger strikes provided a huge public platform for the Provisional movement, and its political wing, Sinn Féin, achieved worldwide publicity when the leader of the hunger-strikers, Bobby Sands, was elected as a British MP in April. His election revealed levels of support amongst the nationalist community far beyond that usually associated with revolutionary republicanism. The prolonged fasting and dramatic deaths of Sands and nine other hunger-strikers in 1981 further increased the publicity for republicans in America and Europe, and greatly increased the level of their support from nationalists.

The Conservative prime minister, Margaret Thatcher, leader of the government elected in 1979, had been determined not to give in to the pressure exerted by the hunger-strikers and their supporters. She resisted their demands until they finally capitulated, but this was a classic case of how to win a battle yet lose the war. Britain's handling of the affair was disastrous. It encouraged the Provisionals to attempt to capitalise on their increased support by entering the political arena and contesting elections. The new Provisional strategy was aimed at taking power in Ireland 'with a ballot box in one hand and an Armalite in the other'. The growing success of Sinn Féin at both local and national elections led to government fears that the moderate SDLP would be replaced as the main voice of Catholic nationalism in Northern Ireland. These fears were increased when Sinn Féin leader Gerry Adams (1948–) won the West Belfast seat in the Westminster general election of June 1983. As political agreement between the parties within Northern Ireland seemed impossible, Britain looked to the Irish government to share the problem, and sought to find agreement between the two governments on the way forward.

On the surface, the years between 1980 and 1985 produced little progress and there was a number of public disagreements between the two governments. To make matters worse, in October 1984 at the Conservative Party conference in Brighton, there was an almost successful IRA attempt to assassinate Margaret Thatcher and members of her cabinet when a bomb exploded in their hotel. However, behind the scenes, officials of both governments had been working together to produce a historic understanding which was signed by the two premiers, Garret FitzGerald and Margaret Thatcher, on 15 November 1985.

The Anglo-Irish Agreement, whilst guaranteeing that Northern Ireland would remain part of the United Kingdom as long as a majority of the population so desired, had the fundamental importance of granting Dublin a permanent consultative role in the affairs of Northern Ireland for the first time since 1921. This willingness to share decision-making powers with the southern government marked a decisive shift in British government thinking. Republicans opposed the agreement because of its continuing support for the Northern Irish state, while unionists were outraged at the way they had been excluded from the two governments' negotiations. In December 1985 all fifteen unionist MPs resigned their Westminster seats in order to fight anti-agreement by-election campaigns under the slogan 'Ulster Says No!' The following March, a unionist Day of Action brought the province to a standstill. The agreement, however, was widely welcomed in the rest of Ireland, Britain and the international world. Despite the widespread, prolonged, and sometimes violent loyalist opposition, the agreement remained secure. This time the British government did not capitulate to loyalist opposition as it had done in 1974.

Despite this inter-governmental consensus, violence still occupied the centre stage. Allegations of a 'shoot-to-kill' policy by the security forces in Northern Ireland were followed by a huge IRA bomb in Enniskillen on Remembrance Day, November 1987, which killed 11 civilians and left over 60 injured. There were also increased killings by Protestant paramilitaries, and three unarmed IRA volunteers were shot dead by British soldiers in Gibraltar in March 1988. However, the appointment of Peter Brooke as Northern Ireland secretary of state in July 1989 produced a fresh political initiative.

Shortly after taking office, Brooke made a number of important speeches in which he indicated that the government would talk to Sinn Féin if the IRA renounced violence; that Britain's role in Northern Ireland was a neutral one; and that Britain would accept Irish unification if a majority of the people in Northern Ireland consented to it. Since 1988 there had also been dialogue between John Hume and Gerry Adams, which attempted to draw Sinn Féin into the political arena. Through its association with the SDLP, Sinn Féin was hoping to establish a broadly based nationalist movement which would have the support of the Dublin government. Furthermore, between October 1990 and November 1993 there were secret contacts between British government officials and leading Sinn Féin figures such as Martin McGuinness, a sign that the British authorities were privately conceding the importance of involving Sinn Féin in political dialogue. Considerable rethinking had also been occurring within the Provisional movement itself, with a growing emphasis being placed on seeking political legitimacy as opposed to a continuation of the armed struggle.

In 1991 Brooke succeeded in getting talks started between all the constitutional parties in Northern Ireland, excluding Sinn Féin. There were three separate strands to these talks: internal relations within Northern Ireland; arrangements between Northern Ireland and the Dublin government; and relations between London and Dublin. These talks continued until November 1992 under a new Northern Ireland secretary, Sir Patrick Mayhew. Although they failed to reach agreement on any of the three strands, they had established an agenda for future negotiations where 'nothing would be agreed in any strand until everything is agreed in the talks as a whole'.

Meanwhile, sectarian murders and bombings continued. The steady rise in loyalist paramilitary violence resulted in the random assassination of Catholics, while in April 1992 the IRA exploded a huge bomb at the Baltic Exchange in the centre of London, which killed three people and caused damage amounting to hundreds of millions of pounds. Despite this violence, the secret and overt political activity of the previous years within Northern Ireland, together with the continuing co-operation between the British and Irish governments, were leading to the possibility of dramatic political movement towards an Anglo-Irish peace process.

"Coming in ? It's terrible !"

14.1 'Coming in? It's terrible!', Gibbard, *Guardian*, London, 5 August 1969

During the early part of 1969 political tension increased in Northern Ireland as civil rights activists continued to clash with the RUC. The beginning of the summer marching season in July led to serious rioting in a number of areas, and the fear that the Protestant Apprentice Boys' parade in Derry on 12 August would provoke serious conflict. Both the prime minister, Harold Wilson, and the home secretary, James Callaghan, were very reluctant to intervene, fearing that once involved it would be very difficult for the British government to extricate itself easily. Callaghan later stated: 'The advice that came to me from all sides was on no account to get sucked into the Irish bog.'

Most British newspapers showed little real understanding or analysis of the issues in Northern Ireland, and often identified religious fanaticism as the source of the problem. This *Guardian* cartoon reflects this British ignorance. Based on the classical legend of Laocoön, who was crushed to death by two sea-serpents sent by Apollo, it shows a helpless Northern Ireland premier, James Chichester-Clark, trying to keep apart two sectarian sea monsters. The diffident, avuncular figure of Wilson is dressed for his swim in the Ulster sea, but is clearly thinking twice about the wisdom of so doing. Not until he was compelled by the complete breakdown of law and order nine days later did Wilson brave the treacherous waters by finally ordering troops into Northern Ireland, thereby directly involving the British government for the first time since 1921.

"We're pagan missionaries come to try to make peace among the bloodthirsty Christians"

14.2 'We're pagan missionaries...', Cummings, *Daily Express*, London,
12 September 1969

When the army first arrived in Northern Ireland the troops were warmly received in Catholic areas, in the belief that the soldiers had come to save them from the aggression of the B Specials and the RUC. However, as the officer commanding British troops in Northern Ireland had warned, this honeymoon period was not to last, and soon Catholics in working-class areas came to see the army as an instrument of the Stormont regime.

British cartoonists in the popular press frequently depicted the army as a benign, dispassionate presence, bemused by the tribal antics of the natives. Religion was supposed to be at the core of the problem, and few in Britain could easily understand why two different strands of Christian belief should lead to such violent conflict. This Cummings cartoon reflects this British incomprehension in its depiction of primitive tribesmen arriving to reconcile the barbarous Irish, who seem intent on tearing each other apart. The racist implication is that black, presumably African, tribesmen are more civilised than the Christian Northern Irish, who have now slipped below even primitive pagans in their innate barbarity. The cartoon thus reinforces stereotypical notions of the Irish as violent and blacks as primitive, and makes no attempt to convey any understanding of the underlying causes of conflict other than religious bigotry.

The Cummings cartoon opposite, published a year later, when Catholic resentment towards the army had increased and Provisional IRA violence had begun, continues to

"How marvellous it would be if they DID knock each other insensible!"

14.3 'How marvellous it would be . . .', Cummings, *Daily Express*, London, 12 August 1970

portray the army as a neutral peace-keeping force. It reflects a growing impatience among some sections of the British public with the conflict in Northern Ireland and their desire for the army to withdraw and leave the Irish to fight it out among themselves. A bruised British soldier attempts to separate two violent Irishmen, whose simian features suggest a direct lineage with the apelike Paddys in *Punch* one hundred years earlier. In fact, Cummings later commented that the IRA's violence tended to 'make them look like apes – though that's rather hard luck on the apes'. The implication underlying both cartoons is that the irrational nature of the Irish question can only be explained through some form of racial madness. Far from helping British readers to understand the complexities of the Northern Irish situation, such cartoons reinforced the growing anti-Irish prejudice among sections of British opinion and so exacerbated the hostile public mood.

14.4 Untitled, Scarfe, *Sunday Times*, London, 14 March 1971

At the end of 1969 a split in the IRA took place, leading to the birth of the Provisional movement. During 1970 relations between Catholics and Protestants continued to deteriorate and IRA attacks on the police and army began. On 6 February 1971 the first British soldier was killed, and a month later three off-duty Scottish soldiers, two of them brothers aged seventeen and eighteen, were lured from a Belfast pub and shot by the

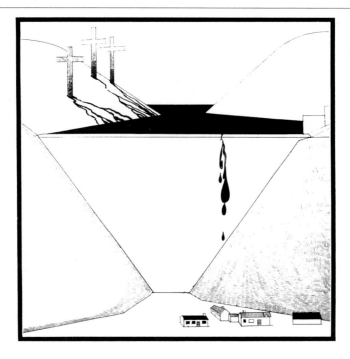

Provisionals. A week later as the security situation worsened, Chichester-Clark resigned and was replaced by Brian Faulkner, who was to become the last prime minister of Northern Ireland.

Gerald Scarfe's cartoon is a powerfully dramatic comment on the killing of these three soldiers on an Irish hillside. He dramatises the popular cliché of 'the rising tide of violence' by showing drops of blood dripping from a crack in a dam onto a peaceful community below. Scarfe's ominous warning of the flood of bloodshed that threatened to swamp the state proved to be chillingly prophetic, as the dam did burst the following year, 1972, when the highest number of deaths during the Troubles was recorded. The parallel between the crosses on Calvary and the three dead Scots adds to the stark power of the image.

14.5 'What was so marvellous . . .', Cummings, *Daily Express*, London, 21 March 1971

As more troops were sent into Northern Ireland during 1971 to deal with the increasing violence, British public opinion fluctuated between advocating a much tougher security policy to 'crack down on the terrorists', and supporting demands for the withdrawal of troops, which opinion polls suggested was the option favoured by the majority of British people at the end of the year. The Cummings cartoon opposite shows a frustrated British prime minister, Edward Heath, and an equally frustrated home secretary, Reginald Maudling, struggling with this dilemma. (Until 1972, responsibility for Northern Ireland lay with the Home Office, and not, as now, with a separate Northern Ireland government department.) Behind them are the different colonial outposts where British troops had once been, but had eventually left or been forced to leave. The advantage of the Commonwealth, which evolved out of the empire, was that Britain could indeed leave those

" What was so marvellous about the rest of the British Commonwealth was that we could always leave it"

countries to their own governments to rule. The problem with Northern Ireland, on the other hand, was that it was an integral part of the United Kingdom, and therefore ultimately the direct responsibility of the British government. Cummings implies that Britain's colonial history amounts to no more than a matter of simply 'leaving' and therefore 'solving' its overseas problems. This is a very patronising imperial view which takes no account of the damaging consequences of colonialism.

14.6 'Paisley . . .', *Izvestia*, Moscow, 10 August 1971

Soviet newspapers followed events in Northern Ireland very closely in the 1970s and were highly critical of the activities of the British army, which it regarded as 'an army of occupation'. *Izvestia*, one of the leading Russian newspapers, criticised the British government for allowing right-wing Protestants to attempt to revive the 'B Special Storm Troopers' in 1971 and alleged collusion between the army and these Protestant groups. Cartoon 14.6 gives expression to these views by depicting Ian Paisley carrying a cross which supports the gun of a British soldier, against a backdrop labelled 'Ulster'. The Russian text at the top states: 'The militant Protestant clergyman Ian Paisley is head of the campaign of terror and intimidation in Ulster', while the caption underneath reads: 'Paisley: "With us is the strength of the Cross"'. This view of the British army as an occupying force in Northern Ireland whose sympathies lay with the Protestant unionist side was a feature of newspapers in the Soviet bloc during the 1970s and 1980s.

14.7 'How to Make the Irish Stew', Scarfe, *Sunday Times*, London, 15 August 1971

As violence increased in 1971, few English cartoonists addressed the complicated nature of the issues which underpinned the Northern Irish problem. This tendency to over-simplify a complex situation was widespread in Britain, and goes some way towards explaining the persistence of the Troubles. Scarfe's work was an exception. In this cartoon he attempts to illustrate some of the historical and contemporary issues which have contributed to the Troubles. He suggests that previous British governments have played a large part in creating the current crisis, and highlights other historical factors, including the Protestant plantations of the sixteenth and seventeenth centuries, the expropriation of land by English landlords, and the Famine. He also implies that the current activities of the British army in Northern Ireland, with its use of rubber bullets and CS gas, are a key ingredient and that the army is not an impartial force. This cartoon appeared six days after the introduction of internment in Northern Ireland, which led to a huge increase in violence and many deaths.

"I suppose, many centuries ago—before the Flood—our English ancestors must have committed a great sin, and this is the punishment that God has visited upon Britannia"

14.8 'I suppose, many centuries ago . . .', Cummings, *Sunday Express*, London, 15 August 1971

On 9 August 1971 the Conservative government finally agreed to Faulkner's demand that internment be introduced to stem the rise in violence. The fact that it was directed solely against nationalists, with no loyalist arrests being made, had disastrous results. Within three days twenty-two people were killed, thousands of Catholics fled to refugee camps in the Republic, and over six thousand people were made homeless as houses were burned down. IRA recruitment soared and the British army came to be seen as an instrument of the unionist regime by most Catholics. The failure of Faulkner's policy and his government's subsequent loss of credibility and legitimacy increased the probability of direct rule from Westminster. This was by no means the preferred option of Heath's government, as this cartoon indicates. Cummings transforms Heath into a modern Sisyphus to suggest the irresolvable nature of Britain's Irish problem. The perplexed prime minister regards Ireland as a punishment visited by God on Britain for some unspecified ancient 'sin'. There is no suggestion that Britain's historical and contemporary role in Ireland's affairs might be part of the problem, but simply that this is a burden which Britannia must stoically endure.

" By Jove, that nearly woke Reggie up!"

14.9 'By Jove . . .', JAK, *Evening Standard*, London, 2 February 1972

One of the key dates in the history of the Northern Ireland conflict is Bloody Sunday, 30 January 1972. During a banned civil rights march in the city of Derry, soldiers of the Parachute Regiment shot dead thirteen unarmed men and wounded seventeen others, one of whom later died. These killings led to a wave of anger and revulsion amongst the Catholic community in Northern Ireland, and feelings in the south of Ireland ran so high that a few days later a large crowd burned down the British embassy in Dublin. Britain was also heavily criticised in the international media, and it was largely because of this incident that the British government finally decided to take over responsibility for security in Northern Ireland and suspend the unionist government at Stormont.

This JAK cartoon refers to the subsequent Commons debate on the event, during which Bernadette Devlin (now McAliskey), MP for Mid-Ulster, accused Home Secretary Maudling of lying to the House and of being a 'murdering hypocrite' when he defended the paratroopers on the grounds that they had opened fire after snipers had fired on them. Devlin, who was an eyewitness to Bloody Sunday, then crossed the floor of the chamber, pulled his hair and struck him in the face. Until the outbreak of violence in August 1969, Devlin had been a popular figure with the British press and had been featured in several flattering cartoon poses. Aged twenty-one, she was the youngest person ever to be elected to Westminster in the modern era and presented a confident, youthful image. JAK reverses this image by depicting her as a impetuous young child who is politically immature and lacking in self-control. As she is escorted out of the chamber, patrician male figures on the Conservative benches regard her antics with humorous condescension. Yet JAK also indicts Maudling for his ineffectual handling of the situation. Well-known for his indolence, he sleeps through this physical assault, and presumably still sleeps while much of Northern Ireland seethes.

14.10 'Now that's what we call . . .', JAK, *Evening Standard*, London, 4 February 1972

After the Bloody Sunday shootings in Derry, Heath set up a tribunal of inquiry under Lord Chief Justice Widgery. However, many northern nationalists argued that a key figure in the British establishment was an inappropriate person to head up such a sensitive inquiry and demanded that a wider, more impartial body be established, which might include international members. This cartoon savagely lampoons this suggestion. It shows Bernadette Devlin and Gerry Fitt, leader of the SDLP, indicating their preferred international inquiry team, comprising an eclectic mix of the biased and the notorious. Edward Kennedy, the well known Irish-American politician, had earlier advised the British government to leave Ireland alone; the Libyan leader, Colonel Gaddafi, was regarded as a dangerous sponsor of international terrorism and chief arms supplier to the IRA; and Dom Mintoff, the Maltese leader, was seen as a leading anti-imperialist as a result of his long

14.11 'And now for . . .', *Irish Times*, Dublin, 5 February 1972

struggle against British involvement in Malta. The figure of Adolf Hitler completes JAK's shocking line-up, thereby suggesting that northern nationalists have lost all sense of proportion in their demands for a different inquiry team.

The *Irish Times* cartoon conveys the scepticism with which many Irish people viewed the inquiry. The image of Maudling preparing to whitewash the British army for Lord Widgery accurately represents the prevailing sense of injustice felt by many nationalists on the publication of the Widgery Report in April 1972. By finding that the army had done its best in difficult circumstances, the judge was widely accused in Ireland of presenting a whitewash. While the report satisfied some in Britain, it left many questions unanswered in Ireland, thereby adding further fuel to the controversy which already surrounded the events of Bloody Sunday.

14.12 'You won't catch us . . .', Waite, *Sunday Mirror*, London, 26 March 1972

On 24 March 1972 Heath suspended the Northern Ireland government after it had refused to give up control of law and order to Westminster. The British government now became directly responsible for ruling Northern Ireland. Ulster unionists were shocked at the removal of what they regarded as their parliament and felt a deep sense of betrayal by the British government, especially a Conservative one. They immediately organised a series of mass demonstrations and strikes in protest at this action. The split between British Conservatives and unionists, who had been close allies for most of the previous eighty years, was soon complete.

'You won't catch us surrendering to the British'

Keith Waite's cartoon reveals British incomprehension at the protests of the Ulster unionists. They are shown carrying slogans which profess loyalty to the British monarchy and waving Union flags, while at the same time proclaiming their refusal to surrender to 'the British'. The cartoon neatly captures the problematic nature of Protestant identity in Northern Ireland. Northern Protestants have traditionally proclaimed their loyalty to the British monarch, while simultaneously being prepared to oppose the actions of the government, with violence if necessary. The lack of understanding and empathy for Ulster loyalists felt by many people in Britain at the time is accurately reflected here. To them, unionists were caught in a historical time warp, and the battle of the Boyne in 1690 had little relevance to the lives of British people in the 1970s.

14.13 'The Professionals', Oisín, *Andersonstown News*, Belfast, 30 November 1974

While most British cartoonists were largely sympathetic to the role of the army in Northern Ireland in the 1970s, it was regularly attacked in the Northern Irish nationalist press, and occasionally in loyalist publications. In this cartoon Oisín, political cartoonist of the republican *Andersonstown News*, parodies the well-known army recruitment slogan of the time, 'Join the Professionals'. The army is depicted as having a bloody record of assassinations in military actions against anti-colonial campaigns in parts of the British Empire, and it is implied that the same tactics are being used in Ireland by the Special Air Services (SAS). Oisín contrasts this bloody reality with the glamour evoked by the slogan, thereby suggesting that the army is little more than a body of mercenaries. Brigadier Frank Kitson was a key figure in the British army leadership in Northern Ireland at the time and was a leading expert on counter-insurgency and covert operations. He had experience of similar campaigns in Kenya, Malaya and Cyprus, and was the *bête noire* of Irish republicans, who accused his troops of engaging in selective assassinations in Northern Ireland.

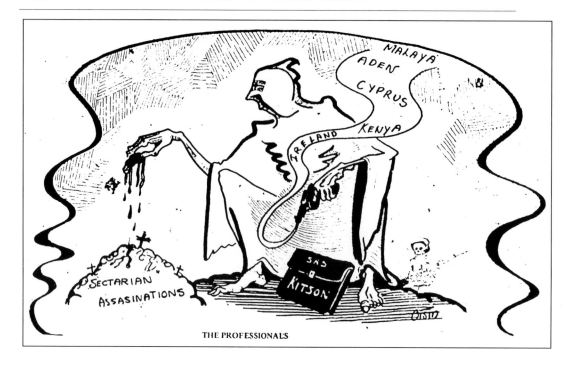

THE PROFESSIONALS

14.14 Untitled, Hill, *Detroit News*, Detroit, 29 August 1979

One of the bloodiest days of the current Troubles was 27 August 1979, when Earl Mount-batten, a relative of Queen Elizabeth, and three other people were blown up on their boat by an IRA bomb at Mullaghmore, County Sligo, in the Irish Republic. Born in 1900, Mountbatten had been supreme Allied commander in south-east Asia during the Second World War, and later the last viceroy of India. On the same day as he died, eighteen British soldiers were killed by IRA bombs near Warrenpoint, County Down, the army's highest loss of life in any single day of the Troubles.

The dramatic American cartoon opposite graphically illustrates how the IRA had that day succeeded in inflicting a deep wound in the spine of the imperial British lion. The lion roars in pain on the cliffs of Mullaghmore, while in the background a Union Jack flies at half-mast on Windsor Castle. Though Mountbatten was not a figure of any real power, to the IRA he was an important imperial and establishment symbol. His death received world-wide publicity and the IRA was widely condemned for its actions that day.

14.15 'Notes', Cormac, *Republican News*, Belfast, 7 June 1980

In June 1972 the Conservative Northern Ireland secretary, William Whitelaw, granted 'special category' status to republican prisoners and others associated with paramilitary or-ganisations. This was a tacit recognition by the government that such people would not be in prison but for the political situation in Northern Ireland. They were not required to work, wore their own clothes and effectively organised their own lives in prison. In March 1976 Whitelaw's Labour successor, Merlyn Rees, announced the removal of this status and decreed that in future all such prisoners would be treated as ordinary criminals. Republican prisoners refused to co-operate with this removal of special status and boycotted prison work and the wearing of prison uniform. Instead they wrapped themselves in blankets and later began a 'dirty protest'. This lasted until March 1981, by which time the focus of republican attention had shifted to Bobby Sands's hunger strike.

Cormac's cartoon strip (14.15) in this staunchly republican newspaper attacks the autho-rities' attempts to criminalise those who regard their crimes as political and who were con-victed in special non-jury courts. He illustrates the inconsistency and hypocrisy of applying special legal measures to such suspects up to the point of conviction, after which they are then categorised as ordinary criminals. Shortly after the hunger strike ended, the govern-ment conceded the right of these prisoners to wear their own clothes and eventually granted virtually all of their other demands.

'Nobody seems to worry about the weight I've lost.'

14.16 'Nobody seems to worry . . .', Mac, *Daily Mail*, London, 24 April 1981

On 1 March 1981 the leader of the Provisional IRA in the Maze prison, Bobby Sands, began a hunger strike aimed at securing for republican prisoners the political status which had been removed in 1976. He was gradually joined by other prisoners, and on 9 April won the Fermanagh–South Tyrone by-election to the Westminster parliament. With a turn-out of over 86 per cent, Sands obtained 30,492 votes to Ulster Unionist Harry West's 29,046. This gave a major boost to the hunger-strike campaign and increased the pressure on the British government to make concessions.

There was little sympathy in Britain for the hunger-strikers' demands, as the *Daily Mail* cartoon opposite shows. It features an ailing Sands, surrounded by grieving visitors, including a priest, while a victim of IRA violence stands alone, his suffering quickly forgotten. Most British cartoons at the time emphasised the plight of victims of IRA violence, rather than that of the hunger-strikers, who were acting of their own free will. Although the British government did not concede the prisoners' demands immediately, and ten of the hunger-strikers were to die, the net result of the campaign for Sinn Féin was a significant gain in electoral and moral support among northern Catholics.

14.17 'Fermanagh South Tyrone . . .', Friers, *Irish Times*, Dublin, 8 August 1981

During the hunger strikes, the SDLP took the controversial decision not to contest the by-election against Sands, so as to avoid splitting the nationalist vote in the constituency and risk losing the seat to the Ulster Unionists. The hunger strikes had become a national election issue and the SDLP believed that it would have been politically difficult for them to have run a candidate against a starving man in a prison hospital. Sands died on 5 May after sixty-six days on hunger strike and a second by-election was necessary. In June the British parliament passed new legislation preventing prisoners from standing for election. Sinn Féin responded by nominating Sands's election agent, Owen Carron, who won the seat with an increased majority on 20 August. Once again, the SDLP did not contest the seat.

Cartoon 14.17 by Rowel Friers, one of Northern Ireland's best-known cartoonists, illustrates the danger which the SDLP was courting by such a policy. Its leader, John Hume, is shown shielding his colleagues Paddy O'Hanlon, Seamus Mallon and Austin Currie, while Carron paddles Sands's coffin through the 'dangerous marshland' of post-hunger-strike politics. The cartoon expresses the fear that Sinn Féin might successfully challenge the SDLP's position as the principal voice of northern nationalism. This did in fact happen soon afterwards when Sinn Féin announced its decision to contest Northern Ireland and Westminster elections. It was the beginning of the policy of 'the Armalite and the ballot box', through which Sinn Féin won significant Catholic support, obtaining over 13.4 per cent of the vote in June 1983, which compared favourably to the SDLP's 17.9 per cent.

FORTNIGHT, OR THE BELFAST CHARIVARI. - DEC.

THE RIGHT LOYAL-PEST

HIBERNIA "O MY DEAR SISTER, WHAT *ARE* WE TO DO WITH THESE TROUBLESOME PEOPLE?"
BRITANNIA "TRY ISOLATION FIRST, MY DEAR, AND THEN ——— "

14.18 'The Right Loyal-Pest', Blotski, *Fortnight*, Belfast, December 1981

In autumn 1981 unionists felt that they were being increasingly ignored, and that the political agenda was being set by the British and Irish governments. They feared that their interests would be sold out by London as part of a deal with the Irish Republic and argued for a much stricter security policy to counter escalating IRA violence. Their anger increased when, on 14 November, the IRA killed Robert Bradford, a staunch Ulster Unionist MP and friend of Ian Paisley. Paisley reacted by setting up a pseudo-paramilitary group called the 'Third Force' to protect the Protestant population, and claimed in December that it had over fifteen thousand men at its disposal. On 23 November his supporters organised a 'Day of Action' to protest against the security policy of Northern Ireland Secretary James Prior, with rallies and work stoppages in Protestant areas.

The Blotski cartoon opposite is a parody of Tenniel's 'The Fenian-Pest' which appeared in *Punch* on 3 March 1866 (see cartoon 5.1, p. 67). Whereas Tenniel demonised the Fenians for their revolutionary presumption, Blotski simianises Paisley's loyalist mob for threatening violent action. The Britannia figure of Margaret Thatcher has no sympathy with their antics and, it is suggested, will crush them if necessary. Thus, militant Ulster loyalism has become just as threatening to the British and Irish governments as militant Irish republicanism.

"Give us the tools – and we'll get on with the job."

14.19 'Give us the tools...', Garland, *Daily Telegraph*, London, 21 July 1982

In 1970 a group of IRA veterans of the Anglo-Irish War, who had been living in America for many years, met with prominent members of the Provisionals in the United States. The result was the formation of Irish Northern Aid (Noraid), whose object was to collect money in America for republican organisations and individuals in Ireland. It won the support of many Irish-Americans and raised substantial sums of money, particularly during the Maze hunger strike, which had a powerful emotional appeal to a large section of the Irish community there. Most of this money was spent on helping the families of IRA activists, although both London and Dublin accused it of being simply a front organisation to enable weapons and explosives to be bought by the IRA. Undoubtedly some of the money was used for these purposes, though most of the money which purchased weapons in America was channelled through other sources.

Nicholas Garland's sketch (14.19) criticises Irish-American financial support for IRA activity by effective use of historical analogy. The cartoon parodies Prime Minister Winston Churchill's request for American money and weapons to aid the fight against Nazi Germany in 1940, prior to the United States entering the war. It shows a blood-soaked IRA gunman issuing a similar request for American aid in 1982, as menacing clouds gather over Ireland. Uncle Sam appears hesitant, however, pondering the potential consequences of his support.

14.20 'The Irish', JAK, *Evening Standard*, London, 29 October 1982

This JAK cartoon caused a great deal of controversy in both Britain and Ireland when it was published in London's *Evening Standard* newspaper in the autumn of 1982. It appeared at a time when paramilitary violence showed no sign of abating and when Anglo-Irish relations were still strained as a result of the southern government's 'neutral' attitude towards Britain during the Falklands War. In July, two IRA bombs in London had killed eight people and injured over fifty others. On 27 October, three RUC officers were killed in a massive explosion in Lurgan, County Armagh. All these events may have influenced JAK's decision to draw this offensive cartoon, though none can excuse that fact that it represents one of the most appalling examples of anti-Irish cartoon racism since the Victorian era.

It shows a man nervously walking past a poster advertising the latest x-rated film from 'Emerald Isle Snuff Movies', 'The Irish', featuring a cast of degenerate nationalist and loyalist paramilitaries, whose initials appear at the bottom of the poster. Not only is there no attempt to explain Irish political complexities or distinguish between different paramilitary groups, the cartoonist irresponsibly homogenises the Irish as a race of psychopathic monsters who delight in violence and bloodshed. No doubt this reflected the attitude of some in Britain who had little interest in trying to understand contemporary Irish politics, and preferred to brand all Irish people as murderous thugs. As a result of complaints made by many people in Britain, the Greater London Council, under its leader Ken Livingstone, withdrew its advertising from the *Standard* and demanded a full apology, which was refused. The Press Council later rejected criticisms of the *Standard* and instead condemned the GLC for attempting to coerce the paper's editor.

"YOU WERE LUCKY THIS TIME . . . YOU WON'T BE LUCKY NEXT TIME" —THE IRA

14.21 'You were lucky this time . . .', Cookson, *Sun*, London, 13 October 1984

One of the most spectacular and devastating episodes in the IRA's bombing campaign in Britain occurred in the early hours of Friday 12 October 1984, when a bomb exploded in the Grand Hotel, Brighton, during the Conservative Party's annual conference. Five people were killed, including one MP and the wife of the government chief whip, while over thirty others were injured. The prime minister, Margaret Thatcher, narrowly escaped injury, as did the rest of her cabinet. British public opinion was outraged at this atrocity, the dreadful reality of which showed just how close the IRA had come to wiping out most of the British cabinet. The bomb had in fact been planted almost four weeks earlier and revealed the increasing sophistication of the IRA's electronic timing devices. Cookson's cartoon in the popular *Sun* tabloid starkly expresses the impact of this attack on the British democratic process by showing the ghoulish spectre of IRA terror slinking away from the scene of the explosion.

In a subsequent statement the IRA said: 'Today we were unlucky, but remember, we have only to be lucky once. You will have to be lucky always. Give Ireland peace and there will be no war.' Margaret Thatcher immediately responded by stating that 'the government will never surrender to the IRA'. However, some of her advisers believed that something more than a security response alone was required, and advocated the renewal of the search for a political solution. Despite her rejection of the main proposals of the New Ireland Forum in November 1984, she and her Irish counterpart, Garret FitzGerald, were to sign the Anglo-Irish Agreement almost exactly a year later.

" I'm afraid they're hard of hearing — all I said was that we would be putting our new guest in the annexe ! "

14.22 'I'm afraid they're hard of hearing . . .', Gibbard, *Guardian*, London,
16 November 1985

The 1985 Anglo-Irish Agreement was an attempt by both governments to bolster constitutional nationalism in Northern Ireland by showing how progress could be achieved through negotiation. This, it was hoped, would reconcile alienated Catholics to the political process and undermine Sinn Féin support. At the same time, the agreement sought to reassure unionists that constitutional change would not happen without their consent. But while many Catholics welcomed the agreement, especially the proposal to allow Dublin a consultative role in northern affairs, unionist hostility was profound and prolonged.

One of the main targets of unionist anger was the permanent inter-governmental secretariat at Maryfield, near Belfast, where British and Irish ministers met regularly to discuss certain aspects of the administration of Northern Ireland. Gibbard's cartoon reflects the depth of unionist opposition to this body. It depicts the occupants of the 'Ulster Lodgings House', Unionist MPs Ian Paisley, James Molyneaux and Enoch Powell, preparing to attack the bemused new guest, Garret FitzGerald, to the horror of housekeeper Thatcher. Most unionists perceived the secretariat as the instrument of an interfering Dublin government and the harbinger of a united Ireland.

Unionist protests continued throughout 1986, spearheaded by Paisley and Molyneaux under the slogan 'Ulster Says No'. Blotski's striking cartoon opposite lampoons this resistance campaign by representing it as regressive and anachronistic. Paisley is figured as a giant dinosaur, fossilised in the stream of history, bellowing dire threats of mass unionist revolt. Behind him lies the UUP monster bearing the head of John Taylor and the tail of James Molyneaux, stoking the inflammatory rhetoric. For all their fierce defiance,

THE DEFIANT DINOSAUR AT ITS DAM

14.23 'The Defiant Dinosaur at its Dam', Blotski, *Fortnight*, Belfast, 8 January 1987

however, they have been bypassed by the British political leaders, Thatcher, Labour's Neil Kinnock and David Steel of the Liberals, who sail blithely on towards the impending general election. Northern Ireland's primitive political creatures, it is implied, cannot and must not be allowed to impede the progress towards a political settlement.

14.24 ' "Shoot to Kill" Inquiry', Garland, *Independent*, London, 27 January 1988

In 1982 the RUC shot dead six unarmed Catholics in County Armagh, five of whom had alleged IRA connections. This incident led to accusations by the Dublin government and the SDLP that there was a so-called 'shoot-to-kill' policy being operated by the RUC and that there had been a cover-up over the killings. In May 1984 Manchester's Deputy Chief Constable John Stalker was appointed to investigate the deaths. Stalker quickly came into conflict with the RUC Chief Constable John Hermon, who, he believed, was obstructing his inquiries. Eventually Stalker was removed from the case as a result of dubious disciplinary charges against him which were later dropped. Stalker subsequently claimed that he was removed from the inquiry because his investigation was about to cause a major political controversy. He asserted that while there had been no official policy to shoot terrorist suspects, special RUC squads had in fact killed these six men and then fabricated a cover-up.

The investigation was continued by the West Yorkshire Chief Constable Colin Sampson in 1986. Although his report was not published, on 25 January 1988 the

attorney-general, Sir Patrick Mayhew, announced that while there was prima facie evidence of attempts to pervert the course of justice by police officers, there would be no prosecutions on the grounds of 'national security'. This decision was widely condemned in many circles. The Dublin government protested, expressing its 'deep dismay' and on 9 February the European parliament asked Britain to reconsider its action. Garland's cartoon illustrates the impact of the decision not to prosecute on the credibility of the whole inquiry. There was a strong feeling among many in Britain and Ireland that the truth had been deliberately obscured, and that justice had been sacrificed for *raison d'état*.

14.25 'As Solid as the Rock of Gibraltar', Turner, *Irish Times*, Dublin, 9 March 1988

The opening months of 1988 witnessed a souring of Anglo-Irish relations. The decision in January not to prosecute eleven RUC officers as a result of the Stalker/Sampson inquiry was followed a few days later by the London Court of Appeal's rejection of the appeal of the six men convicted of the 1974 Birmingham pub bombings, despite new forensic evidence being produced. The Irish justice minister said that he was 'amazed and saddened' by the decision, and when a young Catholic, Aidan McAnespie, was killed at a British army border checkpoint in County Tyrone in February the Irish government set up its own inquiry into the killing.

In March, three unarmed members of an IRA active service unit were shot dead in controversial circumstances by SAS soldiers in Gibraltar. Mairead Farrell, Daniel McCann and Sean Savage were planning to explode a car bomb during a guard-changing ceremony in the British dependency, but for some time had been under surveillance by MI5, the Spanish police and finally the SAS. The killings provoked an enormous controversy, with numerous witnesses challenging the official government version of events. Moreover, a

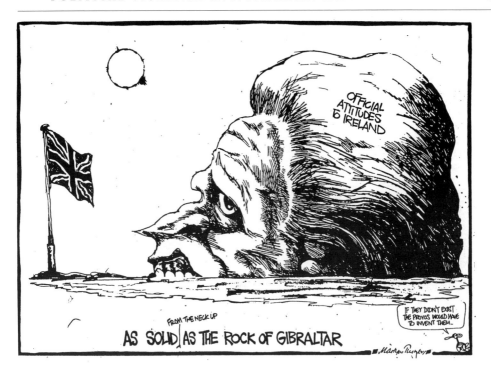

number of British newspapers expressed concern that the use of soldiers rather than police was justifying the IRA claim that they were engaged in a war and not criminal activity. In 1995 the families of the three IRA members won £40,000 from the government for a breach of Article 2 of the European Convention on Human Rights which deals with the use of excessive force.

Turner's cartoon encapsulates the hostile Irish public mood engendered by this series of controversial events. Britain's intransigent response to the Stalker inquiry, the Birmingham Six case and the 'death on the Rock' incident is epitomised by the snarling, gnarled head of Prime Minister Thatcher, rising from the Atlantic like the Rock of Gibraltar itself. The little bird in the corner suggests that British intransigence is ultimately counter-productive in so far as it merely stiffens the IRA's resolve to intensify their military campaign. Indeed, controversial incidents like the Gibraltar killings tended to increase the flow of recruits to the Provisional movement. The sceptical attitude of this Irish cartoon towards official British government policy contrasts sharply with the generally unquestioning acceptance by most British newspapers at the time.

14.26 'Creatures from an Alien World', JAK, *Evening Standard*, London, 21 March 1988

On 16 March 1988, during the funerals of the three IRA Gibraltar victims in Belfast's Milltown cemetery, a lone loyalist gunman, Michael Stone, threw grenades and opened fire on the mourners, killing three and injuring over fifty. Three days later, the funeral of one of these victims, IRA member Kevin Brady, took place in the same area in an atmosphere of heightened tension and suspicion. When a car suddenly drove at high speed into the funeral cortège, many in the crowd thought it was another murder attack. It was in fact

Creatures from an alien world

14.27 'Oh, the horror . . .', Oisín, *Andersonstown News*, Belfast, 26 March 1988

driven by two British army corporals, Derek Wood and Robert Howes, whose presence there has never been satisfactorily explained. Although one of them fired a warning shot, the soldiers were quickly dragged from the vehicle, beaten, stripped and then taken to waste ground where they were shot by the IRA.

The deaths had an enormous impact on people everywhere, mainly because the attack had been filmed by television cameras and by army helicopter surveillance. Television footage of the sheer brutality of the corporals' deaths shocked world opinion, and the picture of a Catholic priest, Father Alex Reid, kneeling in prayer over the semi-naked body of one of the men seemed to encapsulate the tragedy of the Troubles. JAK's cartoon reflects the prevailing impression of the killers as bloodthirsty savages and captures the incomprehension of most people in Britain that such actions could take place in part of the United Kingdom. The simianised faces and apelike gait of these semi-human attackers resemble the grotesque figures in his infamous 1982 cartoon (see 14.20, p. 294) and, before them, the monstrous creations of Tenniel and Boucher in *Punch* and *Judy*.

Oisín, by contrast, views the same incident from a republican perspective, and places the events of that day in a wider historical and political context. He shows a crazed and bloodthirsty Margaret Thatcher wearing the cloak of hypocrisy, surrounded by British weapons of war. The use of CS gas and plastic bullets led to the loss of innocent lives in Northern Ireland, while the missile labelled 'Bulgrano Gotcha!' refers to the sinking of the Argentinian naval vessel, *General Belgrano*, during the Falklands War, which resulted in the death of over one hundred Argentinian sailors. 'Gotcha!' was the infamous headline with which the *Sun* newspaper greeted this news. The cartoon questions the legitimacy of British accusations of IRA depravity by suggesting that Thatcher's government has itself perpetrated acts of horrific brutality in order to defend British interests.

14.28 'Do I know I'm a bloody fool? . . .', JAK, *Evening Standard*, London, 20 January 1992

In spring 1991 the Northern Ireland secretary, Peter Brooke, after much patient work, succeeded in getting talks started between the British and Irish governments and the four main constitutional parties in Northern Ireland. Although these were soon halted, he had high hopes of resuming them after the impending British general election. In the meantime, however, the worst atrocity of the year occurred near Cookstown, County Tyrone, on 17 January 1992, when the IRA blew up a minibus carrying Protestant workers home from the army base where they were working. Seven men were killed instantly, and an eighth died later in what became known as the Teebane massacre. The horror of the bombing appalled most people in Ireland, especially the Protestant population of the north.

Later that evening Brooke appeared in Dublin on one of the most popular shows on Irish television, the *Late Late Show*, his appearance having been planned in advance as part of a public relations exercise in the south. During the show, however, he reluctantly allowed himself to be persuaded by the host, Gay Byrne, to sing 'My Darling Clementine'. Unionists were outraged that the Northern Ireland secretary should have shown such public insensitivity within hours of a grave atrocity and called for him to resign. Brooke did in fact offer his resignation, but it was rejected by the prime minister, John Major.

JAK's cartoon overleaf sums up the acutely embarrassing predicament into which a naïve Brooke had allowed himself to be manoeuvred. Byrne calmly looks on as Brooke happily makes a fool of himself. Many people accepted that Brooke was a decent and well-intentioned minister who had made a silly mistake, and he received considerable sympathy

"Do I know I'm a bloody fool? No! But if you hum it I'll sing it!"

from both government and opposition MPs for his error of judgement. The incident had damaged his credibility with the unionist population, however, and when Major reshuffled his cabinet after the April 1992 general election, Brooke, to his disappointment, was replaced as Northern Ireland minister by Sir Patrick Mayhew. The Irish television authorities later apologised for the incident.

15

THE POLITICS OF PEACE
1993–1998

The year 1993 witnessed continuing violence by republican and loyalist paramilitaries in Northern Ireland, and frequent IRA attacks in Britain. In March an IRA explosion in Warrington resulted in the deaths of two young boys and provoked widespread public revulsion in Britain and both parts of Ireland, though many in Northern Ireland had long since grown accustomed to such tragedies. The following month a huge IRA bomb exploded in Bishopsgate, the heart of London's financial district, killing one person and causing damage estimated at over £1,000 million.

Despite this sustained violence, significant political developments were taking place behind the scenes. Confidential talks began in April 1993 between John Hume and Gerry Adams in an attempt to find common ground on a political settlement. Since the early 1980s the Catholic vote in Northern Ireland had been split between the SDLP and Sinn Féin. Both parties had considerable electoral support, although the SDLP preponderated, and by now Sinn Féin had lost its only seat at Westminster. Hume was attempting to persuade Sinn Féin to use its popular electoral mandate to reject violence and enter the political process, and stressed the significance of the 1990 declaration by the then Northern Ireland secretary, Peter Brooke, that Great Britain had no 'selfish strategic or economic interest in Northern Ireland'. Although Hume was heavily criticised by many on both sides of the water for 'talking to terrorists', he refused to be diverted from his efforts to bring about an end to IRA violence and create a peace process.

The positive response of Taoiseach Albert Reynolds to the Hume–Adams talks infuriated unionists and loyalist paramilitaries. The latter declared their intention to increase their attacks on the nationalist community whose representatives, they alleged, were participating in a pan-nationalist front comprising the SDLP, IRA, Sinn Féin and the southern government in order to negotiate over the heads of the unionist people. The spiral of violence culminated in one particularly blood-drenched week in October 1993 when twenty-four people met violent deaths, including nine innocent civilians who died as a result of an IRA bomb in a fish shop on the Protestant Shankill Road in Belfast. The UVF quickly retaliated with an attack on a public house in Greysteel, County Derry, in which seven people died.

In November 1993 it was revealed that, despite earlier denials, the British government had been having secret talks with leading Sinn Féin spokesman, Martin McGuinness, for three years. This news greatly increased unionist fears of a sell-out and complicated the government's precarious parliamentary position. Prime Minister John Major had emerged from the 1992 general election with a much diminished majority, and his government's controversial policy towards the European Union made it increasingly dependent on the votes of unionists to maintain its authority. Indeed, it was these votes which saved the government from defeat during the debate on the Maastricht treaty in July 1993.

It was important for both the British and Irish governments to win back the initiative from the Hume–Adams negotiations, and from both sets of paramilitaries. Eventually, on 15 December 1993, the two premiers, Major and Reynolds, issued a Joint Declaration on Northern Ireland at 10 Downing Street. This was a complex and finely balanced document which was effectively aimed at bringing Sinn Féin into the realm of constitutional politics. It accepted that a united Ireland could be achieved by constitutional means, though only with the consent of the majority in Northern Ireland. It also signalled that Britain was willing to end the Union if a northern majority wished it, and reiterated that the government had no 'selfish strategic or economic interest in Northern Ireland'. In addition, it offered Sinn Féin an opportunity to engage in peace talks, provided the IRA ended its violent campaign.

While most of the constitutional political parties in Northern Ireland, with the exception of Ian Paisley's DUP, accepted the document as a basis for future political dialogue, Sinn Féin remained hesitant. The declaration placed the party in a difficult position. It had been offered a possible entry into talks, yet there was no indication in the document of an early British withdrawal from Northern Ireland. However, if the violence continued, much of the blame would be placed upon the IRA. Sinn Féin did not reject the declaration outright, therefore, but instead sought 'clarification' from the government on a number of issues in order to buy time. Meanwhile, the bloody cycle of violence continued. In March 1994 the IRA launched a mortar attack at London's Heathrow Airport, and in June UVF gunmen attacked a public house in Loughinisland, County Down, where customers were watching a World Cup football match, and killed six people in retaliation for earlier republican killings.

By now, however, the Sinn Féin leadership had been redefining its political strategy and had established close dialogue with Taoiseach Reynolds and the Dublin government. This was reinforced by new links with the United States when the Clinton administration granted Adams a visa in January 1994 to address a conference hosted by the American Committee on Foreign Policy, despite strenuous British objections. The price of this Irish and American governmental goodwill was that, if Adams was to be accepted as a genuine peacemaker, and the republican movement to be allowed political influence in a talks process, there had to be a commitment to wholly peaceful methods from Sinn Féin and the IRA. Thus, after a long process of consultation and debate, the whole republican military strategy was reassessed, and its supporters required to adopt a 'totally unarmed strategy' (TUAS) in order to achieve a negotiated political settlement. The result came on 31 August 1994 when the IRA announced a cease-fire which was greeted triumphantly in nationalist areas, but also with relief elsewhere in Northern Ireland, however stunned and sceptical.

Six weeks later, on 13 October, after an internal consultative process, the loyalist paramilitary groups, under the umbrella of the Combined Loyalist Military Command, announced a similar cease-fire 'dependent upon the continued cessation of all nationalist/ republican violence'. Significantly, the loyalists went further by offering 'to the loved ones of all innocent victims . . . abject and true remorse'. For the first time in twenty-five years, there was peace. The people of Northern Ireland hardly dared believe that the long nightmare was, in fact, finally over.

The republican cease-fire came about as a result of significant shifts in the position of the Provisional movement and of the British government. Sinn Féin was coming to accept that Britain had indeed little interest in maintaining a foothold in Ireland. The movement also recognised that it would now have to operate its democratic mandate within a loose nationalist coalition involving the SDLP and the southern government, as well as an influential American administration. Similarly, the British government had come to accept the unpalatable fact that the IRA could not be completely defeated in military terms and that Sinn Féin needed to be brought into any effective peace process. It had also accepted the view that the Irish government would have a central role to play in a peace process, and that any long term settlement would have to include a southern dimension.

The Irish government warmly welcomed the IRA cease-fire declaration and within a week the taoiseach met Adams and Hume in Dublin. In sharp contrast, the British government reacted most cautiously and demanded assurance that the IRA's cessation was 'permanent'. Much time was lost in arguments over this issue of permanence, and the position was further complicated when the British insisted that the IRA would have to decommission some of its arms 'as a tangible confidence-building measure' before Sinn Féin could be admitted to all-party talks.

From a British perspective, disarming the enemy through a decommissioning process would ease the problem of dealing with the IRA, by weakening its ability to engage in military activity. Sinn Féin, however, warned that this was a new and unacceptable precondition which, if insisted upon, would threaten the whole peace initiative. It claimed that the government, having failed to defeat the IRA militarily, was now trying to defeat it through peace. It argued that decommissioning was tantamount to surrender, leaving nationalist communities at the mercy of arms held by the Protestant community and by the police and army, whom they could not trust. Many nationalists questioned the motives of the British government and became suspicious of the consequences of Major's increasing dependency upon the unionists at Westminster to sustain his government. Others came to doubt the practicalities of decommissioning and the difficulties of verifying that it had in fact taken place. Nevertheless, for over a year the British government insisted that some agreement on arms decommissioning had to be in place before all-party talks could begin.

Meanwhile, the two governments attempted to move forward the political initiative on 22 February 1995 by issuing a Framework Document, which set out their views on how a permanent peace settlement might be reached. Although it stressed that Northern Ireland would remain part of the United Kingdom as long as a majority of its population so desired, unionists were greatly alarmed, and nationalists heartened, by the proposal to set up a joint north–south body with executive powers over certain issues. While the British government tried to represent itself as a neutral facilitator, saying that the document offered something for everyone, unionists claimed that John Major was now operating according to a nationalist agenda.

The imminent arrival of President Bill Clinton on an official visit to Ireland at the end of November 1995 led to frantic last minute diplomatic activity in Dublin and London to resolve the decommissioning issue. A twin-track strategy was announced, aimed at achieving all-party talks by February 1996, and at the same time setting up an international body to report on arms decommissioning, chaired by former US Senator George Mitchell. It was a useful fudge, which enabled President Clinton to throw his support behind it, and thus make it more difficult for Sinn Féin to reject. Clinton's visit to Northern Ireland, the first ever by a US president, was a triumphant one. He was warmly welcomed by almost all shades of opinion, and seemed to have revitalised the peace process, as well as revealing how much the Northern Ireland question had now become internationalised.

John Major's government had by now lost its overall majority in the Commons and was even more dependent for survival on the votes of the nine Ulster Unionist MPs, and the three Democratic Unionists. When the Mitchell report was published on 24 January 1996 it stated that there was no prospect of the IRA decommissioning its weapons before all-party talks took place, and recommended that this should occur during, rather than before, political negotiations. However, Major effectively ignored Mitchell's key proposals by announcing that there would first be elections for a new Northern Ireland assembly before all-party talks could begin. The fact that this idea had earlier been proposed by the unionists led John Hume to accuse Major and his government of trying 'to buy votes to keep themselves in power'.

The lack of movement towards all-party negotiations over the previous eighteen months, coupled with the government's response to the Mitchell report, caused much dismay in republican ranks and brought to the surface the many tensions within the IRA military command. The tragic result was the ending of the IRA cease-fire on 9 February 1996, when a massive bomb exploded at Canary Wharf in London, killing two people and causing millions of pounds worth of damage. Strenuous efforts were made to try to resurrect the peace process and to maintain the Dublin–London accord, despite disquiet in Dublin at British government policy on decommissioning and the proposed new assembly. At the end of February a firm date, 10 June, was set for all-party talks to begin, and elections to the negotiating forum took place in May. The result provided little comfort for the government, with Sinn Féin winning seventeen seats and over 15 per cent of the vote. This was the party's best electoral performance to date, and its advances were made mainly at the expense of the SDLP, which won twenty-one seats and over 21 per cent of the vote.

When the talks eventually began in June 1996 under the chairmanship of George Mitchell, Sinn Féin was refused entry until the IRA declared an unconditional cessation of violence. A renewal of the republican cease-fire seemed as far away as ever when the IRA exploded a one-and-a-half-ton bomb in the centre of Manchester on 15 June, injuring two hundred people and causing enormous damage. However, in practice, the IRA cease-fire continued in Northern Ireland, as did the loyalist cessation. Nevertheless, great damage was done to community relations during the summer months, the traditional marching season of the Protestant Orange Order. The most crucial incident occurred when the RUC decided to reroute an Orange parade from Drumcree church in Portadown, County Armagh, away from the Catholic Garvaghy Road.

The original plan to march along the Garvaghy Road, an area which had once been mainly Protestant but was now predominantly Catholic, was seen as provocative by the residents. Unionists, however, viewed the police decision to reroute the march through a mainly Protestant area as an act of appeasement to nationalists. This led to four days of loyalist rioting throughout Northern Ireland until the RUC eventually capitulated on 11 July and allowed the Orange march to proceed along the Garvaghy Road. This in turn led to rioting in republican areas, and a continuing series of sectarian attacks on churches, individuals and private property. Cardinal Cahal Daly expressed anger at the reversal of the RUC's decision, claiming to have been 'personally betrayed by the British government', while the new taoiseach, John Bruton, called it a 'mistake'. The whole question of the routing of marches remains a deeply sensitive one, and in recent years it has become an annual barometer of the level of mutual hostility which exists between the two communities in Northern Ireland.

Little political movement took place during the autumn and winter of 1996–97, with Sinn Féin still excluded from a talks process, which, in any case, seemed to be at a standstill.

Major's increasingly weak Conservative government was eventually defeated in the British general election in May 1997, which resulted in a large Labour majority of 179 seats. In Northern Ireland Gerry Adams and Martin McGuinness both won seats, one from the DUP, the other from the SDLP. This was an important advance for Sinn Féin, which had had no seats in the previous parliament. The Ulster Unionists won 10 seats, with the SDLP, DUP and UK Unionists returning 3, 2 and 1 MPs respectively. The following month saw the fall of the Bruton administration in the Republic and the formation of a new coalition government under Fianna Fáil's Bertie Ahern. Thus, in both Britain and Ireland, a fresh approach to the problems of Northern Ireland appeared possible.

Both governments immediately stressed the importance of restoring momentum to the peace process. Prime Minster Tony Blair (1953–) offered Sinn Féin entry to the talks if an unconditional IRA cease-fire was restored and Taoiseach Ahern adopted a more pro-nationalist approach to the process than his predecessor. The British government's large parliamentary majority meant that unionist votes were now of little significance, in contrast with the pre-election situation. This fresh governmental commitment to pursue an energetic joint strategy was soon confronted by familiar obstacles, however. The killing of two policemen in Lurgan, County Armagh, by the IRA in June, and the unyielding determination of Orangemen to march along their 'traditional' Drumcree route in July meant that, on the surface at least, the summer of 1997 offered little hope for the people of Northern Ireland.

The Drumcree march proved to be a crucial flashpoint yet again. After weeks of agonising and trying to find a compromise acceptable to both sides, the new Northern Ireland secretary of state, Marjorie (Mo) Mowlam, finally decided to allow the Orange parade to proceed through the Garvaghy Road. This last minute decision, which was publicly criticised by the Dublin government, outraged nationalists and led to serious rioting throughout Northern Ireland. There was real danger of a major escalation of violence during the Orange marches of 12 July; however, a few days beforehand, Orangemen had taken the dramatic decision to call off some crucial marches which would have passed through Catholic areas, including the lower Ormeau Road in Belfast.

This decision, which was bitterly criticised by some hardline Orangemen, brought about a remarkable lessening of political tension and the marches of 12 July took place peacefully. Northern Ireland had once again pulled back from the precipice of civil war, and the concessions made by the Orange Order led to the republican movement coming under increased pressure from the Irish and British governments, as well as the Clinton administration, to renew the IRA cease-fire. A response came remarkably quickly on 19 July, when the IRA declared a new cease-fire to take effect the next day. Although the thorny question of arms decommissioning remained unresolved, Prime Minister Blair rapidly seized the opportunity provided by the cease-fire to agree that Sinn Féin should be admitted to all-party talks after a short six-week period to test whether violence had really ended. At the end of August Blair accepted that the IRA cease-fire was genuine, and in September Sinn Féin signed up to the Mitchell principles, which committed it to using exclusively peaceful means to resolve political disputes. A few days before the talks were due to begin, however, the IRA stated that it had difficulty with some of the Mitchell principles, and also that it would not hand over weapons.

Despite this setback, the talks began as scheduled on 15 September 1997 at Stormont Castle. At first the various unionist parties refused to sit at the same negotiating table as Sinn Féin, but eventually they did so, with the exception of Paisley's DUP and Robert

McCartney's marginal United Kingdom Unionist Party. The two small unionist parties associated with loyalist paramilitaries, the Progressive Unionist Party and the Ulster Democratic Party, were an integral element in the negotiations. Inevitably there was little sign of progress in the early weeks and much political posturing took place, but at least after many years of frustrated effort and false hope, the different political groupings in Northern Ireland were in the same room together and talking.

A deadline for the conclusion of the talks had been set for May 1998, but by Christmas 1997 there had been little substantial progress, and much time was taken up with endless procedural disputes. Nevertheless, Sinn Féin's growing political acceptance into the Anglo-Irish democratic process was demonstrated by the historic meeting of Blair and Adams in Belfast in October, and the subsequent visit of a Sinn Féin delegation to Downing Street in December.

Later in December, however, the whole peace process was thrown into crisis by the assassination of the leader of the Loyalist Volunteer Force, Billy Wright, in the Maze prison by members of the republican Irish National Liberation Army, and the killing of a number of innocent Catholics by the LVF and the Ulster Freedom Fighters in retaliation. When loyalist paramilitary prisoners threatened to withdraw their support for the talks process, the Northern Ireland secretary, Mo Mowlam, responded by making a dramatic and unprecedented visit to the Maze on 9 January 1998, where she had face-to-face meetings with some of the most hardened gunmen in Northern Ireland. Although her efforts to maintain the vital loyalist prisoner support for the talks process proved successful, in late January the UDP was excluded from the talks for a four-week period because of its links with the UFF, which admitted to having recently killed Catholics.

Despite these setbacks, the two governments urgently attempted to push the process forward by publishing outline proposals for a joint north–south body and a new Council of the Isles which would include England, Scotland and Wales, as well as both parts of Ireland. These proposals were an attempt to offer concessions to both sides, but the crucial question of the powers of these new bodies remained undefined. A new hurdle emerged on 20 February, when both governments reluctantly excluded Sinn Féin from the talks process for a two-week period, despite protests from the republican leadership. This move was prompted by RUC reports of the IRA's involvement in two recent killings, which, if true, constituted a violation of the Mitchell principles. The explosion of a large car bomb in Moira, County Down, later that evening threatened a return to more sustained violence, even though it was alleged that this was the work of the republican breakaway Continuity Army Council rather than the IRA.

These combined setbacks to the peace negotiations led some to conclude that the whole process had become fatally flawed, and that the temporary exclusions were creating a farcical scenario. Certainly much had changed within a year, with principles such as the refusal to 'talk to terrorists' and the insistence that arms be decommissoned before talks being quietly dropped. Nevertheless, both governments remained committed to presenting a settlement for approval by referendum to the people of both parts of Ireland by mid-1998. The search for a settlement acquired fresh urgency in March, following chairman George Mitchell's announcement of 9 April as the official deadline for the conclusion of the talks process. Negotiations became more intensive in the weeks leading up to this date and the political drama deepened as the deadline approached.

With two days of negotiations left, all-party agreement seemed as far away as ever, as unionists and nationalists remained locked in stalemate over two key elements of a political settlement: the powers and structure of a Northern Ireland assembly and a north–south ministerial council. With the fearful prospect of the talks being about to collapse, chairman Mitchell produced a draft document which unionists immediately denounced as 'a Sinn Féin wish-list'. On the night of Tuesday 7 April Prime Minister Blair arrived in Belfast to save the process, where he was later joined by Taoiseach Ahern, in an attempt to resolve these centrally divisive issues. For the next three days the two leaders and the Northern Ireland political parties were locked in intensive, round-the-clock negotiating sessions in Castle Buildings at Stormont, closely monitored from without by an anxious public and expectant world media. News that a historic agreement had been reached eventually came on the afternoon of Good Friday, 10 April, when chairman Mitchell announced that the two governments and the Northern Ireland parties had arrived at a landmark political settlement.

The deal proposed the establishment of a 108-member Northern Ireland assembly with executive and legislative powers, elected by proportional representation and run by a committee of 12 ministers. Key decisions taken by the assembly would require the assent of a majority from both communities, thereby invoking the principle of 'parallel consent'. The first duty of this assembly would be to set up a north–south ministerial council, accountable to the assembly and to the Irish parliament. This body, representative of those with executive authority in Belfast and Dublin, would meet to exchange information, consult and deal with matters of cross-border co-operation. In order to facilitate these new institutional arrangements, the Irish government proposed to amend Articles 2 and 3 of its constitution, which lay claim to the territory of Northern Ireland, while its British counterpart pledged itself to repeal the 1920 Government of Ireland Act, thereby relinquishing the supreme authority of Westminster over Northern Ireland. A further proposal for the establishment of a British–Irish Council, with members drawn from both parts of Ireland, Westminster and the new Scottish and Welsh assemblies, was also agreed upon. Additional articles proposed the establishment of an independent commission to make recommendations about a new police structure for Northern Ireland, and made provision for the release within two years of all prisoners linked to paramilitary organisations on cease-fire.

Despite opposition from dissidents within republican and unionist ranks, the agreement received a muted but positive welcome from most sections of Irish, British and international opinion. The first crucial test came six weeks later on 22 May, when simultaneous referendums on the Easter settlement took place in both parts of Ireland. An overwhelming 94 per cent of those who voted in the Republic supported the agreement, while a substantial 71 per cent of northern voters endorsed it. This outcome represented the most significant political decision of the Irish people since the 1921 treaty, although at the time of writing, June 1998, it is too soon to say whether this hopeful development will be frustrated by political opponents and men of violence on both sides. All realise that the road to peace and reconciliation will be a long and arduous one, with many obstacles yet to be negotiated before what Tony Blair called 'the burden of history' can finally be lifted from the shoulders of the Irish and British people. Meanwhile, Northern Ireland remains poised between the hope of new beginnings and the despair of old hatreds. The emergence of a new and just society will ultimately depend upon the ingenuity, goodwill and spirit of compromise of its people and their leaders. Perhaps, after centuries of conflict, violence and bloodshed, the Irish and British nations are about to arrive at that elusive, longed-for moment when, in the words of the poet Seamus Heaney, 'hope and history rhyme'.

15.1 'Ourselves Alone', Blotski, *Irish News*, Belfast, 7 March 1992

The violent and protracted nature of the Northern Ireland Troubles might lead many to assume that the issue has been a vital preoccupation of British public and parliamentary life since 1969. This, however, has not been the case. Most people in Britain show little real interest in, or knowledge of, the realities and complexities of the problem, and opinion polls regularly reveal a desire on the part of the majority of the British public to be rid of this unpopular and financially draining burden. British MPs have often reflected this lack of public concern by their failure to attend Commons' debates on Northern Ireland, despite criticism from unionist and nationalist members. The very fact that these debates were often scheduled at inconvenient times of the week further underlined Westminster's low prioritisation of the issue.

   This Blotski cartoon represents a stark denunciation of British parliamentarians' indifference to the Northern Ireland political talks process on the eve of the 1992 general election. It shows a lone government spokesman addressing a cavernous Commons during a debate on the talks process. In the foreground sit the SDLP's John Hume and Seamus Mallon and Ulster Unionists James Molyneaux and John Taylor, with DUP members Ian Paisley and Peter Robinson in the background. Several of those present cast bewildered glances at the deserted government and opposition benches, grim testaments to British apathy towards Northern Ireland affairs. The cartoon's title, a common mistranslation of 'Sinn Féin', piquantly underlines the ironic paradox of unionists and nationalists being divided by their political aspirations in Northern Ireland, yet united in their political marginalisation at Westminster. British apathy was again evident during the subsequent general election campaign, in which Northern Ireland scarcely figured as an issue.

15.2 'Northern Ireland', Riddell, *Independent on Sunday*, London, 11 July 1993

The horrific bombs in Birmingham in November 1974 caused outrage in Britain and prompted demands that immediate action be taken to assuage public opinion. As a result, the Labour government rushed through parliament, in forty-two hours, the Prevention of Terrorism Act, giving special powers to the police. Home Secretary Roy Jenkins stated: 'These powers are draconian. In combination, they are unprecedented in peacetime.' Among the key provisions of the Act were the right to detain suspects without reason for a period of two days, with a possibility of extension for a further five days, the exclusion of people from entry into Britain, and expulsion to Northern Ireland.

The PTA was intended as a temporary measure, but has been regularly renewed ever since. It has attracted considerable opposition from civil liberties groups, and in November 1995 the European Court of Justice ruled that it contravened European Union law by interfering with freedom of movement as guaranteed by the Treaty of Rome. One of its most controversial aspects in Northern Ireland was the introduction of 'internal exile' by means of exclusion orders banning people from Britain. Chris Riddell's cartoon aptly sums up the anomalous concept of Britain using Northern Ireland as a political dustbin for unwanted terrorist suspects. It seemed to many that it was Northern Ireland itself that was being excluded from the rest of the United Kingdom in this respect.

15.3 'Oxygen! Oxygen!', Garland, *Daily Telegraph*, London, 1 February 1994

After the Downing Street Declaration of December 1993, persistent efforts were made by all sides to get the Provisional movement involved in the peace process. By now there was an important Irish-American lobby of politicians and businessmen who were influencing

" OXYGEN! OXYGEN! "

American policy at the highest level. They managed to persuade the Clinton administration that granting a visa to Sinn Féin leader Gerry Adams to visit the United States would strengthen Adams's support for a democratic peace process within his own movement and so take the gun out of republican politics. The British government was strenuously opposed to granting a visa to Adams, not least because it would enable him to gain much needed publicity for his cause in America. President Clinton rejected this opposition, however, and Adams arrived in America on 31 January 1994, emerging from the obscurity of domestic broadcasting bans into a blaze of massive international media attention.

This Garland cartoon is highly critical of 'Doctor' Clinton's willingness to provide a gasping Adams with the oxygen of publicity. The cartoon title alludes to a statement made by Margaret Thatcher in the late 1980s, when she justified banning Sinn Féin representatives from speaking on radio and television on the grounds that it would deny the paramilitaries 'the oxygen of publicity'. In actual fact, the increased media attention and heightened American involvement in the peace process did strengthen Adams's position within the Provisional movement and helped him to persuade the IRA to support his non-violent strategy.

Garland's cartoon opposite appeared over a year later, following the announcement by the White House on 9 March 1995 that Adams was to be invited to the President's Saint Patrick's Day reception, and also that Sinn Féin would be allowed to raise funds in America. Since the British government had tried desperately to prevent this, news of the invitation greatly soured the Anglo-American 'special relationship'. John Major refused to talk to the US president for several days, despite Clinton's attempts to contact him. Garland uses a Roman allegory to represent this turn of events, namely, the stabbing of Julius Caesar by his colleague, Brutus, on the ides of March, despite a warning to Caesar that this would happen. It shows the carefully nurtured 'special relationship' between Britain and America lying dead, while Clinton ushers an unrepentant Adams away from the scene of

15.4 'The Ides of March', Garland, *Daily Telegraph*, London, 16 March 1995

the crime and into the political limelight. In reality, the Anglo-American friendship soon recovered from this setback, as there were many other issues and interests which the two countries had in common.

15.5 Untitled, Brookes, *The Times*, London, 8 September 1994

On 31 August 1994 the IRA announced 'a complete cessation of military operations'. The declaration was warmly welcomed by the Irish and American governments, but unionists reacted warily, suspecting that a secret deal had been done between the British government and the republican leadership. John Major's government was sceptical also, and demanded that the cease-fire be shown to be permanent. By contrast, Albert Reynolds, who had played a key role in creating the conditions which led to the cease-fire declaration, immediately invited John Hume and Gerry Adams to Dublin for talks. On 6 September the taoiseach appeared with them in front of the Irish parliament and all three publicly shook hands. This was graphic confirmation of the emergence of a new pan-nationalist front comprising the Dublin government, the SDLP and Sinn Féin, which so alarmed unionists.

Peter Brookes's cartoon (15.5) captures the speedy and positive response of Reynolds to the cease-fire. It shows a dithering Major trapped in the middle of the Adams–Reynolds– Hume handshake, overwhelmed by this sudden nationalist solidarity. At the time, Major's government was under pressure in parliament from Tory backbenchers and unionists to refrain from talking to Sinn Féin, and no meetings took place with its leaders until a 'quarantine period' of over three months ended in early December.

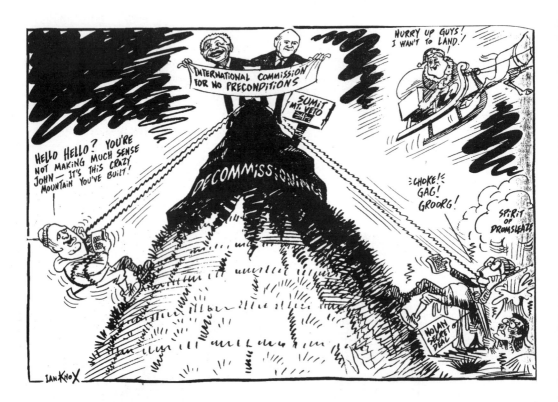

15.6 'Decommissioning . . .', Knox, *Irish News*, Belfast, 25 November 1995

During the period of the first IRA cease-fire, the British government refused to allow Sinn Féin into all-party talks until the IRA began to decommission some of its weapons. This British insistence on partial decommissioning led to serious disagreement between the Irish and British governments in the autumn of 1995, since Dublin believed that this pre-condition was hindering real progress in the peace talks. Knox's cartoon opposite shows Major and the new taoiseach, John Bruton, struggling on the ascent of the steep decom-missioning mountain. There is little communication between them, and Major is choked by the weight of Ulster Unionist leader, David Trimble (1944–), who labours under the 'Spirit of Dromsleaze'. This is a parodic reference to the 'Spirit of Drumcree', a movement which defended the right of Orangemen to parade along their traditional routes, follow-ing the controversy caused by the so-called 'Siege of Drumcree' in County Armagh earlier that year. It also refers to the allegations of sleaze and financial corruption which were then worrying Major's Conservative Party, some members of which were under investigation by a committee of inquiry headed by Lord Nolan.

Standing at the summit of 'Mt Veto' are the exemplary figures of Nelson Mandela and F.W. de Klerk, the black and white leaders of the new South Africa who had recently succeeded in reaching a political settlement without preconditions. Meanwhile, Santa Claus Clinton hovers above, impatient to land. The American president was due to visit Ireland at the end of November, by which time he hoped the two governments would have resolved the deadlock over decommissioning. Eventually, on 28 November, less than two days before Clinton's arrival, Bruton and Major hastily agreed a twin-track strategy of setting a date for all-party talks, while also establishing an international body to assess the decommissioning issue. It was in reality a temporary compromise which enabled the peace process to move forward with Clinton's support.

With an American presidential election due to take place within a year, Clinton was conscious that Ireland was one of his few foreign policy successes. The Irish-American lobby was growing in strength and Clinton certainly wanted to win the support of over forty million Americans who claimed Irish ancestry. Cynics therefore suggested that the real motive behind Clinton's trip was his desire to woo the influential Irish-American vote by means of a well-publicised and successful Irish visit, rather as his predecessor Ronald Reagan had done through a visit to the Republic in June 1984.

15.7 'What Sinn Fein must realise...', Turner, *Irish Times*, Dublin, 9 January 1996

To many people in Ireland, and to some in Britain, the refusal of Major's government to enter fully into negotiations with Sinn Féin representatives on the basis of their links with the IRA was unconvincing. Similar conflicts in other parts of the world had been resolved by negotiations involving all parties and groups, irrespective of their previous associations. In cartoon 15.7 Turner attacks what he regards as the hypocrisy of Major's position by contrasting his unwillingness to talk to Sinn Féin with his eagerness to trade with undemocratic, dictatorial regimes such as those in Saudi Arabia and China, whose disregard for human rights is well known. At the time, many republicans believed that Major's refusal to negotiate with Sinn Féin was influenced by his objective of shielding himself from criticism over the Scott report into British arms sales to Iraq, and his related need to maintain the support of the unionists in parliament.

15.8 Untitled, Schrank, *Independent*, London, 12 February 1996

The IRA cease-fire of August 1994 ended on 9 February 1996 when a huge bomb exploded near Canary Wharf in London, killing two people and causing damage estimated at over £80 million. The IRA blamed the ending of the cease-fire on the British government's refusal to set up all-party talks until paramilitary arms had been decommissioned, and on what it saw as Major's sidelining of the Mitchell report. These criticisms were vehemently rejected by government ministers, who instead blamed the breakdown of the peace process on Sinn Féin's refusal to yield on the issue of arms decommissioning.

The ending of the IRA cease-fire was widely condemned in the British press and led many cartoonists to depict Gerry Adams, who refused to condemn the London bombing, as a mere apologist for the IRA. This *Independent* cartoon by Peter Schrank is something of an exception, however, in that it seeks to represent the invidious nature of Adams's new predicament. By showing him wearing a perplexed and helpless expression as the predatory IRA vulture swoops on the dead dove of peace, Schrank would appear to have some sympathy with the notion that Sinn Féin and the IRA may be distinct movements with separate agenda. His cartoon implies that the Sinn Féin leader, who had played a crucial role in persuading the IRA to abandon violence, had ultimately been let down by the organisation's decision to resume its military campaign. Indeed, some observers began to feel that Adams's influence over the Provisionals was waning. More realistic analysts, however, understood that it was always going to be difficult for Adams to condemn the IRA in public, and that he would be a key figure if the cease-fire was to be restored in the future.

15.9 'It's our Bratash heritage . . .', Turner, *Belfast Telegraph*, Belfast, 10 July 1996

The RUC's decision on 6 July 1996 to reroute the Orange march at Drumcree in County Armagh away from the Catholic Garvaghy Road led to intensive loyalist rioting, prompted by the belief that this decision infringed upon their right to march and thus threatened their cultural identity. The subsequent reversal of this decision by the RUC as a result of loyalist violence led nationalists to believe that they were not receiving equal treatment and status, and inevitably precipitated widespread rioting in republican areas.

Turner's cartoon reflects the widespread incomprehension among the British public of the centrality of cultural symbols and traditions in Ulster loyalist identity. It shows Paisley haranguing a bemused John Major in his thick Ulster accent on the loyalists' right to wear an Orange sash, beat a Lambeg drum (a large war drum supposedly played during William of Orange's victory at the Boyne in 1690) and march along roads throughout Northern Ireland. Major clearly understands none of these traditions; indeed, he cannot even understand Paisley's pronunciation of the word 'British'. Ulster's ancient cultural traditions are a world away from modern British politics, and there is little sympathy or understanding for Orange intransigence in Downing Street.

The dominating presence of Paisley is supported by the insignificant figure of David Trimble, leader of the Ulster Unionist Party, who is allowing Paisley to make the running. On the wall hangs a portrait of Churchill, still muttering his famous 1922 speech in which he spoke of how the Great War had changed the map of Europe and altered the minds of men, yet in 'the dreary steeples of Fermanagh and Tyrone' the nature and integrity of their

15.10 'Phew! For a while . . .', Bell, *Guardian*, London, 12 July 1996

quarrel remained unaltered. The cartoon succinctly captures the continuing weary incomprehension of British leaders when confronted with 'the Irish problem'.

The original decision to reroute the Drumcree march had led to violent confrontations between police and Orangemen over a three-day period. The overturning of the decision brought the RUC into violent conflict with nationalist protesters, many of whom repeated their traditional accusation that this overwhelmingly Protestant force was again failing to be impartial in its policing. Thus, the Drumcree episode served to poison community relations, and led even moderate Catholics to call for the disbandment of the RUC. Steve Bell's highly satirical cartoon shows the police protecting triumphalist Orange marchers as they proceed down the Garvaghy Road, while blatantly batoning nationalist protesters. Bell wickedly suggests that some RUC officers welcomed the opportunity to resume their aggression against nationalists after months of relative peace, since it enabled them to reconnect with their true nature. The RUC defended its actions at Drumcree by claiming that it was in an invidious, no-win situation, caught between two equally uncompromising opponents.

15.11 'Not just now – I'm busy!', Knox, *Irish News*, Belfast, 30 November 1996

The outlook for the peace process at the end of 1996 was bleak. The IRA cease-fire was over and Sinn Féin remained excluded from political talks. To make matters worse, the British government's ability and willingness to manoeuvre at Westminster was greatly hampered by its dependence on the unionists for its overall parliamentary majority.

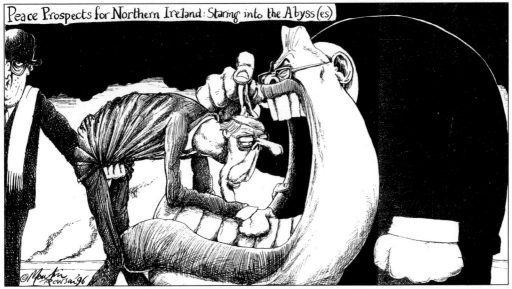

15.12 'Peace Prospects for Northern Ireland . . .', Rowson, *Guardian*, London,
2 December 1996

Meanwhile, John Hume and Gerry Adams were attempting to broker a resumption of the IRA cease-fire in order to help Sinn Féin gain unconditional entry to the talks process, for which they sought a definite time frame.

Knox's cartoon (p. 319, top) comments on this latest Hume–Adams initiative from a nationalist perspective. It casts John Hume in the sympathetic role of a latter-day Sisyphus, tirelessly exerting himself in the cause of peace, while simultaneously vilifying John Major and David Trimble for what it regards as their cynical preoccupation with their narrow political self-interests. While Major is 'too busy' to deal with Hume, Trimble's V-sign is more emphatic. To add to the insult, the scrawl on the bottom of the door indicates that there will be no time frame to the talks. Knox suggests that both Hume's herculean labours and the peace process itself are doomed to failure as long as British Conservatives and Ulster unionists are joined in a mutually beneficial political relationship.

Martin Rowson's cartoon (p. 319, bottom), on the other hand, imagines Major's relationship with the unionists to be a much more uncomfortable one for the prime minister. It shows a bowler-hatted Trimble exerting a firm grip on the more sensitive parts of Major's anatomy, while the prime minister gingerly and gloomily puts his head into Paisley's cavernous mouth to see what the new year holds. Paisley grips Major's left ear, presumably to impart some forthright advice in his own inimitable manner. In the event, Major delayed holding a general election until 1 May 1997, the last possible moment, as he knew that prospects of a Conservative victory were slim. Meanwhile, the unionists were able to exploit their powerful hold over him in order to ensure that no significant concessions were made to northern nationalists.

15.13 'And you can't come...', Turner, *Irish Times*, Dublin, 6 January 1994

The IRA cease-fire of August 1994 created the hope that all-party talks would quickly take place, with Sinn Féin as a participant. In the event, republicans were not invited to talks because of problems over arms decommissioning. This Turner cartoon shows John Hume, a key figure in persuading Sinn Féin to adopt a non-violent strategy, sternly warning

15.14 'All Party Talks...', Rowson, *Guardian*, London, 3 February 1997

15.15 'It is now accepted...', Knox, *Irish News*, Belfast, 31 January 1998

Gerry Adams that he must cleanse himself of all traces of paramilitary association before he can sit at the negotiating table. The marginal voice beneath Hume, meanwhile, suggests that hand-washing alone may not be sufficient to enable Adams and his colleagues to enter talks.

The same theme was taken up by Martin Rowson three years later when all-party talks were under way, but with Sinn Féin still excluded as the IRA campaign had recommenced. Rowson views the issue from a more subversive perspective, however, by highlighting the partiality of those who set the preconditions for entry to political negotiations. His cartoon (15.14) depicts Prime Minister Major nonchalantly walking over the remnants of the 1972 Bloody Sunday inquiry on his way to the conference table. Ahead of him, a sinister figure with bloody footprints and bloodstained hands is about to enter the same room. The clear implication is that some of those already participating in the talks process have dubious pasts, including the British government, whose predecessors have been responsible for bloody deeds in Ireland. Thus, if historic wrongs were considered there would be few participants in the talks. The fine distinction between fresh blood and dried blood strongly hints that British double standards are being applied to the peace process and certain parties involved in it.

Long-standing nationalist demands for a new government inquiry into the events of Bloody Sunday were boosted in June 1997 when the Irish government presented a file of new evidence to the British authorities. As a result, in January 1998, on the eve of the twenty-sixth anniversary of the killings, Prime Minister Blair announced that there would be a full judicial inquiry, headed by Lord Saville, to investigate all the evidence now available. In making this announcement, he accepted that the Widgery report was seriously flawed, thereby confirming a long-held nationalist view. Knox's dramatic cartoon (15.15) graphically illustrates the government's effective repudiation of the original inquiry by showing Judge Widgery, in full legal regalia, lying dead, along with his reputation, in the Derry streets which have come back to haunt him. Whereas many northern nationalists welcomed Blair's announcement as part of a necessary healing process, some unionists condemned it as yet another British concession to republicans.

15.16 Untitled, Bell, *Guardian*, London, 20 May 1997

On 1 May 1997 the Conservatives suffered a heavy defeat at the hands of Tony Blair's Labour Party, which was returned to office with a large parliamentary majority. In Northern Ireland Sinn Féin scored a significant victory when leading figures Gerry Adams and Martin McGuinness were both elected. These gains were seen as a vindication of Sinn Féin's non-violent strategy and strengthened its demands to be admitted to all-party talks on the basis of its democratic mandate.

Bell's trenchant cartoon (opposite, top) shows the victorious duo, encased in the legitimacy of the ballot box, being transported to the palace of Westminster on the shoulders of masked IRA gunmen. The link between the two wings of the republican movement is clearly indicated, as they are confronted by the stern and imposing figure of the Speaker of the House of Commons, Betty Boothroyd, who is shown to be giving the 'Westminster finger' to the newly elected MPs. Following their election, Adams and McGuinness exercised their right to enter the precincts of Westminster but refused to take their seats in parliament and to swear the oath of allegiance to the queen. As a result, Speaker Boothroyd refused to allow them access to office space and other facilities available to MPs, despite their electoral mandate.

15.17 'These are our monsters...', Knox, *Irish News*, Belfast, 7 July 1997

The return to power of a Labour government at the 1997 general election did not produce any immediate amelioration in Northern Ireland. The Drumcree Orange march in July proved to be as dangerous and divisive as in the two previous years. The new Northern Ireland Secretary, Mo Mowlam, appeared decent and well-meaning, and spent some months trying to reach a compromise solution between Orange marchers and Catholic residents. Having failed to achieve this, she made a last minute decision to allow the march to proceed along the Garvaghy Road. She stated that she did this on the recommendation of her security advisers, in particular the RUC chief constable, Ronnie Flanagan, who spoke of there being 'a simple stark choice between two evils'. Immediately afterwards, a strategically timed leak of a confidential government document suggested that the decision to sanction the march had in fact been made well in advance, and led nationalists to believe that the negotiations which had continued up to the last minute were simply a public relations gimmick. The document indicated that the key decision-makers believed that 'if there is no local accommodation a controlled parade on the Garvaghy Road is the least worst outcome'.

Knox's cartoon (15.17) in the nationalist *Irish News* is highly critical of this decision. It shows the chief constable bowing to 'the greater evil' of the Orange Frankenstein's monster, while a member of the death-dealing Protestant paramilitary LVF takes aim from behind. Mo Mowlam and Prime Minister Blair meanwhile contemplate this scenario with growing unease and trepidation. Knox suggests that this Orange ogre cannot be pacified and that political responsibility for dealing with it ultimately rests with the British government.

15.18 'If Northern Ireland was really "British" . . .', Turner, *Irish Times*, Dublin, 11 July 1997

Many people in Britain continue to find it difficult to understand the political culture of Northern Ireland, especially the immediacy of historical events to both communities and the symbolic importance of cultural symbols and traditions. In this cartoon Martyn Turner contrasts British and Northern Irish perceptions of history. He transposes the turbulent issue of Orange parades into a British context, where a sense of mutual tolerance and fairness is supposed to prevail, in contrast to the apparent intolerance of Northern Ireland. He gently pokes fun at Britons' comparative lack of historical awareness, by showing an

Orangeman graciously agreeing not to march where he is not wanted. A local Catholic resident, presumably from the Garvaghy Road or the Ormeau Road area, displays equal consideration, and generously encourages the march to proceed, as it will only last a short time. His son is significantly drinking from a milk bottle, rather than throwing it at his erstwhile enemy. Turner's cartoon also subtly exposes the cherished unionist shibboleth that Ulster is British, by suggesting that some of the very people who claim British identity behave in a most *un*British manner over certain issues. Indeed, the so-called British notion that any problem could be solved by people working sensibly towards an agreed compromise has frequently come to grief in the intractable realities of Northern Ireland politics.

15.19 'Latest Final Comeback Tour', Rowson, *Guardian*, London, 21 July 1997

Shortly after the renewal of the IRA cease-fire on 20 July 1997, Prime Minister Blair accepted that it was genuine and agreed that Sinn Féin would be admitted to all-party talks in September, provided they accept the Mitchell principles on the use of non-violent means to achieve political ends. Sinn Féin duly agreed, but a few days before talks were due to begin the IRA stated that it had difficulty with some of the Mitchell principles, and that it would not hand over weapons. The timing of this statement put pressure on Sinn Féin, which attempted to distance itself from the IRA, emphasising that it had a political mandate to be present at the talks as a result of its recent strong showing in local and national elections.

This Rowson cartoon, published the day after the cease-fire was announced, reflects the scepticism with which news of the renewed cease-fire was greeted by many in Britain and Ireland. Adams is cast as a ventriloquist about to appear on stage for another 'final comeback tour', clutching his dummy, a bedraggled dove of peace which has obviously been through the wars. His chances of entertaining his difficult audience, rows of grim-faced, bowler-hatted Orangemen who look determined not to enjoy themselves, seem slim, and even his audio equipment appears ready to collapse. The only enthusiastic audience member is the effusive figure of Tony Blair, who has already begun to grin and applaud

15.20 'I have problems with . . .', Rowson, *Sunday Tribune*, Dublin, 14 September 1997

even before the act begins. The prime minister's solitary display of approval isolates him in the midst of unionist hostility, and Rowson implies that Adams's comeback show will not run for long, at least not at this venue.

The Rowson cartoon above illustrates the strains caused within the republican movement by the increasing divergence of its two parts, Sinn Féin and the Provisional IRA. He shows a two-headed beast at odds with itself, simultaneously expressing conflicting opinions. One head bears the features of the Sinn Féin president clutching a ballot box; the other is a balaclava-clad, rifle-carrying paramilitary. Each has difficulty with aspects of the other's politics; Adams with the IRA's uncompromising militancy, the IRA with Adams's apparent willingness to compromise. Since they belong to the same body, separation is impossible without mutual destruction.

Northern Ireland Secretary Mo Mowlam and Irish Foreign Affairs Minister Ray Burke stand to one side, both convinced that the beast is as it appears, and that Adams therefore cannot be trusted when he criticises the very movement of which he is an intimate part. Though most people in Britain and Ireland probably regard Adams as the front man of the IRA, the extent of Sinn Féin's influence on the Provisionals remains a matter of debate. However, leaders of all movements, whether peaceful or militant, are often embarrassed by the actions of their putative followers.

15.21 'Tell your friend . . .', Bell, *Guardian*, London, 18 September 1997

The IRA cease-fire of July 1997, coupled with Sinn Féin's acceptance of the Mitchell principles, enabled Blair to admit Sinn Féin to all-party talks on 15 September. However, the unionist parties indicated that they were unwilling to sit at the same table as Sinn Féin. The idea was then mooted of 'proximity talks' at Stormont Castle, whereby all parties would be invited to multilateral discussions in the same building, but not in the same

15.22 'Red white and blue . . .', Knox, *Irish News*, Belfast, 27 September 1997

room. The UUP, led by David Trimble, turned up at the talks, therefore, but initially refused to sit in the same room as the Sinn Féin delegation. A few days later they relented, but Paisley's DUP and McCartney's UK Unionists – a small unionist party with a single Westminster MP – still refused to attend because of the republican presence. Such tortuous political manoeuvring is satirised in Steve Bell's cartoon (p. 327, top) . He depicts a bewildered Mo Mowlam experiencing a fleeting moment of delight, as unionists and republicans are present in the same building at the same time, even though their physical, let alone political, proximity is highly tenuous.

In the same week as the talks got under way, a medical report was published which suggested that people who ate red meat on a regular basis could be harming their health, and advised greater consumption of vegetables. Knox's cartoon (15.22, p. 327 bottom) adapts this theme to comment on the current health of the peace process. He shows a hideously swollen Paisley chained in quarantine, where he gorges on red (white and blue) meat, while a puny McCartney chews a bone. 'Doctor' Blair diagnoses that these are creatures with dangerous political appetites, while Mo Mowlam vainly tries to entice the two carnivores with the carrot of compromise.

Meanwhile, a family of healthy, hippy vegetarians happily pass by on their way to all-party talks, and possibly peace and reconciliation. With delicious comic irony, Knox transforms Adams and Trimble into a couple of peace-loving, nuclear disarmament disciples, gaily frolicking with their children, Ulster Unionist security spokesman Ken Maginnis, and Sinn Féin's chief negotiator Martin McGuinness. The cartoon implies that some form of settlement may be possible involving the Ulster Unionists and Sinn Féin, whereas intransigent reactionaries like Paisley and McCartney will be left to perish in the political wilderness.

15.23 'No Going Back?', Rowson, *Guardian*, London, 14 October 1997

In October 1997 Tony Blair, in an effort to inject new impetus into the peace process, visited Belfast and met the leaders of the various political parties involved. During his visit, he met and shook hands with Gerry Adams, the encounter deliberately taking place behind closed doors, away from prying camera lenses. It was a bold move by Blair, and one which Major had always refused when in office. The Blair–Adams handshake was both historic and symbolic, as it was the first time a British prime minister had formally met with leaders of Sinn Féin since Lloyd George had done so in 1921. While nationalists welcomed the prime minster's initiative, Conservatives and unionists criticised him for what they saw as yet another concession to republican demands for recognition. Anticipating such hostile press reaction, Blair had earlier said of the meeting: 'I greeted him as I would any other human being.' Rowson's cartoon (opposite, top) reflects the potentially irreversible consequences of this handshake for both men. For Blair, the political danger of clasping Adams's bloodstained hand was outweighed by the prospect of confirming Sinn Féin's commitment to constitutional politics; for Adams, the risk of alienating his militant republican support was counterbalanced by the official acceptance of his party as a legitimate element of the peace negotiations.

In a further attempt to bind the republican movement into the talks process, Blair invited the Sinn Féin leadership to Downing Street on 11 December. This was another historically resonant meeting, as the last time such an event occurred was in December 1921, when Michael Collins and Arthur Griffith led the Sinn Féin delegation to London to

15.24 Untitled, Connolly, *Irish Independent*, Dublin, 11 December 1997

negotiate the Anglo-Irish Treaty. Once again, handshakes took place in private, thereby inviting cartoonists to imagine possible scenarios. The *Irish Independent*'s Phelim Connolly responded to the challenge with a provocative cartoon (15.24) of Blair and Adams simultaneously recalling Collins, IRA leader turned statesman, as they shake hands. His acceptance of a compromise settlement with the British government split the republican movement in 1922 and led to a bitter civil war in which he himself was assassinated. As Adams and Blair ponder Collins's fate, the question being posed is whether Adams can persuade the IRA to continue its support for the peace process or if his non-violent strategy will lead to further divisions within the republican movement and bring about his own demise. The breakaway Continuity Army Council had already condemned the whole process, and some new defections had appeared in Sinn Féin ranks.

15.25 'Remember Trimble...', Bell, *Guardian*, London, 7 January, 1998

On 27 December 1997 Billy Wright, leader of the breakaway paramilitary LVF, was shot dead in the Maze prison by members of the republican INLA. Wright, nicknamed 'King Rat', was accused by republicans of orchestrating an assassination campaign against Catholics from his H-Block cell. During the following weeks, eight innocent Catholics were shot dead in retaliation. This sudden resurgence of violent activity by the INLA and LVF, neither of which had declared a cease-fire, threatened to wreck the already fragile peace process and shifted the focus of political attention to the loyalist prisoners in the Maze.

In the days after Wright's death, UVF and UFF prisoners threatened to withdraw their support for their political representatives' continued involvement in the peace talks. This announcement prompted Ulster Unionist leaders to visit them in order to exchange views

15.26 'More Tea, Mad Dog?', Bell, *Guardian*, London, 9 January 1998

on the progress of the talks. Bell's cartoon opposite commemorates David Trimble's meeting with the UVF prisoners in the style of a loyalist mural. It depicts him in a suppliant pose before a group of impassive paramilitary leaders, meekly requesting their continued political co-operation. The accompanying legend is a sardonic reference to Trimble's earlier statement that, unlike Sinn Féin and the SDLP, unionists 'would never sit down with the men of violence'. The uneasy relationship between mainstream unionism and loyalist extremism is clearly highlighted, and Trimble, having spoken directly to these leaders, would find it difficult in the future to refuse similar discussions with republican leaders.

Just a few days after Trimble's Maze visit, the Northern Ireland secretary, Mo Mowlam, also met loyalist paramilitary leaders in the prison. She insisted that the purpose of her visit was not to negotiate, but rather to explain the government's position clearly in an effort to preserve the loyalist cease-fire. She succeeded in her basic aim, but Bell's mocking cartoon above highlights the sheer incongruity of a senior cabinet minister meeting convicted terrorists in their prison cells. To underline the bizarre, almost incredible nature of this development, he imagines Mowlam taking tea with the prisoners, who affect genteel table manners for the occasion. Among the loyalist leaders whom she met was the notorious John 'Mad Dog' Adair, whose fearful nickname is signified by his studded dog collar.

15.27 'Peace Process', Turner, *Belfast Telegraph*, Belfast, 23 January 1998

By the end of January 1998 ten people had been killed in Northern Ireland since the death of Billy Wright, mostly as a result of loyalist violence. The admission by the UFF that it had murdered three Catholics led to the withdrawal of its political representatives, the UDP,

from the talks process on 26 January, before it could be expelled by the two governments for its violation of the Mitchell principles. This development deepened anxieties that the peace process was on the verge of collapse, and that full-scale sectarian violence was about to return to the streets of Northern Ireland.

This latest crisis for the faltering talks process coincided with the release of *Titanic*, the most expensive Hollywood movie ever made. This Turner cartoon draws a parallel between the perilous fate of the peace process and that of the famous cruise liner, which was built in the Belfast shipyards. As the *Peace Process* perishes on the icebergs of loyalist and republican paramilitary violence, the two captains, Tony Blair and Bertie Ahern, are left to contemplate the watery abyss, while Gerry Adams abandons ship and seeks political survival in a lifeboat. In Turner's view, the whole process is doomed and the people of Northern Ireland, like a film audience, are consigned to the role of impotent spectators.

Turner's historical analogy is a piquant one. The sinking of the *Titanic*, symbol of Ulster's strength and invincibility, on its maiden voyage in April 1912 coincided with Asquith's introduction of the third Home Rule Bill in the Commons. To minds disposed to seeing the world in allegorical terms, the ship's fatal loss seemed an ominous portent of Ulster's dire political destiny in a home rule Ireland. It remains to be seen whether the *Peace Process*, a vessel crafted by the Irish and British politicians of today, can yet avoid the *Titanic*'s tragic fate, and safely deliver its passengers and crew to an agreed destination.

15.28 Untitled, Schrank, *Independent on Sunday*, London, 12 April 1998

Hopes of finding a lasting peace settlement were dramatically revived with the announcement of a Northern Ireland agreement on Good Friday, 10 April 1998, following weeks of intensive negotiations at Castle Buildings, Stormont, by representatives of the Northern Ireland political parties and the two governments. Schrank's cartoon reflects the mood of cautious optimism with which news of this historic deal was greeted by many people in Ireland and Britain. His image of the hand of hope dramatically emerging from a coffin with an olive branch, to the alarm and dismay of republican and loyalist extremists, powerfully invokes the archetypal symbol of Christian hope and redemption, the Resurrection. Indeed, the coincidence of the potentially epoch-making agreement with the religious festival of Easter encouraged many to hope that the Christian message of forgiveness and reconciliation might at last be heeded by both communities in Northern Ireland. Such sentiments were most eloquently expressed by Ireland's Nobel laureate, Seamus Heaney, who saw in the agreement the potential for a lasting peace and shared future for all the people of Ireland:

If revolution is the kicking down of a rotten door, evolution is more like pushing the stone from the mouth of the tomb. There is an Easter energy about it, a sense of arrival rather than wreckage, and what is nonpareil about the new conditions is the promise they offer of a new covenant between people living in this island of Ireland. For once, and at long last, the language of the Bible can be appropriated by those with a vision of the future rather than those who sing the battle hymns of the past.

FURTHER READING

Arthur, P. and K. Jeffrey. *Northern Ireland Since 1968*, Oxford, 1988

Bardon, J. *A History of Ulster*, Belfast, 1992

Bowyer Bell, J. *The Irish Troubles: A Generation of Violence, 1967–1992*, Dublin, 1993

Boyce, D.G. *Nineteenth-Century Ireland: The Search for Stability*, Dublin, 1990

Brown, T. *Ireland: A Social and Cultural History, 1922–1985*, London, 1985

Coogan, T.P. *The Troubles: Ireland's Ordeal 1966–1996 and the Search for Peace*, London, 1995

Curtis, L. *Nothing But the Same Old Story: The Roots of Anti-Irish Racism*, London, 1984
 The Cause of Ireland: From the United Irishmen to Partition, Belfast, 1994

Curtis, L.P. *Apes and Angels: The Irishman in Victorian Caricature*, London, 1997

Darby, J. *Dressed to Kill: Cartoonists and the Northern Ireland Conflict*, Belfast, 1983

Douglas, R. *The World War 1939–1945: The Cartoonists' Vision*, London, 1990

Fanning, R. *Independent Ireland*, Dublin, 1983

Foster, R.F. *Modern Ireland: 1600–1972*, London, 1988

Harkness, D. *Ireland in the Twentieth Century: Divided Ireland*, London, 1996

Hoppen, K.T. *Ireland Since 1800: Conflict and Conformity*, London, 1989

Hussey, G. *Ireland Today: Anatomy of a Changing State*, London, 1995

Keogh, D. *Twentieth Century Ireland: Nation and State*, Dublin, 1994

Keogh, D. and N. Furlong. *The Mighty Wave: The 1798 Rebellion in Wexford*, Dublin, 1996

Kinealy, C. *This Great Calamity: The Irish Famine 1845–52*, Dublin, 1994

Laffan, M. *The Partition of Ireland: 1911–1925*, Dundalk, 1983

Lee, J.J. *The Modernisation of Irish Society: 1848–1918*, Dublin, 1992
 Ireland 1912–1985: Politics and Society, Cambridge, 1989

Lyons, F.S.L. *Ireland Since the Famine*, London, 1971

MacDonagh, O. *States of Mind: A Study of Anglo-Irish Conflict, 1780–1980*, London, 1983

Mallie, E. and D. McKittrick. *The Fight for Peace: The Secret Story Behind the Irish Peace Process*, London, 1996

Ó Tuathaigh, G. *Ireland Before the Famine: 1798–1848*, Dublin, 1990

Stewart, A.T.Q. *The Summer Soldiers: The 1798 Rebellion in Antrim and Down*, Belfast, 1995

Ward, M. *Unmanageable Revolutionaries: Women and Irish Nationalism*, London, 1995

Whyte, J.H. *Interpreting Northern Ireland*, Oxford, 1990

INDEX

NOTE: Persons portrayed in cartoons are given roman page numbers for text references, with italic page numbers for the actual cartoons they appear in. General topics and concepts are given roman page numbers only.